REACH THE TOP

YOU CAN, IF YOU PLAN

Y. C. Halan

STERLING PAPERBACKS
An imprint of
Sterling Publishers (P) Ltd.
A-59, Okhla Industrial Area, Phase-II, New Delhi-110020.
Tel: 26387070, 26386209; Fax: 91-11-26383788
E-mail: mail@sterlingpublishers.com
www.sterlingpublishers.com

Reach the Top:
you can, if you plan
© 2012, Y. C. Halan
ISBN 978 81 207 7461 2

All rights are reserved.
No part of this publication may be reproduced, stored in a retrieval system or transmitted, in any form or by any means, mechanical, photocopying, recording or otherwise, without prior written permission of the author.

Printed in India
Printed and Published by Sterling Publishers Pvt. Ltd.,
New Delhi-110 020.

Contents

Introduction v

Chapter 1
Kick-Off 1

Chapter 2
Failure to Success 13

Chapter 3
Success System 24

Chapter 4
A Good Job: How to Achieve 36

Chapter 5
Essentials of Success System 77

Chapter 6
For a Better Tomorrow 101

Chapter 7
Be a Leader 158

Chapter 8
Learning from Peers 232

Chapter 9
Leaders' Legacies 263

Introduction

If you wait for the right time to train, it'll rarely occur. Today is the opportunity to prepare for tomorrow, regardless of how much else is going on.

BERNARD BANKS
Director, Leader Development Science Studies,
Eisenhower Leader Dev Program, West Point,
New York

Social and professional life in India has taken a 380-degree turn in the last 20 years. Businesses have re-engineered their operations to achieve excellence. Many, such as the Life Insurance Corporation of India and the Aditya Birla Group, have already achieved that goal. They have discovered how to achieve success by focusing on their employees, customers, shareholders, and governments. But the number of failures too is large. There is a huge gap between excellence and failure. This book tries to fill that gap. It tries to provide a practical way of identifying what it takes to achieve excellence in life and career and ultimately to "Reach the top".

Life today demands much more from the present generation than it did from the earlier ones. The problem is that though most of us are performing better than the older generation, the performance bar is continuously being raised. This means the employer expects you to do better and give more than what you have. And so in a way you are forced to perform better and in the best possible way just to stay in the competition. It leads to the search for personal success and achievement, and prompts you to think of your life-goal.

In today's times the life-goals motivating a person to work and get ahead in life are different from what they were a few decades ago. When India gained its independence, the operative life-goals, inspiring both the elite and the commoners, were the puritan virtues of work, pride of craftsmanship, thrift, achievement, and the fulfilment of the vocation and tasks to which one was called to. But in the post-liberalisation society of the 21st century, a new pattern of life and a new set of values have emerged. The components of it are success, power, prestige, money, and security. It is known as the "new success system".

This success system is not about some abstract standard; it is about being daring to be different and controlling the future by fighting on your terms and not on the terms of competitors. You have to know the rules of the game and by following them you have to play to "be a winner". In fact, the emphasis of the success system as a whole is on achievement at the personal and team levels to take you to the victory stand. Some known winners, the most talked about and highly respected persons are: Khuswant Singh—the best-selling author; Dhirubhai Ambani—who gave new orientation to the Indian business; Field-Marshal Sam Manekshaw MC—who won the 1971 war and forced the largest military surrender in military history; Lata Mangeshkar—the doyen of Indian music; and Aishwarya Rai—the best known film star who has her pictures on all magazine covers, in India and overseas.

The contemporary society is success-oriented. "Reach the top", is the ultimate ambition of every person. And there is nothing wrong in it. However, the question is how to convert ambition into reality. This book analyses and explains how that could be made possible.

Two significant questions arise at this stage. First, who is a winner? And second, how to survive in a highly competitive world that has come to stay?

First, how to reach the top?

First question first. A winning person is one who may not know all the answers, but he does know the right questions. A wise person will not follow a universal road map. If every one is following the same road map, the road will be congested. We can follow a different path if we train ourselves to ask the right questions, intelligently analyse the answers and create our own road map that helps us to achieve our ambition.

Most of us do not know our future or the direction we are going. Our march into the future can appear to be a random walk when our direction is always changing in unpredictable ways. So we should try to control the future with strategies and plans that prepare us for most eventualities. It is better to have a plan than having no plan.

Most of us live life as if we are moving in a caravan. We join it after it has started and leave it before it has finished. If business is like a caravan traveling towards a decided destination, then when we join the caravan we learn the ways of the caravan. We learn to travel at the pace of the caravan and learn what needs to be done to survive and contribute. We learn it every day, week, month and year. It becomes our normal pattern of behaviour. When we get used to a pattern of behaviour it becomes difficult to break it. This makes any change difficult. The challenge for you is to make changes faster than the caravan and initiate changes in operations and make people who work with you to accept it.

How to survive in a highly competitive world

There goes a story. After the Third World War, that was nuclear, civilization was wiped out. The only survivor was a monkey couple who came out of their hideout, looked around and said with great concern: "Oh God, we have to start it all over again".

The story points out the predicament the survivors of the 21st century may find themselves in and the attitude they should develop to face such a situation coolly. But before that we should analyse the factors that have led us to an all-round deterioration.

At the global level, the law of the jungle prevails. The powerful nations are ruthless and follow only Darwin's theory—survival of the fittest. What happened in Iraq and Afghanistan and may happen in Iran is a testimony to it. After the Second World War and before the fall of the Soviet system, the two superpowers did not allow any third nation to become powerful enough to challenge their superiority. Today the only superpower, the United States of America, wants to remain the only powerful country in the world. Unfortunately, the remaining developed countries are fighting for the largest share in the world markets, leaving the developing economies with just peanuts. This law operates at the national level also where different tiers of society fight bitterly to retain their positions in the national economy. This operates at the levels of regions, communities, families, and individuals.

Wars and widespread turbulence, particularly in Asia, are causing untold misery and suffering. India has its own set of problems thrown up by circumstances peculiar to this country. To begin with, the breakdown of the law and order machinery is a major issue to worry about. Then the value system is declining and corruption has acquired a veneer of respectability. Even the rich and influential are forced to pull strings for day-to-day requirements. A survey by *Transparency International* shows that India is the world leader of corrupts societies. India tops the list of countries whose companies pay bribe to clinch overseas deals.

What chances does this leave to the man-on-the-street with? Contact with the Western culture and the coming of channel and cable TV has resulted in the emergence of strong individualistic and smug feelings. The family as a unit is beginning to break. From joint to micro-family and finally to micro-individual is slowly becoming the history of the Indian family system. This phenomenon was confined to urban areas but now is spreading to even small towns and villages. The fallout is the increased number of pampered and undisciplined children, divorces, alcoholism, and drug addiction occurring at a rapid rate.

All these factors may deteriorate in the coming decades, making life difficult and even harrowing. Education is supposed to prepare the youth for a better future but most of our educational institutions are incapable of doing so. Most of them are becoming irrelevant and therefore redundant. In fact, colleges and universities are de-educating boys and girls. Whatever education they receive during the first 12 yeas of their schooling is forgotten in the universities and colleges, not to mention acquiring new knowledge. The job market, leaving apart some scarce specialised skills, is rapidly becoming a buyer's paradise as hundreds run after one job. The employer, therefore, demands the very best and is willing to pay a price for that. It has created tough competition in the employment market.

Your road map

Considering the trying times ahead, the well-educated youth of the 21st century might suffer more than the sufferings of the 20th century youth. However, the situation is not as bad as it was for the past-century youth. With a number of new scenarios emerging and new markets being created, there is great scarcity of a number of skills. In Bangalore, a reputed company displays a line at the reception. It says, "Trespassers will be recruited".

Those who want to benefit from a situation where there is scarcity of talent must develop that skill-blend and a personality that is in greater demand. What is that?

The first need is to *become a fine human being*. You have to prove that you have humane personality that is ready to help those in need. The Lal Bahadur Shastri Institute of Management in New Delhi gave priority to the son of a bank peon while admitting students for the MBA course. The boy deserved to be there but had certain handicaps. But in no time he became the most popular with the students and faculty, as he was always there whenever there was any need for help. The boy was the first to be picked up by a reputed company at a good salary during the campus recruitment.

You can become such a person only when you are modest. Your learning process stops when you are arrogant, because you think you know every thing and the others are wrong. This is the end of growth and development. You should think like Bertrand Russel who believed that his learning process never stopped. "I feel I am collecting shells at the shore of the sea of knowledge", he used to say. Broaden your horizons by becoming well read, up-to-date and knowledgeable. Be a realist and do not live in a make-believe world of the past. Avoid being dogmatic. Promote yourself in a legitimate and honest way.

Second, is to develop the art of time and crisis management. Time is more valuable than money. Those who cannot manage it, continue to swim in the backwaters of their career. Crisis management brings the hidden qualities of a person to the forefront and gives an opportunity to move upwards. Be clear-headed and not a confused person. Do not remain in suspended animation. Take quick decisions, develop sharp reflexes, and don't behave like a failure. In fact, persons with quick reflexes live longer. About a dozen attempts were made on the life of General Charles de Gaulle but he saved himself because of his quick reflexes. Develop the habit of speedy analysis of situations. It would help you in taking quick decisions.

Lastly, *be grateful to someone* whom you feel indebted. Have a value system; even animals have one! So why don't you have one?

In the years to come only those who are fighters will reach the top. The world has always loved a fighter and only he gets a cherished place in society and history. Mahatma Gandhi, Winston Churchill, Abraham Lincoln, Charles de Gaulle, and Indira Gandhi were all fighters and winners in their respective fields. They have created a place for themselves in history. Read about them; their biographies can bring you closer to your winning post.

Chapter 1

Kick-Off

After having established itself as a global leader in IT and pharma generics, India is not only poised to emerge as the world's auto factory and medical tourism hub, but also as a global peacemaker as it can offer the world the great Indian dream that strikes the ideal balance between materialism and spiritualism.

PHILIP KOTLER,
Management Guru

What awaits you & how to prepare for it?

India during the past 20 years has moved from poverty to prosperity and from tradition to modernity. Today it is a spirited, dynamic, vivacious and vibrant free-market democracy. The markets are expanding as high purchasing power is being generated because of the boom in certain sectors. It has resulted in reduced percentage of the poor and an increased size of the middle class. A new class of millionaires, those who can purchase the most expensive goods, is increasing at a very fast rate. In 2008–09, India had 84,000 millionaires, and this number grew by 50.9 percent to reach 1,26,700 in 2010. More than that, out of the total 1,210 billionaires in the world, as per the Forbes Billionaire 2011 list, 50 are Indians. This, however, is not the real indicator of prosperity, because the wealth measured includes only financial and real estate assets and excludes self-occupied houses. Most of the new millionaires and billionaires did not inherit wealth, but created it with their talent, hard work, and professional skills. Today India has the fastest wealth creators through all income levels. In 1999 a total of only 740 Mercedes-Benz cars were sold, but by 2011, in just one month (January), 640 cars were sold. Another luxury carmaker, Audi, sold 480 units in January 2011 – the highest-ever monthly sales in India – as against 306 units in the same month in 2010. Booms and unprecedented prosperity has unlocked a sea of opportunities to the present-day youth. Nevertheless, such opportunities are not scattered on streets. You have to prepare yourself to step into the wonderland of money, power, and status. But before that it is necessary to know what this wonderland is all about.

What awaits you

The working world, particularly the corporate and other elite services such as the civil service, that you intend to enter, is fiercely ruthless, highly competitive, and extremely demanding. Nevertheless it ensures high rewards, a satisfying career, and develops rare skills in an individual. It gives you money, power, and status. But it is a difficult world to work and live in. Let us find out more about this world. This world is:

Fiercely Ruthless: Markets are ruthless. You have to survive in the most difficult and demanding environments. If you are gentle in your approach and attitude, the rivals will not allow you to exist. The competitors always try to edge others out of the market. Every business house attempts to grab the existing market from the others and expands its own share. Those who are not able to do so are pushed out of the market – the Modis, Sri Rams, and many other such business houses have failed. On the contrary, there are many others who did not exist earlier in the industry are ruling the market, such as the Jet Airways, Maruti, Whirlpool, and Airtel. Some of the brands failed terribly too—Ovaltine, Fiat car, Lamberta scooter, Sunlight soap are some such brands that do not exist any more. Mobile phones have replaced the landline phones. PCs and laptops are being used instead of typewriters.

Highly Competitive: Competition is the market force, the main motivating power, and a powerful engine. The Kirloskars remained a small company by international standards in the absence of competition. Toyota, merely a car dealer in the early 1950s, became a multinational company. Competition is the name of the game.

Indian markets have become highly competitive since 1991, even though, some were competitive earlier too, such as banks, soaps, and cosmetics. Bajaj, the leading two-wheeler manufacturer, survived because it decided to face competition boldly.

Till the eighties, India was a "scarcity" economy—it did not care for cost, customer, quality, or price. The consumers and their needs were taken for granted. But, the present India has a "surplus" economy. Companies now have to produce larger quantities at a lower cost. In the past 15 years alone, the companies have reduced their costs, lowered prices, and improved on customer care and the quality of their products. They are working on much lower margins than before. For instance, the highway construction companies work on zero margins and earn through claiming a bonus by finishing their client's projects before time. This is only possible when companies have dedicated managers who work for them, and who are quality conscious and believe in the high production of products.

Extremely Demanding: The corporate world demands the very best from you because of critical market compulsions. It demands high quality and productivity from managers so that they can survive and prosper in the market. With a view to achieving this, they involve them in risk-taking by giving them profit incentives and rewards like equity participation.

When working in a cut-throat competitive environment, every company wants to produce quality products at a minimum cost and keep its customers happy. These companies have to be one-upped by providing good quality goods and satisfying services at a low price. They have to increase their market share so that they can have the economies of the scale. To keep their customers happy they have to be demanding on their employees. Therefore, "deliver or perish" is the present day catch-phrase for managers. Those who perform well in their jobs move up the ladder fast, and those who fail are given the pink slip. Nevertheless, the corporate world is highly rewarding, satisfying, and may develop rare skills in you, providing you financial independence, power, and social status.

How to prepare

You are expected to be a leader and an innovator (thinking out of the box), a magician (providing solutions at the drop of a hat), a dynamic motivator, a stern but fair judge, a diplomat, a politician, a protector.

If you want to be a leader you have to be a planner, a strategist, an executor, a performer. You have to get along with people, wear the right clothes, have the right set of friends, and possess agreeable personalities. You must work hard and responsibly represent your the corporate pride. You should develop the rivalry that a player develops to become number-one. Remember, sense of power flows from success and achievement. Power is not something that is given to you on a platter. You have to acquire it by your determination, wisdom, and strength. The more you use it, the more you will get.

Ayn Rand shares an appropriate incident in her novel, *Atlas Shrugged*.

She had fallen asleep and she awakened with a jolt, knowing that something was wrong. Before she knew what it was; the wheels had stopped. She glanced at her watch: there was no reason for stopping. She looked out the window: the train stood still in the middle of an empty field.

"How long have we been standing?" She asked the fellow passenger.

A man's voice answered indifferently: "About an hour."

She leaped to her feet and rushed to the door, as the man looked after her astonished.

She saw the figures of men standing by the engine and above them the red light of the signal.

She walked rapidly towards them and asked, "What is the matter?"

The engineer turned, astonished. Her question had sounded like an order, not like the amateur curiosity of a passenger.

"Red light, lady," he said, pointing up with his thumb.

"How long has it been on?"

"An hour."

"We're off the main track, aren't we?"

"That's right."

"Why?"

"I don't know. I don't think we had any business being sent off on a siding, that switch wasn't working right and this thing is not working at all. I think it is busted."

"Then what you are going to do?"

"Waiting for it to change. Last week the crack Atlantic Southern got left on a siding for two hours — just somebody's mistake," interjected the fireman.

"This is the Taggard Comet. It has never been late."

"The only one in the country that hasn't," said the engineer.

"There is always a first time," said the fireman.

"If you know that the signal is broken, what do you intend to do?" she asked.

> *"My job is to wait for orders."*
> *"You job is to run this train."*
> *"Not against the red light. We're not moving till somebody tells us to."*
> *She looked at the red light and at the rail that went off into the black, untouched distance. "Proceed with caution to the next signal. If it's in order, proceed to the main track. Then stop at the first open office." She ordered.*
> *"Yeah? Who says so?"*
> *"I do."*
> *"Who are you?"*
> *"Dagny Taggard. Proceed to the main track and hold for me at the first open office."*
> *"Yes, Miss Taggard."*

She was the daughter of the owner of that railway system in the United States.

Preparing for the corporate world requires developing five attributes. These are: **Courage** to say, in a diplomatic and articulate manner, what you feel; **Conviction** to believe in what you say and make others believe that you are correct; **Clarity** of what you believe in, and then convey it in a simple, concise, and understandable language; **Credibility** that people trust you and what you say; **Wisdom** to understand and know your argument and then defend it effectively.

To possess these five attributes you have to develop a winning personality. And what is a winning personality? It is a mix of qualities and skills exhibited by a person that distinguishes them from others. It is the totality of an individual's behaviour and emotional characteristics. These are—authenticity, character, vision, will, and wisdom.

Authenticity: Do what you say and do the right thing. It leads to honesty, an appropriate attitude, and an action which others follow. Jack Welch of GE says, "have a soul" (emotional and intellectual energy) so that the mind, body, and the heart resonate. A synchronised reaction of the three should produce a justified reaction to a problem.

Character: A spectrum of traits that include integrity and compassion. It is a value system that consists of morality in one's actions, good intentions, and working in the interest of the organisation and for an individual.

Vision: It is the awareness about perspective and viewing things in their true relations or relative importance. It needs openness of mind and creativity in work. It means living in the real world and arriving at pragmatic solutions. Similar to the commander of a ship who must have a helm to grasp, a course to steer, a port to seek so that the ship sails on the right course.

Will: Visions remain empty dreams if they are not achieved. They need a will and an attitude — passion and determination. You should move on and should not stop till the vision is fulfilled. It requires courage and ability to take risk. This does not mean foolhardiness, like Lord Cardigan who in 1854 led his 600 soldiers of the British Light Cavalry directly into the face of the Russian field batteries and were decimated by the Russians during the siege of Sevastopol.

You ought to have a strong will to win the losing game. If you are not getting the desired result, modify your thinking, and bring in organisational and strategic change. Ask one question — what difference would an incremental improvement in energy, time, money, or any other resource make, and how would you accomplish it?

Risk taking is implicit in any desire to win at a game. Delegate decision-making and share power. Aim at high performance and develop an optimistic outlook. Always believe that bad events are temporary and are caused by bad circumstances, and that they will be over if you continue to fight. All this needs is a positive attitude. It was with this attitude that Churchill won the Second World War. Pessimism is the state of helplessness that makes one dependent on others in the face of adversity.

Wisdom: This is the common sense that reflects the condition in which thinking, feeling, and action is synchronised. It means balancing reality with aspirations. It is integrating conflicting goals effectively, and understanding the importance of moderation. You should know when to act and when not to. It is about making difficult decisions in ambiguous circumstances or in situations where data is incomplete and lacking.

Wisdom is taking decisions after careful thinking, introspection, and considering all the aspects of a situation. The following is a true story of a farmer as told by Dr. Russell Conwell, founder of Temple University in Philadelphia, PA:

> *A farmer became excited about tales of other farmers who had made their fortunes from discovering diamond mines. He sold his farm and spent his life unsuccessfully searching for the prized game. Eventually impoverished, desolate, and alone he took his own life.*
>
> *The new owner of his farm had in the meantime discovered an attractive stone in the riverbed of the farm. He placed it on the mantelpiece. A guest one-day saw it and picked it up to examine. He could not believe what he was holding – one of the largest diamonds ever discovered. The farm that had been sold off in order that the first farmer might find a diamond mine, actually turned out to be the most productive diamond mine on the continent. The first farmer had already owned acres of diamonds but he had sold them for practically nothing in order to look for them somewhere.*

The moral of the story is that diamonds, like opportunities, are disguised. Diamonds in their rough state do not in any way look like diamonds. They require preparation. Similarly, study and preparation have to go in before opportunities can be capitalised on. All the talents, skills, and abilities required for whatever you want are already present in you in an undeveloped and unprepared form. Everything you require is under your feet or at least within your reach; so do not waste your precious time trying to look elsewhere to realise your goals.

If the first farmer had studied and prepared himself, to understand what diamonds look like in their rough form and thoroughly explored his own farm before looking elsewhere, all of his dreams would have come true. Each of us is standing on our own acre of diamonds. Before you go running off to greener pastures, make sure that you have explored your own green pastures. If someone's pastures are greener it may simply be because it is getting better care and attention. Remember, while you are looking at the other greener and fresher pastures, other people are looking at yours.

> Diamonds, like opportunities, are disguised—each of us is standing on our own acre of diamonds.

Wisdom can also be learnt by playing sports such as golf, tennis, hockey, or football. Team games teach strategy and teamwork. Board games such as chess are good for strategy. Playing a game or sport should not lead to empty pride; the lessons of the game should be applied to life too. Adopt the scenario technique. Involve yourself in simulation exercises. Be conscious of the dynamics of learning. Read biographies of successful entrepreneurs. Surf the Internet. Legend has it that a Chinese wise man, setting off on a pilgrimage at the age of 60, declares: "If I meet a 3-year-old child on the path who knows more than I do, I will learn from him. If I meet an 80-year-old sage who knows less, I will teach him."

If given the opportunity to lead you will fail in the long run (regardless of your skills as a manager), unless you cultivate these five cardinal leadership virtues—authenticity, character, vision, will, and wisdom. These will not be sufficient unless they are augmented by a set of practical skills and competencies.

In real life, when you come across doors that are shut on you, you will have to open them. Those who learn to open the closed doors will leave behind those who cannot open closed doors. Here let me share with you the story of a bellboy who was fired by the church but became one of the richest persons of London.

> Charles was crestfallen. He couldn't believe his ear. The priest called him and told that his services were not required any longer.
>
> "But what is my fault?" He inquired with anguish in his tone.
>
> "You are illiterate," replied the priest.
>
> "But how does that matter?" I have been pulling the bell of the church for the last 40 years. What education is needed to pull the chain?"
>
> "I wish I could help you, but I am helpless. There is a new law which requires minimum literacy even for your job," the priest replied, throwing up his hands in despair.
>
> With tears in his eyes and hope in his heart, Charles left the church where he had been pulling the chain of the bell every day for 40 years. He had an urge to smoke but could not find a shop to buy a cigarette. He started walking and found one after walking about one-and-a-half kilometre.
>
> Charles cooled down after a smoke and started thinking about the future. He realised that there may be many more persons who wanted to smoke after the church service and had to walk a kilometre-and-a-half to get one. He decided to sell cigarettes on that stretch. Soon he started earning well, much more than what he was earning as a bellboy. He decided to look for places where stretches were long and there were no cigarette shops.
>
> Soon Charles became the leading tobacconist of London and one of the richest persons in London. A tabloid decided to develop a story on him. The reporter who came to interview him asked: "What would you have been doing if you were literate?"
>
> "Ringing the bell at the church," was the answer.

You do not need a prominent degree for success. What you need is a down-to-earth approach and an active mind. Also, you need to be grappling with the problem at hand and facing it head on rather than merely sulking. Problems are a reality of life; no one can escape them. Anyone who tries to escape gets entangled even further.

Norman Vincent Peale, the author of the well-known book, *The Power of Positive Thinking* was once asked if there was any place where a person could live in peace. Peale replied that there was one—"Right down the alley there is the cemetery where 100,000 dead persons live without any problem."

The next 50 years will present extraordinary challenges to you. You will experience major demographic changes—shift from a manufacturing to a service economy, increasing importance of entrepreneurism, and the overpowering impact of technological revolution. If you want to succeed, and that is not difficult, you have to evolve a self-organising system, not dependent on your natural growth, but one that also encourages mutation (significant and basic change). You will have to understand the community—why its members want to work together and what they will try to do together. Teamwork must replace a self-centered working system. Satisfying the needs of all should replace the search to satisfy your own singular needs. This is the ultimate challenge for you in the 21st century.

When you move ahead in the real professional life, which may run for around 35 years you will find yourself in gloomy situations. Do not just knock on doors; try to open them yourself. Learn from the following Zen story:

One stormy night a man came upon a monastery in the forest. He knocked at the thick door and shouted to be admitted for quite some time, but no one responded. Finally, he found a heavy stone and pounded on the door. A monk appeared and directed him to a room containing only a sleeping mat. Exhausted, and relieved to be out of the rain, the traveller put his stone on the floor and fell sleep.

In the morning when he awakened, he tried to open the door of his room to ask for food, but the door was locked. He shouted, but no one answered. At last, he picked up the stone and pounded on the door. A monk soon appeared and led him into another room, in which were waiting food, water, and a pallet. The traveller bathed, ate, and rested.

When he sought to leave, he found the door locked and no one answered his call. When he pounded with the stone, he was again answered and taken to a more comfortable room.

And so he lived like that for a number of days, carrying his heavy stone from room to room, and using it to open each succeeding door. Ultimately, he no longer shouted or tried to open the door, but immediately pounded with his stone when he wanted to leave.

One day, when he was pounding heavily on a door, the monk on the other side said to him, "Why don't you try the door yourself?" The man pushed against the door, and it opened easily into the next room.

The monk said, "Is it always necessary to carry your heavy stone and beat upon the door? There are many that are not locked."

India since 1991 has moved from poverty to prosperity. A new middle and millionaire class is growing fast. The entire business scenario is changing and the system is demanding efficient, skilled, and productive managers with leadership and entrepreneurial qualities. Nevertheless, the business world is becoming fiercely ruthless, highly competitive, and extremely demanding. Today's managers need to be planners, strategists, executors, and performers to not only survive but also prosper in this new world. This requires the development of five attributes — courage, conviction, clarity, credibility, and wisdom.

Chapter 2

Failure to Success

*If we all did the things we are capable of doing,
we would literally astound ourselves.*

THOMAS A. EDISON

One can say with surety that a person does not have much control on external factors and environment. Even then one not only has to survive but also move horizontally and vertically to prosper. This is possible only when a person keeps on progressing continuously in his life and career. If you lead a sheltered life, you soon become frustrated. You have to understand the system and its limitations, and learn how to overcome these obstacles to become more successful than others. This is the way people who do not control the levers of power and money create a way for themselves. Some of such well-known examples of individuals coming from weaker sections of the society are Abraham Lincoln and Lal Bahadur Shastri — both attained the highest position in their countries. Coming from modest backgrounds, both changed the course of the history in their countries — the United States and India, respectively. However, one should not forget those mighty ones who fell from high pedestals to very low levels. Harshad Mehta and King Gyanendra of Nepal are examples of two such persons.

To convert failure into success what is required is a continuous momentum and motion in efforts.

Prepare for the market

Here is a story of a student that may be a similar story of a majority of Indian students today. Rajan was a smart young boy who joined the CCS University, Meerut for a graduate degree. He came out of the high portals of the University with a first-class degree in his hand and high aspirations in his heart. He was confident of getting a lucrative job and dreamt of settling down in life comfortably. However, he was crestfallen when he was forced to face the existing market realities. Running from pillar to post, he realised that he would not be successful in getting a good job because the education he had acquired was not accepted in the field of his choice. The knowledge that he had gained during his stay in the university was suddenly of limited use to the changing markets of the 21st century global India.

Rajan is not an isolated example of the frustrated youth of today. Hundreds and thousands of Rajans find themselves in the same situation year after year. The reason being the fantasy they develop in the university of a lucrative job awaiting them when they step into the real world.

Such a fantasy is caused by two factors. First, a student assumes that the life in the real world would be similar to that which existed in the university. He also assumes that he is being properly trained and impartially evaluated. But that is not the reality. Unlike the advanced countries, learning in India is not a creative exercise. The student does not play an active role while learning in the class. He is also not evaluated properly at the end of the course. Therefore, students are not able to develop a well-trained and disciplined mind that should contain the core faculties of comprehension, analysis, and rational thinking. Unfortunately, not many educational institutions are backed by wisdom to provide creative teaching. Instead of developing problem-solving techniques, students are taught "plug-in formulas'. Teachers find it easy to spoon-feed them rather than pushing them to think and apply their mind. The lesser said the better about the evaluation system in Indian schools and colleges. Therefore, a university degree is merely a farce and in no way bears the mark of quality education imparted to students.

Second, educational institutions, particularly the ones involved in higher education, exist in isolation and do not have close links with the community, the society, the polity, or the employment market in the country. In countries like the United Kingdom and the United States, the educational institutions have a close link with the community. Students and teachers voluntarily involve themselves with community work and to solve its problems. They also react to the basic problems arising out of the government policies. In India, students are insensitive towards social and community problems like corruption, rape, dowry deaths, female infanticide, murder, or child abuse. Such topics remain confined to their classrooms for discussion.

Theoretical teachings have little relevance to the real world which students enter after completing their studies. They are also indifferent to the political process. Only a small fraction of the students' community is involved in political activity but that too is strongly controlled by the political machine. Unfortunately, these rowdy political figures become the sole representatives of these student communities to express their own party's opinions and to also plan their agitations, to which the majority may not even agree!

Besides training students to apply their minds to various situations and problems, schools and universities also need to educate, train, and prepare today's youth for their future journey in life. They should develop such skills in them that can provide them with resources for earning a living and to prosper in their careers. However, they have failed to do so because they have not established connections with markets that provide jobs and careers to their students. In most of the countries, developed and even not so developed, educational institutions restructure and update the curricula keeping in view the market requirements and the professionals needed for that. They upgrade curricula with the changing markets and advancements in knowledge and technology. The teacher is given complete freedom to re-design the syllabus and update it. Such is the unawareness in these countries, that if a teacher is teaching their class according to an old syllabus, students do not join the course. Therefore, everyone as a unit has to pull up their socks. In India, syllabus revision is a rarity. For years, the development model of the USSR was taught to the Economics (Honours) students even when it had failed and collapsed. The Chinese model is still not being taught. Being a lengthy and often frustrating process, universities do not encourage curriculum revision. Modern academic systems are opposed by teachers in the University of Delhi, though it is being followed in the leading universities of the world and also many in India.

The end result is that universities are far away from the realities of life. The market does not require what universities teach and universities do not teach what the market requires. A student in turn does not develop a personality of one that represents a successful person with a career. Such a situation has created a dichotomy in the society. What is needed today is close understanding and synergy between universities and markets. Universities should develop a mechanism to find out what the market requirements are, and then re-design and re-structure courses according to its findings and research. If such a situation could be achieved, university education would become an asset for today's youth. Only then would they be able to get suitable jobs when they graduate. The present day youth, therefore, in their own interest should demand a system of education that is relevant for their professional life and markets. Till that is possible they have to make their own efforts to develop a market- and career-oriented personality.

Avoid being a failure

In the early months of 1986, a widely circulated magazine for the university students from the Times of India Group of publications asked its readers to nominate the successful Indian of the Year, 1985. The then Prime Minister, Rajiv Gandhi received an unprecedented 65 per cent nominations. Ace runner P. T. Usha had managed a merely six per cent score. The golden girl, however, overtook the Prime Minister next year by bagging a thumping 88 per cent of the nominations—an all-time record. You can guess the percentage nominations received by the 1985 winner.

> **Winners are masters of communication who deliver the hard truth effectively and face problems head on.**

The descent of a mighty Prime Minister, who till then was the "heartthrob" of the youth, in less than a year is something that calls for a serious analysis. The most relevant question is why did a winner plummet to such low levels on the popularity scale within merely 12 months? Analysing the issue was interesting and serious.

The then Editor of *TOI* magazine decided to discuss the issue with a cross-section of the society and the government to find out why the once-popular PM's image crashed in such a short period. People from different strata of the society, particularly the youth, were contacted and the issue discussed. We give here the main findings by the Editor.

Rajiv Gandhi took over the command of India at a very critical time—right after the assassination of the then Prime Minister, Indira Gandhi—on 30 October 1984. India at that time was reeling under the worst crisis in its political history. Confident, optimistic, witty and candid, he inspired hope in all sections of the society. In him the masses found a hope, the dawn of a prosperous and powerful India. Like the majority of the youth, he too had dreams—rosy ones. The result was that everyone gave him a helping hand. But "all these assets now stand considerably depleted and the image possibly, irreparably tarnished," said Jaswant Singh an MP from Bhartiya Janata Party (BJP).

Now the question that arises is, what happened between January 1986 and January 1987 to merit such a drastic change of attitude? During those 12 months, Rajiv moved from the sea of confidence to a crisis of credibility. *India Today* believed that "the overall impression was of government at odds with itself". This was felt because Rajiv Gandhi stumbled from gaffe to political errors to major policy bungling in the domestic as well as in international arenas. *The Hindu* found Rajiv Gandhi a failure on the domestic front as well as in the foreign policy areas. On the domestic front, he displayed a prolonged drift over the destructive Punjab crisis, and the initial handling of the Gorakhnath affair was not only irresponsible but also clumsy. The manner of announcing major funding decisions on his political visits to states was arbitrary and amateurish. The decision to shift the most outstanding member of a quite undistinguished Cabinet, for no credible reasons, from Finance to Defence was unreasonable and did not find favour with the nation. All this caused unfavourable political implications. On the external front, "major weaknesses are the superficial, unfocused and compromising policy towards the Sri Lankan crisis, the inept handling of the border-military crisis with Pakistan and less coherent approach to uneasy relations with China," were the reasons for the falling popularity of Rajiv according to *The Hindu*.

The people did not like his deep distrust of the democratic institutions, the efficient bureaucrats, and of the persons to whom he owed his power. According to *The Illustrated Weekly of India* (now not being published), "Pliable civil servants are rewarded; independent ones are discredited, everyone around is used." A few examples were given to substantiate the view of *The Illustrated Weekly*. The first was the all-time sunken relationship between the Prime Minister and the President. The second was the vesting of extra-constitutional power with Romesh Bhandari. The third was the public humiliation of A. P. Venkateswaran, the then Foreign Secretary, in a press conference that he was being dismissed. Moving his best Cabinet minister from a job where the minister was needed to one where somebody less capable could have done it was the fourth one.

Whimsicalness and eccentricity demonstrated by the chief executive of the country did not go well with the people. The youth did not appreciate all the decision-making process of Rajiv Gandhi and it was expressed in the elections. Not less than 28 secretaries of the Government of India were transferred in a single major reshuffle. Transfers continued and eventually almost 40 of the 80 secretaries at the Centre were shifted. In just a period of two years, he reshuffled the Cabinet six times. All this raised doubts about the PM's maturity. It was thought that power would make him mature but it did not. "It only emboldened him in his way", wrote A. G. Noorani in one of his articles.

His snide school-boyish style was unbecoming of the high office held by him. "It demonstrated petulant arbitrariness, not firmness of command," said Jaswant Singh. The episode connected with Venkateshwaran, C. Srinivasa Sastry, Agriculture Secretary, D. Bandyopadhyaya, Rural Development Secretary, N. R. Reddy, Deputy Director, Special Protection Group, and Sarla Grewal, his own Secretary, proved that he had no real understanding of the political and democratic processes. "And that style of government is a potential threat to Indian democracy", opined Noorani.

The administration cannot be allowed to get perverted to the extent that it is totally subjected to the whims and fancies of the PM. Almost everyone took an adverse notice of his way of dispensing vast sums of public money in those states that were going in for elections. People across the country asked the question: How could the public exchequer be considered the PM's personal property?

Thus came down the image of the most popular person in the country in just a few months' time because the people did not like the leadership style.

Individual vs. institution

Institutions in a country are the backbone that provide foundations to the social structure and family life. Therefore, every civilized society gives higher priority to institutions than individuals. If in a country individuals keep themselves above institutions, neither they nor the institutions prosper. History is a witness to it, and what is going on in India since 1969 proves it. Unfortunately, no efforts are being made by leaders and people to rectify that situation.

If we look back we find that leaders who founded great institutions and respected them not only became great but have acquired a permanent place in history. Jawaharlal Nehru was one such leader. No doubt he is an example of a successful political leader and statesman of the world order. Lal Bahadur Shastri was another such person who gave less importance to self and more to institutions. Unfortunately, leaders who acquired power later gave more importance to themselves and less to institutions. With that began the decline of institutions.

Indira Gandhi became the Prime Minister after the death of Lal Bahadur Shastri in 1966. She found that certain powerful leaders were against her and were using the established institutions to control her working. She decided to destroy institutions that were not to her liking. The first institution that she demolished was that of the Chief Minister. The process gained momentum after 1969 when she acquired absolute power and most of the institutions became defunct. It was a sheer power game in which the established structure of the oldest political party was demolished and the national institutions were made subservient to the political power centre. Whatever was left of institutions was finished during the Emergency. One heard about committed bureaucracy and judiciary. That made civil servants subservient to political leaders and their portages. With the acceptance of that famous slogan, "India is Indira, and Indira is India", the difference between the individual and institution totally disappeared.

Ultimately, neither she nor the institutions survived. Today the Congress, as a political party that dominated the scene for more than 125 years, is in a pitiable condition—almost in shambles. The country too is without a strong and stable leadership. The outcome is that the nation is suffering.

Next was Rajiv Gandhi. He appeared on the political scene as a messiah and swayed everyone at that time. He became the symbol of youth, dynamism and modernisation. Everyone including the Opposition felt that a new era had begun, and it was felt that institutions would be revived. But Rajiv soon developed a deep distrust of the democratic institutions, efficient bureaucrats and the very men whom he owed his power to. He rewarded pliable civil servants and discredited the independent and efficient ones. We all witnessed his great fall from grace.

Introspection needed

When a person proves a failure, it is time for him to do some introspection and find reasons. In the case of a public figure, others should learn from his failures and avoid repeating those mistakes.

President Abraham Lincoln of the United States, who changed the course of the American history by abolishing the slavery system, once said, "you can fool all the people some of the time, but not all the people all the time". You can displease a few and get away with it, but you are bound to suffer if you offend everyone. It is because when you annoy a small group or just one person, a few persons around you are antagonised. Those outside this group who have not been affected badly do not feel unhappy and become your supporters. But if you annoy everyone, you would be left with no friend, only enemies ready to pounce on you each time you are vulnerable. Rajiv Gandhi unfortunately offended everyone, the bureaucracy, the opposition, and even his own party people.

One can't please everyone. Not even Lord Krishna could do that. But also one should not displease everyone and make him or her feel unwanted. During the last three years of his regime Rajiv made everyone feel unhappy by his actions.

One should do one's homework perfectly and avoid being caught on the wrong foot. Rajiv was slipping at every step. In his speech on Independence Day, he repeatedly referred to it as Republic Day. During his visit to Andhra Pradesh in August 1980, he accused N. T. Rama Rao of cheating the tribals of 20 paise on every kilogram of rice. The fact was that the state government was spending 20 paise more on the rice sold to those with an annual income of less than Rs. 6,000. Incidents like these spoiled the image of the former Prime Minister.

Finally, you have to stand by your friends. Rajiv Gandhi dropped every close friend who was helpful to him at one time or the other. The fall of the two Aruns is a classic example of throwing off the best people available to him and depending on cronies and sycophants.

If we want we can be a winner by learning how not to lose the ground on which we stand.

Essentials in a winner

The winner has to be a charismatic, big-picture visionary, and a catalyst. He has to be a manager as well as a leader. There are lots of people who have excellent managerial skills but fail to be great leaders, while a great leader might fail to create a sense of stability in an organisation and not measure up as a manager. Increasingly, Management Gurus have come to believe that the most effective are those who essentially are both managers and leaders. They suggest that to be both they should develop the following skills:

Effective communication

Communication with the larger audience is a must for a manager as well for the leader. **Winners are masters of communication** *and can reach people by appealing to their sense of what is rational. They spend most of their time* communicating. *They are able to formulate their message, however complex it may be, to something that is accessible to those who may not be as knowledge as they are. They believe in simplicity and can say things in a few words. General Electric's Jack Welch is one such good example. He is amazingly articulate and able to convey complicated concepts in just a few phrases.*

Delivering the hard truth

Winners are pragmatists who can deal with difficult realities but still have the optimism and courage to act. **They are able to communicate facts that are difficult to deliver.** *Winston Churchill was one such individual. During the First World War when the Allied forces faced a devastating defeat at Gallipoli (Turkey), resulting in over 100,000 Allied casualties, Churchill took complete responsibility of the defeat and was able to move forward to lead his country to victory in the Second World War.*

Facing problems head on

Successful managers have the positive potential of facing problems head on. **Managers and leaders who are winners do not run away from reality.** *Hard situations demoralise the weak personalities, but winners have the stamina to bear difficulties. In those situations they can inspire people to take action that will enable them to come out of it.*

Though you do not and cannot control levers of power, you have to not only move upwards fast but faster than others otherwise you will be left behind. Therefore, you have to prepare for the market and train yourself in applying your mind in solving situations and problems. You have to make extensive efforts to develop a market- and career-oriented personality by ensuring that you are not at odds with yourself and do not shift from the sea of confidence to crisis of credibility. You have to develop an institutional approach in which institutions and not individuals grow and strengthen. This requires introspecting and finding reasons for your failures. The bottom line is to stand with your friends because it is only they who will come to your support in times of crisis.

Chapter 3

Success System

Every man is a fool for at least five minutes every day; wisdom consists of not exceeding the limit.

ELBERT HUBBARD

If you want to be successful you have to develop a success system. How can you do that? A former Chief of the Army Staff suggested one such system that has been discussed later in the following text. You can also benefit from a research by the Gallup Organization in the United States by adopting the suggested five basic steps to success. Moreover, you can take the help of powerful writers who write on success and lay down ten commandments to move to the fast lane. Finally, do not run away from problems but tackle them by the horn, as suggested by our silver-tongued Lalu Prasad.

Mettle matters

An Indian is a top-grade worker outside India but does not prove his worth within his own country. Why this dichotomy one wonders? Is it because he moves and acts as a team when he works in a foreign country? His hundred per cent attention is towards his work and his wholeheartedly cooperation with his colleagues in carrying out the leader's instructions to achieve the targets and numbers. His participation in strikes, go-slow movements, and *gheraos* is zero. Hence, almost nothing obstructs his climb up the professional ladder. The fact that Indians are the richest community in the United States proves this.

The situation is different when it comes to office work in India. Back home he neither moves nor acts as a team. Much of his time is spent participating in agitations and finding ways of getting more pay for less work. Consequently, he becomes a stagnating, non-thinking worker who is more an individual than a team worker.

General K. Sunderji, a former Chief of the Army Staff, analysed the entire situation and told his officers this: "We have everything—brains, bravery, technology, skills, and ability—all we have to do is to get moving and get our act together and there is no stopping us". He found that the answer lay in increasing interest in careerism, opportunism, and sycophancy amongst Indians responsible for the falling standards of integrity, honour, and patriotism in the country. The General came down heavily on sycophancy. "There is nothing as disgusting as a person who boot-licks the senior, boots the junior and cuts the throats of his peers", said Sunderji. These in fact are the qualities typically characteristic of a sycophant.

If anyone wants to reach the top of one's career, there is no harm in praising his superiors on whom his elevation depends. But seeking advancement by any possible means, rightful or dubious, is not only unethical but also unreasonable and degrading. In India, a crop of opportunists have sprung up who want to get to the top without furthering their capabilities—both in terms of efficiency and knowledge. Such unscrupulous people resort to dubious methods and even indulge in sycophancy to get promotions. However, the worst suffering in the workforce are those who cherish honour and do not compromise with their value system. The number of such persons is miniscule and, therefore, they are unable to protect the integrity of the system and the safety of the nation. But can individuals prosper if the nation's integrity is at stake? In the short run, may be, but in the long run, never!

An interesting question arises here: Why then do good and well-meaning people become sycophants? Perhaps it is due to an ardent desire for comforts and luxuries and a yearning to adopt the five-star culture. There is no harm in aspiring for a good living and a high-profile lifestyle. But one should get it through honest means and hard work. A person who remains unproductive throughout the year—what we call "zero-productivity'—has no right to expect good rewards from life. Sunderji described the phenomenon realistically when he said, "Some have perhaps unthinkingly developed a yearn for five-star culture and ostentation, which flows from neo-rich values in our society, where money is the prime indicator of success and social position. This adoption of mercenary values is disastrous for the self-esteem of the individual…"

Sunderji rightly held the senior officers responsible for the growth of sycophancy in the country. They "have obviously not set the right example. Many of us have not professionally kept ourselves up to date, doctrinally or technologically; we have felt that we have got it made, and rested on our oars; we do not read enough, we do not think enough, and some, of course, have been promoted well beyond their capability." The Army Chief expected seniors to be leaders and pathfinders rather than becoming prisoners of circumstances, a complacent and complaisant person. It is the first category of persons who become Rakesh Sharmas (the first Indian to go into space) and Kiran Bedis, whereas the second category become the 2G and Commonwealth Games 2010 bureaucrats.

Sunderji besides finding faults with officers also gave them tips on how to become more efficient. One way to remain up to date professionally is by meeting experts in their respective professions and learning from their experiences. Attending seminars, workshops, and lectures can also be helpful to pick up a few things that may be useful professionally. Reading magazines and books is another way of improving professionally. Few of us realise that one who does not read enough is like a marooned person, an ignorant literate. Reading is like intoxication—a habit that grows on you. Those who develop interest in reading cannot live without it; but those who do not read find it cumbersome even to lift a book.

> A problem must be dealt with whenever it arises; it can be postponed only temporarily, not permanently.

Sunderji did not appreciate the old British tradition of sticking to the rank level on social occasions like marriages, birthday parties, and cocktails. In fact, in a democratic society, the environment should be more open, even in offices. In the U.S. everyone, even the boss, is called by the first name without using a "mister" or "sir" before the name. In India the practice of "sir"-ing is increasing. In fact, one who does not use the word "sir" while addressing the boss is considered impolite and impertinent. Such a practice is no more relevant with changing times, as it does not encourage the developing of a friendly atmosphere. We should avoid the frequent use of "sir". Seniors should be treated with respect and courtesy, but cringing must be avoided.

Finally, the selfish attitude of officers, who do not care enough for their juniors, is the main cause of the rot in the work system in our country. It is rather unfortunate that heads of institutions and departments do not care for those working under them. This attitude alienates the workers from the institution. Naturally, they try to do work without any serious involvement and shirk any kind of responsibility that comes their way.

The effort of General Sunderji to analyse the attitude of the stagnated and indifferent leaders during his time is relevant even today. In fact, we should all try to imbibe the meaning and spirit of Sunderji's sayings and help in building a respectable and reliable society for a prosperous India.

The success formula

Success is most difficult to achieve. It often eludes most of us. Why only a few are successful while most are not is a billion dollar question often asked by all but seldom answered satisfactorily. Three researchers in the United States working at the Gallup Organization took up the challenge to find reasons for success. They conducted a research on 1,500 prominent men and women. The persons were selected not because of their wealth or social position but because of their achievements.

The Gallup Organization found that the secret success formula contained five traits — common sense, knowing your profession, self-reliance, general intelligence, and the ability to get things done.

Common sense: Seventy-nine per cent of the respondents in the survey said that common sense was an important factor responsible for their success. Though difficult to define, they associated it with the ability to make sound and practical judgements in day-to-day affairs. This helped them arrive at the heart of the problem. They were able to simplify complex problems and explain them clearly to others.

Those who have common sense do not live in ivory towers but in the real world. They move out to see and hear things for themselves. Many people are born with common sense. But many others develop it. You too can acquire it by participating in activities like group discussions, debates, and public speaking. It can also be learnt by observing others —

your friends, your boss, your colleagues. Find out why they committed mistakes and how they could have avoided them. Try and learn things everyday from people who know the best and from people who are on the job. Learn how to set things right and make improvements.

The secret: Respect the knowledge, experience, skills, and wisdom of those around you.

Know your profession: Seventy-five per cent of the respondents were successful because they had acquired specialised knowledge in their own area of activity, learnt the tricks of the trade through observing people at work, through discussions, and so on. They had acquired practical understanding of the crafts in their business. Many had even acquired specialised knowledge through self-education — not merely by going to schools and colleges. The man who had designed and supervised the construction of the Bhakra Dam was merely a matriculate.

Acquiring knowledge to understand your work better cannot be a learn-a-minute phenomenon. It is also not a one-day affair. Learning is a continuous process. Those who have been successful in their life, consider themselves to be students their entire life — always eager to learn more. They never presume to have achieved perfection.

The secret: Never stop learning and never stop wanting to learn. Learning is exciting and generates interest in work and life.

Self-reliance: Seventy-seven per cent of those interviewed said that they had always depended upon their own resources and abilities. They relied on their will power and the ability to do their work. They had known and been aware of what they wanted to achieve and so had made deliberate attempts to achieve what they desired. They had the guts and stamina to work for longer hours and to never feet defeated. They always sought new ways of getting the work done effectively and always worked hard at meeting deadlines.

Self-discipline is necessary for self-reliance. Successful individuals not only discipline themselves but also encourage those who work with them to practice discipline. They review discipline in their organisation from time to time.

The secret: Depend on yourself and be strong. You can bargain only from a position of strength and not when you are standing on weak ground.

General intelligence: About fifty per cent of the respondents believed that the ability to comprehend difficult concepts quickly, and to analyse them clearly and incisively played an important role in their success. This ability is nothing but general intelligence. Many may not agree that those with a higher IQ have better access to success. However, there is no doubt that successful persons have higher IQs than others. They are able to understand situations and things quickly, clearly, and easily. The level of IQ and the general level of intelligence can be enhanced by developing the habit of good and extensive reading and the skill of effective writing. Needed for that is extensive vocabulary. It helps in understanding and expressing situations accurately and effectively. Those who had been interviewed for the survey had read, on an average, 19 books in a year. Having an inquisitive mind, which helps a person to think widely, can raise the general level of intelligence.

The secret: Have multifarious interests in life. It leads to success faster.

Ability to Get Things Done: Seventy-five per cent of the respondents had the capacity to complete their tasks efficiently. They could do it because of three qualities: organisational ability, good work habits, and diligence. They were all solution-oriented and quickly got on the job to complete it. They did not waste time in looking for excuses and avoided rushing blindly in different directions for help. They understood the job and finished it on schedule.

Good communication skills help a person to do things better. These skills also provide specific guidance and instructions so that everyone is able to complete their job as planned. An environment climate of trust and mutual help is created. A successful person ensures that everyone works hard and achieves the desired results. He sends a message across the board that only high standards at work will be accepted. Thus a warm, supportive, and cooperative environment develops at the workplace. Once this is achieved everyone becomes committed to work and all work hard towards the achievement of a common goal.

The secret: You cannot be successful unless you are willing to sit down by yourself and study hard. The best way to improve and became an achiever is to learn from the experience of others. You too can. Can't you?

Ten tips to success

Mark H. McCormack, the author of the bestseller, *What they Don't Teach You at Harvard Business School,* is a highly successful businessman. Known as the most powerful person in sports, he was able to transform sports into a big business. Mark was consultant to more than 50 of the *Fortune* 500 companies, and on his suggestion these companies combined leisure with business and made it an interesting and profitable activity. He also wrote another bestseller and shared his success formulae with others. Of all the success tips that he mentioned, we have picked up ten most important that may be suitable and useful to the Indian youth. Here are the tips.

Never underestimate the importance of money: One must remember that though money is down-rated by most of the religious leaders, it, in fact, is the most important asset that really gives value and respect to a person. Therefore, it is necessary to be concerned about money. It is, after all, the way most businesspersons keep up the score. McCormack accepts that he has always been grateful to his mother for cleverly letting him know this fact.

Don't overestimate the value of money: Money is important but it is not an essential requirement for success. Cash, after all, is by no means the only currency in business. There are other factors that are equally responsible for the success of a person. These are a job well done, respect for others, and the thrill of developing something out of nothing. If you follow these tips and pursue your goal, the success will follow.

You cannot have too many friends in business: Friendship is a rare phenomenon. A true friend is one who derives as much pleasure from your success as you do. But such friends are rare. Nevertheless, they are your best and solid support. One way of developing such persons is to give friends top preference in business, even though you may make more profits from others.

Don't hesitate to say: "I don't know": Do not pretend to know every thing. If you don't know something, say so. No one can know everything. In fact, there is a subtle form of flattery and ego stroking at work when you plead ignorance and ask the other person to educate you. If you are going to bluff, do so out of strength, not ignorance. You can very often say, "I don't know", even when you do know. This could be to find out how much the other person really knows about the subject.

Don't be big mouths: Talking too much and all the time is not a good habit. If you do that and try to speak all the time, you may often put your foot in your mouth. But you would not blunder if you were not speaking. Flapping gums dull your two most important senses—your eyes and ears. It always helps to read the constantly shifting rhythms of your listeners.

Keep your promises, the big ones and the little ones: If you do what you say, you would impress people who matter. On the contrary if you do not keep your promises and forget what you said you would do, you put off people and they do not depend on you. It affects your credibility. Make trust and not suspicion the starting point of any relationship.

Every relationship has a life of its own: Some relationships need tender loving care, some need to be forgotten soon. Once you understand that, be adaptable. Go into a negotiation with as few pre-conceptions as possible. It will not depress you if you get less than what you expected. Also, it will not gladden you if you secured more than what you were bargaining for.

Have eyes for quality: Every work must be taken seriously, whether unimportant or significant. Concentrate on each task, whether trivial or crucial, as if it's the only thing that mattes. If you feel you cannot do a job, do not accept it. It is better not to do a task at all than doing it badly.

Be nice to people: Being sensitive to other people's feelings always yields handsome results. It has an uncanny way of (*i*) alerting you to their business need; (*ii*) sharpening your sense of timing; and (*iii*) getting you out of awkward situations. All things being equal, courtesy can be most economical as it costs nothing but pays high dividends. Be kind to people not because you may need them as you move on in your business and career, but because it is the most pleasant route to the top.

Share credit with others: If you think you are the smartest guy in the town, do not tell the world how smart you are. You may not be that smart as there may be smarter persons in the city. Do not live in a fool's paradise; live in the real world.

McCormack's ten tips may not be the last word on success. But if you keep these in mind, your success graph may be higher than others. Why not give it a try.

Keeping off problems, adds to them

"I want to talk to you," said the stranger as the man opened the door.

"But who are you?" inquired he, a rich man of Isphanhan whose greatest desire was to have a long life.

"I am *Yamdoot*..."

Before the sentence was completed the man slammed the door in Yamdoot's face. Rapidly he got out of the back door, picked up the fastest horse, and fled. For three days and nights he galloped restlessly to find a safe place to hide. Finally he found an inn on reaching Samarkand, a tiny town amidst dense forests. Knocking at the door of the inn, he asked for the safest room. He heaved a sign of relief on getting the keys to one such room. As he turned the key and opened the door to enter, he froze. Yamdoot was sitting on an easy chair.

Rising from his chair, the God of Death spoke, "I am glad you have come here. I wanted to tell you that day that we would meet here in this room at this time 3 days later. But before I could finish my sentence you slammed the door. The appointed time has come. Let us go."

The story is known as "The Appointment of Samarkand". The moral is that a problem can be postponed only temporarily but not permanently. The rich man could have lived in peace for three days if he had not tried to run away from the situation. Most of us react like our friend in the story. We assume that deferment is the solution forever. But the ostrich approach does not solve the problem. On the contrary it complicates the problem further. Once postponed, its handling becomes much more difficult and a heavy price may have to be paid. This is true at the individual as well as the community level.

Life is full of problems: some major, some minor. A few affect our lives seriously, others may not. All of us tackle them either the Kamraj way or the Indira Gandhi way. The former is the *pakaren* approach, while the latter is taking-the-bull-by-its-horns approach. Kamraj has disappeared in oblivion while Indira Gandhi shot into global limelight. She is still remembered for solving the most difficult problems well in time.

The pakaren approach is not the right strategy for solving any problem. In fact, a problem must be dealt with whenever it arises. It may be difficult to solve it at that time, but it is the only way to have a lasting solution. The only requirement for this approach is a positive attitude. To develop it, the first requirement is an understanding of the problem's nature and its origin. Persons associated with the issue should be contacted to find out the root of the problem. A discussion with these persons will give an insight into the reasons of the problem.

Once the problem has been understood, it has to be grappled and handled to solve it permanently. The emphasis should be on finding out the best way of tackling it. This should be an interesting exercise, as various persons will give various suggestions. Some of them may be contradictory. But you will be able to have a number of alternatives to choose from.

The final stage is to mentally analyse and evaluate the whole situation. By this time you are aware of the exact nature of the problem and the possible ways of solving it. Make a thorough appraisal and decide on the best solution. Once a decision is made, implementation in the best possible way must be ensured.

What we have just offered is a general pattern. You don't have to follow it rigidly, as no two situations are similar. You may have to choose the best way of handling the situation according to its nature and severity. Some problems demand quick and immediate action while others give you sufficient time to think and act. How you handle the problem and come out of the situation is a test of your personality.

If you want to reach the top you have to develop a success system. What is essential is to help develop a healthy society in which leaders are pathfinders and not prisoners of circumstances. An effective success system depends on developing traits like common sense, knowing your profession, self-reliance, general intelligence, and having the ability to get things done. Finally do not develop a "pakaren" approach of postponing the problem but adopt the taking-the-bull-by-its-horn approach of solving any problem when it is occurs.

Chapter 4

A Good Job: How to Achieve

Always look purposefully in front.
Don't waste your time looking in the rear view mirror.

H. P. NANDA

A good and satisfying job, whether wage or self-employment, is the test of the success system. Everyone aspires to be employed in the best job, acquire money and status, and enjoy all the comforts that life can offer. In a business, everyone wants to be at the top in terms of turnover and profits. The focus of this chapter is wage employment. Therefore, we will discuss how to prepare to get in to a good job and have a satisfying career.

You have to take the whole process seriously, from the first stage of sending the application to the final stage of attending the interview. Prepare your application carefully and meticulously. Work hard and put your best foot forward. Develop a wide-angle approach. Attend lectures; they are the best way to widen your knowledge base. It is essential to have an effective personality for getting selected in an interview.

Once you find a good job, you enter into the success system, and with planned and intelligent efforts you can end up at the top of your career.

Now read the following carefully.

Preparing for a career

It's a winner's world. In every field of life — games, elections, exams, wars, or career — it is important to win. It is the winner who gets all the attention, appreciation, and applause. The loser falls in the "also- ran" category; just one in the crowd. **You, naturally, would like to be a winner, a successful person**, wouldn't you? Let us find out how you can try and be one.

Begin the campaign by reading the biographies and autobiographies of successful people. And then explore and analyse how different they were from the others of their times; what special qualities they had in them that made them great.

The first thing that you might observe is that were all clear-headed and knew what their objectives were in life. President Abraham Lincoln of the United States, Winston Churchill of Great Britain, General Charles de Gaulle of France, Mao Ze Dong of the Peoples Republic of China, and our own Mahatma Gandhi, Jawaharlal Nehru, and Lal Bahadur Shastri were all-time successful persons. They all had a clear vision of what they wanted to achieve. Interestingly, Lincoln and Shastri were born in extremely poor families. Yet, not only did they achieve their goals but also shaped the destinies of their nations.

In present times Jack Welch of General Electric had established new standards for business performance. Steven Spielberg changed the style of movie-making and Phil Jackson set new standards for coaching basketball teams in Chicago and Los Angeles. In India, we can identify with late Dhirubhai Ambani, K. R. Narayana Murthy, A. P. J. Abdul Kalam, as universally acceptable icons of success. Images of these leaders come readily to mind whenever one thinks of successful persons.

You also should be clear of your objectives in life and make sure that you sincerely endeavour to achieve them. Develop a strategy and a plan to implement it. However, it is suggested that you decide early in life that you want to be a successful person.

In the initial stages of life most of us are undecided on the choice of a career. One way to decide is by appearing in competitions and accepting whatever you get first. This does not naturally ensure you the best, and may cause wastage of precious time and resources also. A friend's son appeared in the engineering and medical exams. He cleared the former but could not pass the latter. He joined the B.E. course. But he was more interested in medical and so appeared in that test again next year. This time he was selected. He left engineering and pursued his medical career. A more positive approach is to have a definite plan. Decide as early as you can about the career you want to take up. Make a list of all the existing training institutions and give priority to top institutions. Nevertheless, other institutions should not be left out. Collect all information regarding training, salary, work benefits, and potential of growth in that particular avenue.

Then start preparing on a war footing. Settle down with the syllabus and the previous year's question papers; try to assess the important topics likely to be asked in the exam and prepare them thoroughly. As a second line of defence prepare yourself for the unexpected questions. Therefore, study even unimportant topics, though not as thoroughly as the important ones. Read through the remaining syllabus casually.

You must start preparing for the competition well in time. If you start preparing much in advance, the chances of success would be higher. If you happen to know much more than others do, selection becomes a surety. You should try to get the maximum marks and not just be satisfied by a passing grade. It is not an exam where you care to pass. In competition there are no pass marks. You have to score high to be selected for the job.

> **Remember, it's a winner's world!**

The preparation should depend on the type of exam you want to take. If it is an objective test, you have to read a lot to fully and clearly understand concepts and all other information. For an essay type test, more importance has to be given to expression and analysis than to information and facts. For it you have to read comprehensively and systematically. Prepare notes and arrange them in such a way that you are able to find the information you need without wasting any time. A strategy prepared on this model would equip you for every situation.

Be confident on the day of the exam. Reach well in time, find your seat in advance and settle down 10 minutes before the starting bell. Last-minute confusion causes mental imbalance and affects your performance in the test. Once the exam starts, keep your cool. Do not panic if you cannot remember things. If you maintain your composure, you will be able to handle difficult questions easily.

Preparing for exams

Examination (exam) is an essential part of life. Though not liked by any one, everyone has to accept it right from one's school days. Even after entering a career, promotional exams are part of most careers.

Exams cause a fear psychosis that leads to nervousness and anxiety. But why should any one dislike exams and fear them? Why can't appearing in exams be a pleasant experience, like participating in a game? Undoubtedly, there will always be excitement and apprehension before the exam. But why should it lead to tension and restlessness? The reason is the lack of correct attitude.

The normal attitude is negative and escapist. We feel the exam is to fail us and, therefore, we want to avoid it. If you could develop a positive and healthy attitude towards exams and decide to achieve excellence through it, you can convert it into an interesting game. The emphatic need is to understand that the exam is not your enemy and you are not its victim. You should regard it as a means by which you can obtain essential qualifications. Let us see how successful persons have made their exam easy during the pre-exam days and the techniques adopted in the exam hall. We give you a plan based on that.

1. Pre-exam days

Develop a positive attitude towards exams by not resenting, fearing and avoiding it. It would be unnatural to say that a feeling of stress should not be in you. It has to be in an average person. Some stress must be felt, as it is useful by fueling your preparation. What is to be checked is the feeling of anxiety, because it reduces your power of concentration and makes preparation difficult. It also affects your power of registration and, therefore, your ability to grasp.

The feeling of anxiety can be avoided by taking three simple steps. *One*, the preparation for the exam must *start well in time*. Do not keep on postponing it till the last minute. Make it an ongoing process. *Two, recreate and refresh* yourself physically and mentally during the preparation and exam days. Recreational activity, however, should be of a short duration and physical exertion should be avoided. *Three, accept exam-preparation as an enjoyment* and not a suffering and distressing experience. Do not think it to be boring.

Understand the exam and its requirements. Get the latest copy of the syllabus. Go through it carefully and see what all it requires. Procure exam papers of the previous few years. See the type of questions that have been set and the topics on which they have been framed. Make a list of such topics and refer to it during the course of your study. Note how many questions have been set in each paper, what choices are provided, and how the marks have been allocated.

You must revise your studies at regular intervals. You should regularly repeat what you want to memorise with the active involvement of the mind. Have a five-step strategy for revision:

Step one: Read your notes carefully and refer to the book when in doubt.

Step two: Revision should be with the recitation method. Recall major points and compare them with your notes to find out how well you remember what you have learnt.

Step three: On the basis of the previous years' question papers and contemporary happenings, prepare a few expected questions.

Step four: Consult your notes and books to prepare answers to the questions selected.

Step five: Share your answers with your friends and classmates and, if possible, with your teachers.

2. Exam hall techniques

The exam hall is the real battleground. You have to fight it out and get the maximum score. An eight-step strategy is suggested:

Step one: Carefully read all the instructions and questions. Mark those that can be best answered by you.

Step two: Plan your time on each question intelligently so that you can answer all the questions. Give time according to the weightage of the question in terms of marks.

Step three: Read the question carefully before answering it. Write only what is required. Do not write what has not been asked from you.

Step four: Organise the answer mentally before you write it.

Step five: Do not spend much time on one single question. Marks in one question do not determine your result; the total marks from all the questions do.

Step six: Do not scribble. Write in a legible handwriting. If you are not understood correctly, you will not be evaluated properly.

Step seven: Keep sufficient time for revision and questions you decided to attempt later. Do not make wild guesses if you are solving objective-type questions, as you can never be sure of negative marking. Revision does help in detecting some minor errors.

Step eight: Do not get tense in the exam hall. To avoid it, do the best you can and leave the rest to God.

If you plan well and develop a positive attitude, you can have a pleasant exam experience and an excellent result. Remember that everybody makes the best effort, but some fail while others succeed and only a few excel. It all depends on the timing, methods and intensity of mental involvement. It is only these three factors that tilt the balance in favour of those who surpass others.

Looking for a job

A good job is the final objective of academic and professional education and training. It is an essential requirement in the pursuit of happiness, social status, and prestige. No doubt, everyone after completing their education seriously look for an appropriate job that can give them a handsome wage and a respectable position in society.

The job market is like any other market where the value of a commodity is determined by its scarcity. That may be the reason why some get more than one job, whereas many may not be able to get even one. The lucky boys and girls graduating in engineering, computer science, medicine, and management are able to get quick employment. Those graduating in other areas may not be as lucky as jobs may not be as many as the number of graduating students. Therefore, the latter category cannot afford to sit back and wait for employers to approach them with an offer of a job. Jobs are there and employers, in their own interest, have to fill them up, you have to make an effort to present yourself, market your personality, and impress the employer to offer the job to you. What should you do to get it? That is what we will discuss in the following text.

> But wait. Before we start on a job hunt, let's make one thing very clear — be ready to receive a large number of rejections. Some organisations may not even reply to or acknowledge your letter. It is part of the game and should cause neither disappointment nor frustration.

Job hunting is a six-step operation: self-analysis, job search, gathering information, formulating strategy, preparation of a resume, and facing the interview.

1. Self-analysis

It is an attempt to know the self — you. It, in fact, is basic to any career planning. Before you enter the job market, you have to find answers to two fundamental questions: The first being, what is your personality? The second being, what are your weak points? This entire exercise is for your benefit and has to be undertaken seriously, thoroughly, and honestly. It involves a bit of research about your background and psychology, and your relationship with others. Some of the questions you may ask yourself can be:

- What are the things you can do best and what are they related with — people, machines, nature and environment, money, or material wants?
- Can you express yourself clearly to others?
- Can you lead a team and get work done or do you just follow directions and do things as you are told to do?
- When you are under pressure, do you manage to work in a normal way or do you become tense?
- Can you work fast with accuracy?
- Do you enjoy new ideas, people, and situations, or are you comfortable with known routines, people, and places?

- Do you wish to work only in your own city or can you go anywhere in India or even abroad?
- Do you prefer a low-salaried secure job or a high-salaried risky one?
- Are you a clock-watcher who likes a ten-to-five job or would you like a job, which does not go by the clock?
- Do you love travelling or do you want to be tied to one place?
- With what kind of people do you feel most comfortable — educated, illiterate, rural, urban, men, women and children, young, old?
- Do you want to work for a large organisation or a small one?
- What are your weak areas?

If you answer these questions honestly and prepare an essay, you would be able to open up to yourself. This exercise will help you analyse things that are important to you, jobs you are interested in, and organisations where you should try applying for a job. You will realise the kind of individual you are, and this piece of information will be invaluable when you prepare your resume and appear for an interview. This inventory on yourself will help you answer several questions that your prospective employers may ask you in the interviews. Such an analysis will serve to be a good memory aid to ensure that you do not forget important details about yourself.

After self-analysis comes career awareness. At first you may not have a clear idea about the various careers available, the nature of work in certain careers, and promotional prospects. Do not hesitate to discuss the subject with your relatives and friends.

You should know that you are in a buyer's market. Being the seller of your service, you are in a weaker position unless you have rare skills. Therefore, make sure you do not concentrate on one type of career or job. Identify at least three alternatives for which you are qualified and are willing to work. If you can afford to have more options, you improve your chances in the job market.

2. Job search

The second equally important step is to understand the job market. Searching for a job means sifting through advertisements in newspapers and magazines. Your job search has to be wide and not confined to one or two newspapers. Many advertisements that appear in *The Hindu* may not be in the *Deccan Herald* and may never be found in *The Hindustan Times*. Dailies such as *The Times of India* and *The Telegraph* may not carry the same advertisement. So you have to develop the habit of going through several newspapers and magazines from different parts of the country to narrow down on a satisfactory job of your choice.

How should you go about doing this? No one can afford to buy all the newspapers and magazines. The best way is to visit a library once a week and go through the files of newspapers and magazines. You must go through advertisements and note down the vacancies, qualifications needed, job-profile, and expectations from the person selected for the job. You should also note down names and addresses of employers, the last date for sending the applications, and the names of the relevant newspapers and magazines and dates of the advertisements.

3. Information gathering

The third step in the job-hunting operation is the collecting of information on jobs connected with your qualifications. You must start from the first important question: Would you like to go in for a government job or a private one? Before you take the final decision, find out the major differences between the two and also the promotional aspects and prospects in each area. It would be better to find out as much as you can about various employers. This part of the operation is rather difficult because the sources of information may not be clear and known. Sometimes you would be groping in the dark and may not be able to find much information. However, you should not be discouraged. Try to get as much information from various other sources. You can talk to your relatives, friends, teachers, and others who may be working in such organisations and companies. Knowing somebody who knows somebody helps, and can sometimes be the most effective way of collecting information. The point is that no single opportunity should be overlooked.

4. Strategy formulation

Developing the best strategy is the fourth step for job hunting. For this it is necessary to make a thorough research on your employer in order to know whether it is worth going in for an interview. This reduces your options and saves a lot of time. Knowledge of your employer is necessary because they may lose interest in you if they realise that you know very little about them. Normally an interview takes 20 to 40 minutes. If you show complete ignorance about your prospective employers, they may not like it and your chances of selection will be reduced. If, on the other hand, they realise that you know quite a lot about them they may feel embellished and your impression on them will be good.

Much before you go for an interview you should try to collect information on things like: Where are the offices of the employer located? What are the major activities in which they are involved? How they are doing in their business? What major problems are they are facing currently? Who are their major competitors and how these competitors are affecting their business? What were the major problems the company was facing in the past? How can you help with the activities of the company in promoting its further growth and progress?

As preparation of a resume and the interview are important we will deal with them separately.

Resume: the first step

The success of a business undertaking primarily depends on the quality of its human resources. This fact has become all the more important in the present-day knowledge companies and learning societies. However, the old misgiving of the colonial times persists—employment could be gained only through the back door. The fact today is that a company, in the face of cut-throat competition, can survive only if it is producing the best at the lowest cost. Only a skillful, knowledgeable, and dedicated team of employees can achieve that. Determined to find out the reality, we met the personnel manager of a reputed company.

Relaxing in the back lawns of this manager's residence, I asked him, "If you don't consider recommendations, how can you call just ten persons for an interview out of hundreds of applications?" He smiled and said, "If you are really interested, come to my office tomorrow and see how we select the ten out of the hundreds of applications."

Next morning I was in his office. He asked his secretary to bring the applications file. Soon she was there with the thick file of applications. The two started going through the applications. The personnel manager would pick up an application, give it a quick glance, flip through the pages, and would either hand it over to the secretary or keep it aside. The process continued for less than two hours and he disposed of about five hundred applications. The secretary was left with only about fifty in the end. After putting aside the last one, the manager looked at me and said, "This was the first stage of selection."

The second stage started soon after. The secretary handed over the fifty applications to the manager. This time he gave each application a few minutes and selected ten for the interview. The secretary then left the room leaving me staring at the manager as puzzled as before.

The manager looked at me and said, "Have you realised how I select candidates for an interview?" I frankly said that I couldn't.

"Very simple," he said. "We want to earn money. So we are always on the lookout for smart, talented, and well-organised persons at the junior as well as the middle levels."

He had two opportunities to assess the personality of the candidate. One was when he was looking at the resume and the other when he was talking to the person at the time of the interview. I could understand the interview stage, but how could he find out from the resume whether the person was organised and efficient? In reply to my question, he asked his secretary to bring back all the applications and asked me to "have a look" myself. A quick glance at each application revealed that it reflected the personality of the candidate.

A resume *is the first encounter of the candidate with the selector*. This piece of paper represents the candidate. Therefore, a candidate who presents his resume in an impressive style stands a better chance of being short-listed for an interview. Many a times a good resume is set aside only because it is unable to create the right kind of impression on the selector. We could see several good applications rejected only because they were either not neatly typed or the information was not properly presented. The manager told me that if a candidate could not send a presentable resume or could not present facts of his life in an impressive way how would he take his job seriously?

After making a careful survey of the selected and rejected applications, I came to the conclusion that the entire operation of sending applications should be divided into four stages — collection of information, drafting the application, getting it typeset, and forwarding it to the concerned person. This has been discussed in detail in the next section.

Resume writing

A resume is a marketing tool used to secure a new job, a promotion, or an increase in salary. A typical resume contains a summary of relevant job experience and education. It is typically the first thing that a potential employer encounters regarding those interested in the job. It is typically used to screen applicants.

1. Preparing a resume

You should prepare your resume, also known as a bio-data or personal profile, as a statement of your personality and qualifications. That's why your resume should present facts in such a way that they promote your personality. Remember it would be your first introduction to the company. It should attract their attention, arouse their interest in you, and prompt them to consider you for the job. They should feel that only you are the right person they were looking for.

To create a good impression make sure your resume is simple, lucid, and packed with relevant information. It should be accompanied with a covering letter. Maximum care should be taken to see that the contents of the covering letter do not repeat the data in your resume. The resume has to be prepared and revised thoroughly and carefully. It must be shown to two knowledgeable persons and then typed neatly and carefully on a computer. It must briefly present your educational qualifications, professional experiences, your interests, and most importantly your goals. In brief, you should write on the following points:

Who you are?
What do you know?
What have you done?
What would you like to do?
What can you do for the employer?

The first content in your resume should be your personal information. Therefore, compile correct and detailed information about your age, academic qualifications, co-curricular activities, work experience, visits abroad, honours bestowed upon you, publications, seminars attended and papers read, public offices held, and membership of professional associations. Do not leave out any information even if you think it is not important.

Collect all the relevant information in one place. Once it has been collected, categorise it as experience, education, and other interests. While listing your experiences, also include the jobs you have performed but were not paid for.

The academic section should be in a tabular form containing the following details:

Name of institutions:

Degrees/certificates:

Specialisation:

Performance:

Honours, awards, and scholarships:

The description of each work profile must include details of your position, employer, location, and duration of work. It is easier to map your career path if you ask yourself relevant questions. How did you accomplish your role? Why did you choose this method? What were the results of your choice? The answers will help you emphasise your responsibilities better and define your accomplishments with numbers and specific skills.

The last section should be an additional information section. It should include positions held in professional and student associations, participation in sports, extracurricular activities, special skills, interests, and similar activities.

Your resume should not be a detailed description of you. It should be brief and indicative of what you have done in the past. A good-sized resume should not exceed two pages. You must be precise and provide all the information regarding your education, work experience, and career objectives.

Always keep in mind that the purpose of the resume is to introduce yourself to an employer who may not have seen you at all. Do not include your photograph unless you are applying for a job as a model or an actor.

Equally important is to understand what not to include in the resume. Never mention your weaknesses, be it poor academic scores or unflattering performance at work. Also, it is not advisable to include details of your income and reasons for leaving previous jobs, unless there have been far too many job-hops.

Resume writing should not be done in a hurry. You should spend sufficient time to select information for the resume and read it carefully in its prepared form. You can organise the information in a chronological or reverse chronological or a functional format. Each has its own advantages.

Reverse chronological format is widely used because it helps employers to understand a candidate"s growth along a timeline. On the contrary, the functional format aims at targeting specific and relevant skills that a recruiter is looking for.

You should be extremely careful in ensuring that there are no spelling and grammatical mistakes in your resume.

The resume should be typed and spaced properly and a good printout should be procured on a quality bond paper. Use a business font, such as Arial, in 12 point size, and use bulleted points with sufficient white spaces to avoid clutter. The last page of a multi-page resume should be at least two-thirds full. Unless specified otherwise, use a PDF file format for attachments and text format (ASCII) in online text boxes. Avoid fancy designs and special effects; simplicity and professionalism are the cornerstones of an effective resume.

The entire text should be set in an impressive format. Leave appropriate margins on the left and the right side of the paper. The left-hand margin may be four centimetres and the right hand margin two centimetres. The top and bottom margins should be four and three centimetres, respectively. Your name and the position for which you are applying should be boldly typed at the top of the first page. Each heading should be in bold and the details should start from the next line. Leave some space between the two headings. Number all the pages before stapling them.

Every page of the resume should carry your name.

The final resume should be carefully read for corrections. You should be extremely careful in ensuring that there are no spelling and grammatical mistakes in your resume. The ideal application should have no corrections. Avoid edits and alterations.

The last step is forwarding the application. Send the application in an A-4 size envelope so that there are no folds. If that is not possible, fold the application neatly and choose the right-sized envelope. Write the address and affix stamps of correct value. Better if you send the application by courier service.

Send a fresh printout and not a photocopy with your application. If you send a photocopy, the impression would be that you are sending it by the dozens. It does not create a good impression on the person who would be reading your resume and making the final selection.

These days the employers do accept applications by e-mail too. Some insist on e-mails and do not accept applications through postal mail. In that case prepare the resume on the pattern discussed above and send it as an attachment. Text gets gobbled up and the employer may not like to look at such a resume. That is why these days many companies want it via e-mail only. In that situation, do not send your resume by postal mail. But if there is an option, send by both.

You should make the work easy for the HR person by incorporating job-specific keywords. You can consult your teachers, senior students, and friends for words and phrases related to your domain. The HR Manager involved in campus recruitment opines that he always looks for keywords to select the best resumes before short listing candidates for interviews. So never undermine the power of the right words.

One thing should be clear to you that your resume serves as a sales pitch for your capabilities. You cannot get a job only because of good resume. It can only help you in getting shortlisted for the interview. Therefore, the resume should be aimed at this goal. The next step, which is the interview, will only convince the recruiter whether you should be offered a job or not.

When you are sending an application, you are taking your first step out. Put your best foot forward. You will surely succeed.

2. Have brand differentiation

Both Pepsi & Coke are sugar-water syrups. Yet both are different brands and have the perception of being different products, though similar.

In the same way you can write a resume to make you a brand different from other similar professionals. It is like your personal advertisement enticing your potential employer to look at you as a good candidate. Therefore, it is the most important document on your personality. Remember the selector has not met you face to face and so does not know who you are. But he still develops a perception about you by just reading what you have written about yourself.

If you want to develop a positive perception about you, plan your resume keeping in view the following four things:

One: *Understanding the recruiter psyche when he reads your resume.*

Two: *How to design a resume that sells. Remember your resume is your first battle.*

Three: *How to bring out the REAL YOU through the resume.*

Four: *How to differentiate yourself through your resume.*

The battle begins: the group discussion

At ten in the morning, a group of final year students of MBA are sitting in a small placement room of a reputed business school. They have gathered here to be considered for their first job in a big multinational financial company. They are waiting to be called for the Group Discussion (GD).

The HR manager arrives and takes the group to the discussion room. They are seated around a horseshoe shaped table and briefed on the pattern of the discussion and the rules to be followed. The HR manager asks one of the candidates to come and pick up a chit from a heap. It mentions the topic for discussion. The manager announces the topic from the chit and takes a back seat. Seated in front are the interview board members.

The discussion starts. It's a free-for-all with several students speaking at the same time. Feeble voices are drowned in the din created by more vocal ones. One boy is dominating the discussion, cutting all others to pieces. Another aggressive fellow is trying to dominate the discussion. Everyone feels that one of these two would be selected. However, in the final list of selected candidates, both are no where.

Group discussion, of late, has become an important tool for selecting persons, particularly for well-paid jobs. Good companies in the private and public sectors are using this technique widely for selecting management trainees and business executives. The Services Selection Board (SSB), that selects officers for the Indian defence services, seems to have introduced and developed this method of eliminating candidates. It is still using this technique in its selection process. Its usefulness has been accepted now by and large by all corporate selectors.

Why has GD become an important tool for selection? The reason is that GD is a complete personality test. After a 20-minute discussion of this kind, the varied personalities of the group members are exposed. The selection board can judge whether the person has self-confidence, tact, a cool temperament, or an alert mind. Can he convince others that what he thinks is right? In a way it is a supplementary technique to personal interview to test how the interviewee would behave in a group. So let us discuss how you should participate in a group discussion.

Group discussion is a favourite test used by most selectors to test six skills:

Leadership qualities
Interpersonal skills
Ability to work in team
Clarity of thought
Logical thinking
Tact

You might ask a question: How can somebody judge as many as six attributes in a 30-minute GD? This remains a secret but what is important is how you can create an impression on the mind of the selector that you possess all the six qualities in abundance.

1. Dressing for the occasion

The clothes you select to wear to the group discussion should give you a cool, calm, and composed look. It is not necessary that you should be formally dressed either in a business suit or safari suit. However, the choice of clothes, colour, and combination should reflect some degree of sophistication. For boys, the choice is extremely limited namely shirt, trouser, coat, or jacket (though optional) along with a necktie. Some of the colours such as blue, grey, black, and their different combinations do give a more formal executive look. Jeans, T-shirt, or kurta-pajamas are never to be worn for this occasion. The choices are wide ranging for girls as they may choose to wear a saree, kurta-salwar suit, or a business-suit. The key consideration should be the comfort level one gets in a particular outfit.

You should always carry a folder or file that must contain a writing pad, pen, certificates (photocopies or original) as per the requirements or any other document mentioned in the call letter. Don't carry bulky notes for reading. One should make sure that he reaches the venue at least 15–20 minutes in advance, because the traffic situation is unpredictable especially in metropolitan cities. It is better to wait there for some time and get acclimatised rather than getting tense on reaching late.

2. GD in action

After some initial formalities you will be directed to the venue for the GD. You may have to wait for some time before actually being called for the GD. This waiting time can be utilised to acquaint yourself with the other members of the group. This activity helps you in overcoming the initial hitch and creates a comfort level. Building a rapport with the team will surely help you at the time of the actual discussion.

On reaching the designated room for the GD, you may find the seating arrangement may be circular, rectangular, or semi-circular. Usually the seats are allotted by the person who conducts the GD. However, in case you are given the choice to select your seat, occupy a seat that gives you the chance to address the maximum number of members in the group. Whichever place you occupy, make yourself comfortable at the earliest. Wait for the instructions to be explained about the topic and do not get into a rush or panic.

3. Play your role

During the GD you can play different roles. Which role has to be played when, is a key issue that one has to understand. Judith Dwyer in *Business Communication: Strategies and Skills* has mentioned different roles that one can play.

During the GD one should adopt a positive role that can be presented in different ways. For a simple understanding of this let us take the following topic:

Should IIT Graduates be made to sign a bond to serve their country for 5 years so as to limit brain-drain?

The positive task roles can be played in one of the following ways:

Initiator: *"Let's try to understand and debate upon the quality of IIT graduates and their possible contribution to this nation in case they do decide to stay back."*

Information seeker: *"Can anyone give some statistics about the number of IIT graduates who have gone abroad in the last few years?"*

Information giver: *"As per the estimates of IIT, Kanpur, 30 per cent of IIT graduates move abroad within three years of completing their education."*

Opinion seeker: *"Don't you think that they can contribute to the nation even when they are abroad."*

Opinion giver: *"Surely, I agree, because many of the IIT alumni have contributed significantly to their institutions as well as the country in a variety of ways."*

Clarifier: *"We need to get hold of the data to understand the different ways in which IIT graduates have contributed to the nation."*

Summariser: *"As the time to summarise is only two minutes, I wish to say that the group is divided with respect to the topic. But many of us agree that signing a bond may not be a solution to the problem of brain drain."*

Along with these task roles, there are a number of maintenance roles that may be played by the participants as the GD develops further and opposing points of view start trickling in. Given below are some of the positive maintenance roles that can be played accompanied with their typical dialogue:

Social supporter: *"I think our discussion has generated some valuable points."*

Harmoniser: *"No. 7 and 8 have analysed the topic from different perspectives. Let us see if we can gather something* *from both points of view."* (*In a GD the participants are allotted numbers and they are not supposed to use personal names even if they know it*).

Energiser: *"It's nice that No. 3 has put forth the foreign exchange inflow in the country as one of the benefits our country gets from these IITians working abroad. Let's explore this point further."*

Compromiser: *"Our group is clearly divided on the topic. It would be pertinent in case we look at the relative merits and demerits of all the arguments."*

Gatekeeper: *"May we have the opinion of No. 5 on this issue? It may add a new dimension to our discussion."*

4. Act as situation demands

After understanding the different roles that can be played by a GD participant, one should choose the role one wants to play and this should depend upon the stage and manner in which the group discussion is flowing. In case the situation is too tense and a lot of argumentative encounters take place, one should immediately play the role of "Harmoniser" to diffuse the situation. In case your knowledge on the topic is very limited, do not hesitate to assume the role of an "Information seeker" or "Clarifier". If you find one of the participants could not get the chance to contribute then get into the role of a "Gatekeeper" immediately, it would reflect positively on your interpersonal skills.

Similarly, take the initiative to start the discussion and set the tone carefully elucidating the different sub-themes for deliberations. If you do not have much idea about the topic and could not contribute effectively during the GD then it would be advisable to note down points given by others to play the role of "Summariser" at the end. When you find the discussion to be monotonous and the participants unenthusiastic, play the role of "Energiser" to fuel a new leash of life in the GD.

5. Never adopt a negative role

One should never adopt a negative or disruptive role in a GD as this reflects an unconstructive impression about the personality of the candidate. In case you have a point of view, wait for the opportune moment to get into the discussion. The best time to get in is, when the other person is nearing the end of a sentence. Sometimes, the other person may not let you to present your point of view. Raise your voice a bit at times to show assertiveness but avoid aggression. Maintain eye contact with the group members. Do not create sub-groups within a group and try to address all the members. Avoid personal attacks and do not show off during the GD. Avoid too much interruption and be a good listener also. There is no need to monopolise the GD because it is a discussion among equals.

6. Imagining the role

When you are participating in a GD imagine yourself in the role of an executive in a corporate meeting and act accordingly. There are no marks for demeaning or insulting others. How passionate you are in terms of building the discussion, taking the group members along, arriving at the conclusion, resolving the conflicts, diffusing the tense situation among others, are the key criteria for evaluation. Be a group member but also retain your identity as an individual so that the selectors can rate you. More importantly, keep track of time. Though there cannot be a single yardstick in a GD of 20 minutes comprising ten participants, one should speak for around 2 to 3 minutes. So prepare well, put your best foot forward and hope for the best.

7. What to avoid in a GD

Most of the candidates who participate in a group discussion do not understand the real purpose behind this test. They think that their debating quality and ability is being tested.

Therefore, they try to prove themselves as effective and aggressive speakers. Everyone shows that he has the capacity to dominate others and tries to score debating points. All these notions are erroneous. The result is that many good candidates, who are intelligent otherwise, do not get selected because they make some common mistakes. The most common one is the desire to dominate the discussion. In fact, one should try to speak effectively. It does not mean speaking exclusively and not allowing others to speak. You must listen to others and understand their points of view. Only then can you argue convincingly.

It is important to argue each point logically. Most of the participants make a point but cannot substantiate it properly. Many times they contradict a certain point without explaining why. A few can be seen raising their voices during the discussion, using their vocal cords rather than their minds. Many keep changing sides frequently. A good number of participants keep interrupting while others are speaking, thus not allowing other participants to complete their point.

A Group Discussion mimics a battlefield in which you fire arguments instead of bullets. Therefore, you must enter into a GD as a soldier would enter into a battlefield. This implies that you should have a strategy and should know how to implement it. Immediately after the topic is announced you should decide your strategy—whether you plan to agree or disagree. You have to think fast and decide within a minute. You should also think of arguments, examples, and views that can help you substantiate your strategy.

You must have a basic stand on the issue that should never be changed drastically. However, this does not mean that your approach should be rigid. During the course of the GD when you find that other person has a good point, you should accept that and modify your view.

Your behaviour and body language during the discussion should be sophisticated and serious. You should not be frivolous. However, this does not mean that you should be poker-faced throughout the discussion. Your behaviour should be normal. You should show all niceties and must have a positive approach. For example, there is no need to say, "You are wrong." Instead you can say, "Yes, you may be right."

You must know when to support and when to oppose. It is not good to keep supporting or opposing others. If you are criticising an argument extended by another participant, do not make fun of them. Do not try to prove that what he was saying was worthless. Be courteous and say a good word about their views. Then keep your arguments to prove that their views were wrong. Similarly, do not provide total support when you agree with an argument. When you are giving your view you must mention the reason of supporting the view or the argument. Your view should not be similar to the one extended by another candidate.

The preparations for a GD cannot be overnight. It has to be done over a period of time. You have to develop certain traits, mannerisms, and a pleasant way of speaking. There are no easy lessons and you can only learn by experience. The best way to learn is to participate in discussions whenever you get an opportunity. Organise small discussions and meet frequently in small groups to discuss various topics and issues. Whenever it is possible invite knowledgeable and experienced persons to be present during the discussion and give an assessment of your performance.

The interview

An interview is an essential part of a job-selection. In today's selection process the interview has become far more important than the written test. The written exam can judge only your academic knowledge. Your personality can only be assessed at the time of the interview. It is therefore imperative that you take an interview seriously and give more importance to it than the written test. Any one who wants to get an employment — whatever may be the level —

has to face an interview. No job is offered to a person without it. In fact, the final selection of a candidate depends on the impression he creates on the person on the other side of the table during an interview. Therefore, you must know what an interviewer expects from a candidate who wants to become a prospective employee in that organisation.

An interview can be formal or informal. In the formal interview, a board of experts interviews the candidate. All the board members jointly assess the candidate. In an informal interview, popular in developed countries but gaining importance in India too, the candidate meets each person connected with his work separately. This is a lengthy process and is normally adopted for very senior level positions.

Normally a successful interview lasts for about 30 minutes. During this period the interviewer wants to know as much as possible about the candidate. On the basis of the experience of being on the interview board of various selection processes it can be said that an interviewer wants to examine the personality of the interviewee on four counts — appearance, behaviour, expression, and knowledge.

1. Appearance

As you enter the interview room, the members of the interview board watch you. They have a complete view of you and this initial impact is important and lasting. If you are properly dressed and well groomed, it is likely to create a positive impression. Candidates appearing either overdressed or wearing casual clothes make a poor show. If you wear a suit and tie in sultry weather of July or August you may not be able to create a good impression. Similarly appearing in jeans and a T-shirt with *Kolhapuri chappals* would definitely not give a serious impression. Therefore, you should be dressed in such a way that it looks formal and is in accordance with the weather of your city and the current fashion. You should always look smart in whatever outfit you wear.

2. Behaviour

After appearance comes behaviour. Your behaviour becomes conspicuous the moment you establish contact with the interview board. The way you move yourself, sit in the chair, place your hands and your briefcase and talk to the board members reflects your behaviour. If you walk in a sloppy way, talk either loudly or slowly, get irritated on small points, start showing documents and books without being asked, you exhibit bad behaviour. You should enter the room smartly, move towards the chair in a dignified way, wish the board and sit in the chair when asked to do so. Thank the board at the end of the interview. During the interview you should place the briefcase close to the chair, sit cross-legged and hands on your lap and talk to the board members in your normal way.

You should always be careful about your behaviour. You should have an impressive style that carries a mark of distinction. It should be the distinctive way in which you behave, appear, and express yourself. You should show that you are cooperative, disciplined, hard working, positive, and constructive. In all, display an outgoing style and an open mind.

3. Expression

An important aspect of the interview is the way you express yourself. You may be with board members for about 30 minutes to answer their various questions. Your expression conveys your views and opinions. The first important factor of good expression is clarity of mind and speech. You should be able to show that your thought process is balanced and that you can convey your views clearly to others. This requires choosing your words carefully. You should not use words that express contradictory meanings. Never use bombastic words, clichés, or flowery language. The language used should also not be slang or lifted from popular films or novels. The terminology should be of normal usage and relevance. Ambiguous statements should be avoided. If you are not aware of the correct facts and information, it is better to confess rather than guess and give wrong information. Always be sure that your facts and information are correct when you are talking to the board.

The second aspect of expression is that you should be able to convey your point of view. In the interview you may be asked questions where you have to either agree or disagree with the view. You should have an opinion on the issue and should be able to convince the board members about your views. They may not agree with your view and argument. But you should not feel offended. Even if you feel so, do not let it be expressed on your face.

You should be able to create an impact by using correct expressions. Give an impression of being a leader. Show that you can cooperate and get cooperation; that you can share views and make people accept your authority and decisions, and also that you can implement them. Show that you have convictions. A good candidate would not prove the interviewer wrong with a grin.

4. Knowledge

Appearance, behaviour, and expression are all superstructures. The foundation is the knowledge that you acquire during your school and higher education. Knowledge has two aspects — width and depth. Wide knowledge means that you know much more than your own area of specialistion. Besides knowing your subject you should be aware of the major happenings around the world, your nation, and your city. You should have interests in other subjects like environment, wildlife, culture, and history. Develop hobbies like films, reading, music, and theatre.

Deep knowledge means that you know your subject in great detail. For example, if you are discussing the Indo-Pak relations you should know about the geography, history, socio-political aspects, international implications, and the contemporary problems being faced by the two countries.

Wide and deep knowledge is gained through reading and listening. Be a serious, voracious, and avid reader, and devote three to four hours every day to reading. Your readings should include books, newspapers, and magazines. If you do not get much time every day compensate it on Sundays and holidays. Never justify your ignorance by saying that any subject other than your own does not interest you. Read on various topics and select a few topics for developing continuing interest.

Listening, at times, is more important than reading. Be a keen listener and listen attentively to assimilate major facts. Store them in your brain without conscious effort. Make use of them at appropriate times. Do not interrupt others while they speak and learn even as you listen.

Finally, never consider yourself to be perfect. You are a human being and, therefore, susceptible to flaws. However, try to conform to the highest standards and reach as close to perfection as possible.

Preparing for an interview

The interview is the final stage of the entire selection process. Therefore, your performance determines your fate. As stated earlier you are operating in a buyer's market. Hence, you have to project yourself as the most suitable person for the job. The process of an interview, let there be no doubt, involves creating an impression on someone superior to you. Your personality, knowledge, and behaviour should impress the interviewer.

Homework: The first step to a successful interview is doing some serious homework. The moment you get the interview call your preparations should start for it. Find out about the organisation and the type of work that you would be asked to do. Collect all the information about the job—the nature, salary, training, and growth prospects. Try to get in touch with some of the employees of the organisation to learn about the company's activities. Also try to find out the problems being faced by the organisation and plan how you would handle some of them.

Organise your material: The second step is to collect all necessary papers that you may need during the interview. These could be your credentials, degrees, certificates, testimonials, and copies of your writings. Carry a copy of the book if you have authored any book or have contributed to a book. All these must be properly arranged and you must remember the order in which you have kept them in your briefcase.

Mock interview: Much before the interview, may be a few days before, you should have a mock interview. You can request one of your friends or parents to act as an interviewer. He could question you on your studies, current happenings in the national and international scene, problems the country is facing, and your interest in sports and your hobbies. Later when the mock interview is over, analyse your replies and what were the shortcomings or what more could have been said. The mock interview would reveal your weak points and help you improve them before the actual interview.

You may be given the option to ask questions after the board members have finished. You should ask relevant and intelligent questions on the type of work you would be asked to do, your training programme, future plans of the company, and the future prospects in the job.

On the D-day make sure that you reach the place of interview much before the allotted time. Often persons get late because they do not know the exact location and take more time than they initially thought they would take. You should go a day earlier to know where the exact location of the interview place is. Reaching late is worse than not reaching at all. It shows you in a poor light as the interview board may develop a feeling that you are neither responsible nor organised. You feel frustrated and confused and that may affect your performance during the interview. You may falter in your replies or give wrong information.

When you are called in, enter with confidence and poise. Look at the key person on the board – the chairman – who is responsible for conducting the entire interview. Follow his instructions relating with handshake and seating. The chairman will set the ball rolling or may ask another member to begin. When the chairman or any board member is speaking, do not interrupt him. Listen carefully and look at the person when you are reacting. While replying remain cool, organised, and responsible. Give brief and precise answers. If your opinion is asked, express the one that you can defend, if need be.

It is a wrong impression that you have to always agree with the interview board. If you have different views, you can express them but do not be dogmatic. You should be realist and practical. Show perception and a wide outlook in your answers.

Sometimes the interviewer may ask questions that you may feel are absurd. Do not get irritated. Such questions may be put to see how you would react in unexpected situations. For instance, take a question like this: "What would you do if your shoestring snaps on your way to interview?" You would not create a realistic and good impression if you say "I keep a second pair of shoestrings with me." No one keeps a second pair. You can say that you would tie up with the torn shoelaces and buy a new set later.

When the interview is over, thank the chairman and the board members. Move out of the room confidently and gracefully. Back home, have a post-interview analysis to see where you went wrong. Find out how you could have fared better. Learn from your mistakes. Improve upon them in your next interview if you were not lucky this time.

The interview is the final stage of the entire selection process. Therefore, your performance determines your fate. Remember, that most of you are operating in a buyers' market. Hence, you have to project yourself as the most suitable person for the job.

About the interview

The interview aims at judging you in a face-to-face discussion. The selector is looking at the following:

Content offered by the candidate

Attitude – How does the candidate react to unfamiliar circumstances

Creativity

Logical thinking ability

Communication skills

Clarity of thought and purpose

It might sound confusing as to how would one present all these at the same time. There is nothing to fear, because you can prepare yourself to acquire all these qualities, as most of the interviews follow some typical formats. It, therefore, becomes possible to equip oneself with all these qualities to make a lasting impression.

Know...

How do they judge you in an interview? The psyche of the interviewer.

What are the different types of interviews – the content interview, the HR interview, and the attitude interview and how to handle them.

Frequently asked questions in the interview? How to handle them?

How to impress the interviewer in your domain?

Why do the brilliant in academics not get selected

Every placement session leaves certain trails that the students are not able to comprehend. One is that many times those brilliant in academics do not get a good job while those not very brilliant or not having high scores get good jobs. I know a number of students who were outstanding throughout their academic career, but were not able to get the best jobs. Why does this happen?

Wrong perception

The main reason is that those who are involved only in academics have a wrong perception of the job market. They believe that big companies are interested in highly academic candidates. Therefore, they concentrate only on studies and withdraw themselves completely from the non-academic life on the campus. They take no interest in dramatics, music, sports, or films. They also do not read widely on history, current problems, philosophy, and international relations. The result is that though they can explain the complicated problems of marketing or finance, they fail to discuss why the Indian hockey is being pushed out of the international arena. No doubt they are excellent in their own subject, but are totally blank when it comes to finer things in life, such as art, culture, and entertainment.

Just to know more on this, I met the Vice-President (HR) of a company that had rejected such a person. I discussed with him the reasons why brilliant candidates like him were left out while others less brilliant were selected. The VP told me that he was definitely interested in intelligent people but preferred those who could approach a problem from various angles—social, political, economic, psychological, and cultural. And he tested them in different ways to find out how wide-ranging their thinking was. Written tests, group discussions, and personal interviews were the different tools to find out whether the person carries a wide-ranging personality? What he wanted to test was how a candidate would react in critical situations in real situations.

The selection strategy has changed during the last few years. Top managers have learnt from experience that those who are good academicians may not necessarily prove to be good managers when involved in a job. The VP gave an example. There were frequent breakdowns in one of the shop floors and the manager was perplexed. He got the equipment repaired but it broke down again. As he was not able to solve the problem, a senior manager was called to handle the situation. This manager was able to solve the problem and the breakdowns stopped. The senior manager did not perform miracles. He only talked to workers who were handling the machines. He found out that they had some long-standing grievances that were being ignored by the previous manager. To show their anger and discontentment the workers were not operating the machines carefully. He investigated the complete problem, took certain steps to remove the workers' grievances, and the situation became normal.

Read widely and think broadly

Unfortunately a large number of young boys and girls do not realise the importance of reading widely and thinking broadly. When they do not show these qualities at the time of placement and miss out on being employed in high-profile companies, they feel dejected and complain of favouritism. One who is entering the job market must know that the top management does not like to be disturbed for petty and routine problems. Therefore, anyone holding a responsible position should take care of problems at his level. A wide perspective enables you to achieve solutions to difficult and complicated problems and situations.

The time you spend at the business school is the best period to broaden your outlook and perspective. Reading general books, discussing political developments, analysing contemporary problems, organising cultural events, going on treks and tours, are a few different ways in which one can learn what books and classroom lectures do not teach. You can learn only when you come face to face with problems and meet different types of people. It helps you in learning the different aspects of life. You become a realist and not a theorist.

Make sure that you develop all aspects of your personality rather than only one. You then possess a well-rounded or a balanced personality.

> **Blurb 1**
>
> *You should be able to create an impact by using correct expressions. Give an impression of being a leader. Show that you can cooperate and also get cooperation; that you can share views and make people accept your authority and decisions, and that you can implement them. Show that you have convictions. A good candidate would not prove the interviewer wrong with a grin.*
>
> **Blurb 2**
>
> *One who is entering the job market must know that the top management does not like to be disturbed for petty and routine problems. Therefore, anyone holding a responsible position should take care of problems at his level. A wide perspective enables you to achieve solutions to difficult and complicated problems and situations.*

Developing a wide perspective

Vikas has been an outstanding student throughout his academic career. Always a topper, he never secured less than 98 per cent marks. He was in the first ten in the IIT-JEE and was able to choose his first choice—electronic engineering. During his 4 years at IIT-Delhi he was the front-ranking student, good in every subject taught to him. No doubt everyone envied him. It was a common belief that he would get the best job once he graduated. He too was sure that placement would be no problem to him. In fact, he was so sure that he presumed having at least half a dozen appointment letters in his pocket. But at the time of placement, students much lower than him in rank were able to get better jobs than him and also much before he was able to get a job. He did get a job but not the best one.

Why could Vikas, the best student of IIT-Delhi, not get the best job? The reason was that Vikas had a wrong perception of the job market. He had believed that big companies were interested in highly academic candidates for their companies. Therefore, he concentrated only on studies and withdrew himself completely from the non-academic life of the campus. He took no interest in dramatics, music, sports, or films. He also did not read widely on history, current problems, philosophy, and international affairs. The result was that though he could explain the complicated problems of electronic science, he could not discuss why Indian hockey was being pushed out of the international arena. He was excellent in his own subject but was totally blank when it came to finer things in life, such as art, culture, and entertainment.

Just to know more on this, I met the Vice-President (HR) of the company that had rejected Vikas. I discussed with him the reasons why brilliant candidates like Vikas were left out while others less brilliant were selected. The VP told me that he was definitely interested in hiring intelligent people but also preferred those who could approach a problem from various angles—social, political, economic, psychological, and cultural. And he tested them in different ways to find out how wide-ranging their thinking was. Written tests, group discussions, and personal interviews were the different tools to find out whether the person possessed a wide-ranging personality? What he wanted to test was how a candidate would react in critical situations in real life.

The selection strategy has changed during the last few years. Top managers have learnt from experience that those who are good academicians may not necessarily prove to be good officers or managers. Having a broad perspective on various matters enables you to achieve solutions to difficult and complicated problems and situations.

The time you spend at the college or university is the best period to broaden your outlook and perspective. Reading general books, discussing political developments, analysing contemporary problems, organising cultural events, going on treks and tours are a few different ways in which one can learn what books and classroom lectures do not teach. You can learn only when you come face to face with problems and meet different types of people. It helps you in learning different aspects of life. You become a realist and not a theorist.

As young people, you are still in the learning stage. Make sure that you develop all aspects of your personality rather than only one. You then are able to possess a well-rounded or a balanced personality.

Learning from lectures

More often than not, when we talk about studies, we refer either to reading a book or to making notes. The habit of thinking, discussions, application of mind, and attending lectures seldom come to our mind as tool of study. However, we should give adequate importance to the non-reading tools of learning that can improve learning in more ways than one. Going to listen to lectures is one such method. Lectures are frankly expository, that is, their purpose is to convey information, subject-matter, or techniques.

Lectures are not popular with most of us because these are considered passive learning. One person speaks and a large audience listens and takes notes. This may not be true. A lecture cannot be passive learning, though it may be dull at times. In fact, a well-delivered lecture can initiate an intense thought process in the listener's mind if he is really attentive and interested. You can involve yourself in the lecture if you are thinking about what is being said, thinking examples and applications, reacting in a critical fashion, or trying to link what is being talked about with your existing body of knowledge.

If you are serious about effective thinking, deep analysis, and an enriched thought process, you will find lectures have an edge over books. Given a choice between reading a book and listening to a good lecture, I would prefer the latter, any day. The impact of a lecture is usually greater than that of a book, because enthusiasm and attitudes are more readily communicated when a person speaks to you.

The former President of India, late Giani Zail Singh, believed that listening to a good lecture was like reading several books. It contained views and thoughts from various books and journals to which many of us have no access. A good speaker will organise and integrate the various aspects of a subject more efficiently than a book. He can adapt his talk to the needs of the audience and can provide information and analysis that would be available in books several months later. Even if you don't understand much of the lecture, it at least exposes you to your areas of ignorance. With the help of this limited understanding of the subject (picked up during the lecture), you can make a beginning in learning more on the subject being discussed.

Much depends on how you get the best out of a lecture. You have to be careful about two things—where to sit and how to takes notes.

1. Where to sit

The best place to sit is in the middle towards the front, from where you can see and hear the speaker easily. In many lecture theatres, the acoustics are bad. So if you sit at the back, you may not be able to hear the lecture clearly. Your attention may become intermittent. Moreover, having the rest of the audience in your field of view may distract you. A middle-front seat will make you feel more involved with the lecture. You will be in the company of keen and serious-minded listeners. Those sitting at the back are usually the disinterested lots who might be there just because they want to be a part of the audience.

2. Taking notes

There are two ways of making notes. You can make copious notes taking down as much of the lecture as possible; or you can take outline notes including definitions, main points, arguments for and against, data and main conclusions. Taking copious notes may not be possible for everyone because to note down every word, you must know shorthand. However, you can take outline notes because many of the words spoken by the speaker may not be relevant. Speakers also include in their speech much redundant material, like thanks giving, some words about themselves, introductory remarks, stories, and anecdotes. They also tend to repeat and emphasise many points and ideas. Such things can be ignored.

Long notes are not advisable because if you were taking complete notes you will not be able to follow the lecture. Your concentration will be on words and you may miss ideas or even the general argument. It also becomes difficult to revise and re-learn copious notes, as many pages of continuous writing are hard to organise and equally hard to commit to memory. However, if the notes are prepared in bullet points they stand out. They can then be easily visualised in memory, when indented, numbered, or labelled, well spaced out and interspersed with diagrams.

Not taking notes is also not advisable, particularly for those lectures that are full of facts and arguments. However, if the subject of the lecture happens to be your area of specialisation, you may ignore notes. As you have an extensive background on the topic, you can follow the argument closely. You can think simultaneously on the issue being discussed so that you can put questions to the speaker at the end of the lecture. But here too, some skeleton notes may be necessary as impressions fade quickly, and brief basic notes will not distract your attention. If you do not take basic notes, certain details will fade completely and inaccuracies and over-simplifications will occur. The experimental psychology of memory has demonstrated the limitations of human beings as recording instruments. You cannot afford to not make notes.

During the final analysis, jotting down main points is the best option. You can visualise these notes more usefully and effectively. These can be easily reconstructed in memory. As you are not writing all the time, you can carefully concentrate on the lecture and assimilate ideas. If you have followed the structure of what is being spoken and have made good outline notes, you can reconstruct the entire lecture at a later time. However, in outline notes, ensure that the transition from one topic to the next is well emphasised in the spacing of notes. Use headings and sub-headings, and leave plenty of room for elaboration or expansion after the lecture. In taking notes, a single word will be enough to remind you of the complete idea or the argument. You can later reconstruct the major part of the lecture with the help of a few key words.

> The process of acquiring a good and satisfying job should be taken seriously. First you have to prepare for your career by reading biographies of highly successful persons. Then prepare seriously for the tests and examinations that may be required for the profession. Also you have to analyse yourself and find out your strengths and weaknesses. Resume creation is the next priority. Then prepare for group discussion and personal interview if it is needed. For both you should develop a positive attitude, a pleasing and confident personality, and a good recall system. You must do your homework diligently and intelligently, and do a few mock interviews. Right from the beginning you should try to develop a wide perspective. This can be done by attending lectures and taking notes for future reference.

Chapter 5

Essentials of Success System

> *One must forever strive for excellence or even perfection, in any task however small, and never be satisfied with the second best.*
>
> J. R. D. TATA

A long new journey begins once you are selected for a job. You look for a fruitful and rewarding career that can provide you money, status, and fame. Once employed you are in the saddle, riding the horse. Before you put the spurs on, make yourself comfortable. Have a feel of the job and prepare yourself for trotting. Be ready to ride on a new road, in a new environment, and on your own. Stop depending on others, particularly your parents. Try shifting from home culture to institutional culture. Market yourself for wider exposure and greater acceptability. Develop certain traits like building a sound memory, learning how to maintain deadlines, and managing time efficiently for better functioning and enhanced returns. Soon you would be galloping on the road to success.

Develop an institutional culture

Samir, an MBA graduate, got a job in a multinational company in Delhi. After joining, he had major differences with his boss, Amit who was not an MBA like Samir. Amit was an "honours graduate" in commerce from Sri Ram College of Commerce, Delhi. He had joined the company as a management trainee and had climbed his way up the corporate ladder to a senior middle-level position due to his hard work and diligence. Now he was Marketing Manager.

Samir, after joining the company, thought that the company was not being managed on the models taught to him in his Business School. As Samir was intelligent and fresh from academics he argued and challenged his boss. He wanted to have his way and work independently. Thinking that he was a great manager Samir talked to the International Manager during his visit to India and explained how the company was not working on sound lines. He gave his strategy and plan of action. But he was surprised; rather than getting a pat on the back he got his marching orders. Though Samir's plan was sound, the company was working well under the leadership of Amit, increasing its market share every year and earning handsome profits. The corporate policy, as the Americans say, was "not to repair unless broken."

Samir was like thousands of fresh MBAs who think of themselves as part of an elite group of young managers. Their objective is to head straight to the many cushy marketing or financial jobs. They see themselves as thinkers, but not as doers; analytical, but not skillful; managers, but not leaders; Indian, and not global; limited, and not diverse. Consequently, they become rigid and highbrow like the IAS officers

One must remember that when a new person joins an organisation—government office, private sector or public undertaking—he has to adjust to its culture. For this he has to change his perceptions, attitude, and approach. Large organisations do not change their cultures to accommodate every individual who joins them, whatever may be his level of intelligence or position. Only that person who adjusts to the organisation's culture has the possibility of moving upwards. Any one, who wants to change the organisation's culture according to his thinking and perception, either resigns or becomes frustrated.

The Japanese are quite particular about cultivating institutional culture. They use various ways to inculcate it in their new internees. First, they infuse in the person those skills that are necessary to make him a good employee. Every one is acquainted with the work and the system prevailing in the company. After that the person is integrated into the fraternity of the organisation. The integration into the company is done through several methods such as prominent display of company slogans at different places so that everyone gets familiar with them. Singing of company songs every morning before the work starts and delivery of lectures by senior officers on company philosophy and its importance to the company's functioning are some other such methods.

Management innovators as they are, the Japanese have during the last 20 years adopted a new technique of spiritual training for inculcating right attitudes known as *Seishin Kyoiku*. It contains a number of mechanisms and exercises aimed at bringing the individual face-to-face with a spiritual struggle within himself. It helps him to have a deeper insight into his own motivations.

Seishin Kyoiku in more ways than one draws heavily from techniques for development used by Zen, a sect of Buddhism that has had a deep influence on the Japanese culture, personality, and psyche. The focus of Zen is to change the attitude of an individual. It does not believe in using words and expressions but uses the basic strategy of "directly pointing to reality". The newly appointed persons, called trainees, are introduced to group living and group responsibility.

Each one has to participate in housekeeping chores and adhere strictly to a routine. Diaries have to be maintained which are discussed periodically. Sometimes they are asked to maintain a public garden near the company. A few days in the month senior managers of the company join them and talk to them about the symbolic importance of their work. The trainees are sometimes exposed to disconcerting situations. Roto is one such exercise.

The trainees are taken to a new town about which they know nothing. They are asked to wear odd white uniform and go from door to door. They ask for work without any payment from the one who opens the door after the knock. The person is always a stranger. They are forbidden from revealing their identity. They just offer their services and accept any task given to them.

In a country where strangers are always viewed with suspicion and even mistrust, the chances are that the trainee would be met by stoic silence. Once a trainee leaves a group and moves alone, he has to muster courage to approach a stranger's door. In most cases, no work would be offered; many a times the trainee is rudely asked to leave. After a few refusals the trainee may get some work from a benevolent housewife. The trainee would feel an overwhelming sense of relief and gratitude and would put in his best whatever may be the status of the job.

These exercises are aimed at completely destroying the ego of a person. His perception of the concept of work undergoes a sea change. Says an expert: "After such an experience, it is difficult to deny the assertion that any form of work is intrinsically neither good not bad, satisfying nor unsatisfying, neither appropriate nor inappropriate. Pleasure in work, it must be conceded, varies according to the subject's attitude and circumstances." It is true that the work itself does not determine whether or not one enjoys it, but it is the attitude of the person that makes it enjoyable or boring.

In India, incorrect attitudes towards work are the main cause for the absence of a healthy work culture. As Tomas

Rohlen has written in his book, *For Harmony and Strength:* "The basis of a proper attitude is acceptance of necessity and responsibility. Instead of fighting life's requirements, it is better to acknowledge and accept necessary difficulties. Complaining, criticising and other forms of resistance are examples of actions that reflect improper attitudes."

The TATA Group experiments

In India, we desperately and urgently need such types of training to inculcate correct attitudes and approaches. The TATA Group realised the need to change their corporate culture and designed a programme as the concept of manager changed as India entered the 21st century. It felt the need of changing its corporate culture by introducing a programme to train the elite Tata Administrative Service (TAS) managers to learn to roll up their sleeves to meet the new global-rural requirement.

Tata Administrative Service (TAS) was conceived by JRD Tata, the late chairman of the Tata group, in the 1950s to select and groom the best young Indians and use their talent as a group resource. They were to be utilized by companies across the Tata organisation. Each year 20 to 30 from among 1,500 applicants from the best institutions were selected for TAS who became members of an elite corps among the group's 3.6 lakh employees.

But this perception of the Tata Group has undergone a change with the turn of the century. They realised that they were still getting the same calibre of people who were extremely analytical but not really developed in a broad manner so as to work in either rural areas or in other countries. This was adding to the elitist perception. To change with the changing times Tata decided to reinvent its corporate culture. It was to begin with TAS managers. Therefore, in 2009, it tied up with Sir Dorabji Tata Trust (SDTT) to get TAS managers to work directly with the NGOs associated with the trust for a 49-day period. The Group decided to experiment with unconventional measures in order to change the perception of the TAS from "elitist" to "realist".

The 35 recruits of the 2009 batch were put through a 3-day training module at the National Police Academy. The module dealt with issues like discipline, planning, managing with or without structures, effective communication, decision-making, decisiveness, and managing ambiguity.

It also included leadership talks by senior police officials, including an overnight experience of conducting an anti-terrorist operation with colour pin-ball guns. One of the things the TAS members became aware of was that they have to be prepared to lead in any situation, such as 26/11 that can come in many forms and everyone should be able to handle it.

In the second part of the programme each of the 35 members was clubbed into small groups and sent to remote villages and denied access to nearby company facilities such as guest houses, vehicles, and easy communication. They were hooked up with Sir Dorabji Tata Trust and were asked to work on rural development projects. One group found out that the villagers had a problem of not being able to crop vegetables throughout the year due to water shortages. So, the group taught the farmers how to dehydrate surplus fruits and vegetables and store them for future use. They showed the farmers how the vegetables could be used for up to three months after re-hydrating.

The rural exercise showed them the reality that exists in their own backyard that they had never experienced. The decision to throw its new recruits into difficult rural environments was the best way to turn the thinkers into doers. At the same time, this sensitised them to the company's responsibility towards the society.

After two months in the villages, the 35 new TAS members were dispatched to many corners of the globe. The next couple of months were spent on projects in the operations of group companies such as Tata Beverages or

Tata Communications in countries like South Africa and UK. This "village-and-the-world-in-120-days" break-in drill is a recent introduction to the 53-year-old programme and part of an attempt to reinvent itself to meet the group's new talent requirements.

TAS trainees are now given a real view of life. There are no think-tank jobs for them at first go. In the first year, each TAS trainee is now put through four cross-functional, cross-business, and cross-located assignments, including three 15-week stints in business functions in three companies. The fourth, a seven-week rural assignment, exposes the trainees to the Tata corporate social responsibility programme and philosophy. It introduces them to community work in rural India, and enables them to understand the ethics of the Tata Group — of giving back to society.

This helps them develop real leadership traits and in turn makes them an ideal leader. This new breed of managers is likely to be globally intelligent, have multi-cultural skills, and be rooted in universal humanistic values like joy, peace, and creativity.

Market yourself

If one were asked to define business in one word, probably the best definition would be "marketing." This in a broader sense means developing a market for your product, your ideas, and your services. Therefore, techniques and strategies developed by experts to create, regenerate or expand markets, and promote sales can also be used with some modifications in other areas, particularly in selling one's services. One can learn from Tony Harrison, a marketing expert who worked in Switzerland to design the training of marketing and advertising professionals.

Harrison developed many ideas with the objective of formulating systematic advertisement strategies. He offered a number of working methods that he renovated while working with various organisations. Trial and error helped him to perfect his models. These have proved their feasibility. He learnt the basic principals in the consumer goods field and successfully transferred them to selling "high-ticket items, selling investments, persuading people to contribute to charities…. They work because the essentials of human nature are the same everywhere."

Methods suggested by Harrison are found to be effective on a wide range. The important point to consider here is: "Can these methods be used to market your ideas and services?" To put it more directly, can they be used to develop a better and effective personality (which is a high selling point of any service)? If yes, how?

Harrison suggests a 6-step formula to achieve market success. One, understand your product; two, understand your competition; three, understand your customer; four, develop a unique promise; five, communicate it effectively; and last, communicate it to the right people.

And now let us see how these steps can be used to shape a winning personality.

Understand your product: The first basic principle of management is to understand your product in and out. Interpreting it broadly and using it on personality means that you must understand yourself. If you are producing an item you know all the weaknesses and strengths of your product. In the same way you should be aware of all the positive and negative aspects of your personality. You should know what your areas of strength are. It implies that you should be aware of your positive qualities that give you an edge over others. Moreover you should be aware of your weaker aspects that may be the cause of your failure. A successful person understands his personality intensively and tries to prevail over the weaker aspects. If you really understand yourself you can effectively project yourself to your maximum advantage. Exposing and exploiting your positive qualities and improving the weak points can do this. This way you can improve your salability.

ESSENTIALS OF SUCCESS SYSTEM 85

Understand your competition: Every producer first has to understand fully the market of his product. Whatever is the nature of the market—commodity or service—a certain amount of competition prevails. It puts every seller under pressure. Every producer, therefore, operates in a competitive market. The higher the competition, the greater will be the pressure. As you are also a seller of your services, you should understand the market where your services are needed and valued. Here, knowing the strengths and weaknesses of others will help you to understand the totality of the market. It will enable you to sell yourself better. An interview helps you to score over your competitors.

Understand your customer: A successful seller understands his customer and services him to his total satisfaction. As a seller of your service you should also understand your employer who is the buyer and user of your service. He in fact is your customer. If you know the type of customer he is and you are able to find out his liking and disliking, your relationships would be better with him. It will make you a better acceptable product and your market value will also increase. It is similar to developing brand loyalty. When a customer becomes used to a particular brand, he does not mind paying a higher price for it. You too should become a "brand" for your employer.

Develop a unique promise: Every producer tries to develop some unique features in the product so that it becomes different and better than others do. This is called "unique selling proposition" or USP. Any product that becomes unique, like the Maruti car when it came on the streets; it became a highly saleable product and was even sold at a premium for a very long time. It still is the market leader. Similarly, if you become a unique product by acquiring rare skills and high efficiency, you develop a better market for yourself. For example, if an engineer becomes a management expert, his marketability improves over a person who is simply an engineer.

Communicate effectively: Effective communication is essential for capturing the market for your product. A manufacturer communicates with buyers by advertising his product in the print media and on television. He makes efforts to tell his customers that his product is better, more economical, useful, and beneficial than the other competitor products in the market. One who communicates in a better way with the customer is able to sell more than other producers of the similar products are. The example of *Nirma* washing detergent is often used to prove that effective communication enables a manufacturer to capture the market even though the competitor may be a multinational giant.

You, as a seller of your service, should also communicate effective and widely. It means that you must have effective public relations. You should find effective ways to communicate with your employer to be one up on others. In fact, your work is the most effective communication medium. Therefore, you must put in your best, develop contacts in various organisations, maintain good relations with them, and be popular in your group. Never take a back seat. Be in the forefront if not at the head of the line. Do not injure the pride of a person unless your self-respect has been wounded. Even an insignificant person may become important in a democratic setup. There are instances where persons who were working at the lower end became important political figures. The former Vice-President of India, Bhairon Singh Shekhavat was initially a *havaldar* in Rajasthan Police. Lalu Prasad Yadav and Mayavati are other such examples of those who have risen from very low levels to high political positions.

Communicate with the right people: Only communicating effectively is not sufficient. It should also be done with the right people. A product has to be communicated to the targeted buyer. If you advertise for a high priced product in the middle class market, your entire expenditure would be a complete waste. Buyers in that market do not have enough purchasing power to buy expensive products, though many might long to own them. Similarly, a low-priced product like *Lifebuoy* soap cannot increase its sales by advertising in the up-market section. You not only have to find out the right people, your communication channel too should remain open with them. You should communicate with those people who really matter in your life and career. You should be in touch with those from whom you can benefit, especially in the long-run. Communicating with the wrong set of persons would create an adverse effect and prove to be a total waste for your precious time and efforts.

> Gallop on the road to success— develop certain traits like building a sound memory, learning how to maintain deadlines, and managing time efficiently.

The 6-step strategy to ensure successful marketing can be easily adapted by you to market yourself. So put on your thinking cap, forget your laziness, and do not waste time on unnecessary activities.

Sound memory helps

The history teacher was giving a lesson on the epic of *Mahabharata* to his class VI students. At the end of the lesson he asked a student, "How many brothers were the Pandavas? Name all of them."

The student began: "One was Bhim, the second was Arjun, Nakul was third, there was a fourth brother too, and… I have forgotten the fifth one."

Then there was the famous British spy-catcher, Lt-Col Oreste Pinto, a wartime Allied counter-espionage expert. Lt. Col. Pinto was responsible for the arrest of several Nazi intelligence officers as he was able to identify them in a crowd of hundreds. The reason — his excellent memory. As a child he could repeat a whole page of the telephone directory just after one reading.

A sound memory is an important personality trait. If you can recall important facts, information, anecdotes, and stories at the appropriate moments, you can succeed where others fail. But if names and facts cannot be remembered at the relevant time then they are of no use to remember. You may have to cut a sorry figure many a times. A sound memory is God's gift and everyone is not endowed with a Pinto-type memory. Can an average person improve his memory? If yes, how?

First, let us find out what memory is? Memory is the faculty by which things are called to or kept in the mind. It has three parts — learning or memorising, retention, and recall. The three are inter-related because you cannot recall anything that you have not retained. Also you cannot retain anything that you have not learnt. Therefore, if you want to improve your memory, improve all the three — your learning, retaining, and recollection.

Improvement in memory is, in fact, the betterment of your methods of learning. Your first task should be to examine your present methods and find out what are the shortcomings in them. Only after that will you be able to decide on better methods to improve your memory system. No universal method can be suggested because every individual is a unique personality and has his own way of handling information and situations. However, certain principles can be followed that can help you in developing a good memory system.

The first principle is concerned with our senses. All individuals do not have all their senses of the equal strength. Some persons may have a powerful visual imagery while others may have a good auditory imagery. If you have strong visual senses than the other senses, make more use of your eyes while learning. Those who have strong auditory sense should make better use of their ears. If you really want to achieve better results, use both the senses and supplement one with the other.

Next you must learn to concentrate. It means that you must focus all your attention on what you are reading. An hour of study with concentration is better than several hours of study when your mind is wandering and wavering. Concentration is largely an art. You can concentrate better if you try to establish similarities and comparisons.

Interest is another fundamental factor to memorising. When you have an interest in something you would like to know more about it and also often discuss it. This helps you in remembering those things easily. Anything that is of less interest to you, hardly matters to you in your priority system. You give no attention to it. Therefore you may not know elementary facts about it. Those interested in cricket would always be interested in reading about it and watching the game whenever it is played. But those who do not have any interest in it just ignore it and do not retain any of the facts even when they are in the company of such cricket enthusiasts. So it is important that you develop an interest in those topics which are important to your career.

Research has proved that the "whole method" is better than the "part method". In the former we read the entire material in one go rather than dividing it into sections. This makes comprehension far easier than reading in parts. It can be applied to any kind of reading. This method is simple. Make a general survey of the entire book when you pick it up to read. Read the jacket and the preface. It would give you a bird's eye view of the complete book. You can decide to read it in detail if it interests you. Otherwise you can leave it and choose another book for reading. Next, you should go through the book quickly turning pages as you glance at the whole page in one look and trying to find out the matter on the page. Give special attention to chapter headings, sub-headings, and the treatment of the subject. In short, make an outline and then fill in.

The recitation method — reciting what you are reading — is also considered to be effective. It enables you to comprehend various points quickly. It also breaks the monotony that is sometimes generated while reading.

Some break in reading is essential. Before you start a new chapter or subject, give yourself an interval. This will prepare your mind to receive new ideas.

The second stage — retention — is a difficult one. Psychologists do not agree whether the capacity of a person to retain can be improved. Some believe that our genes determine the retention power. However, the efficiency in retention power depends on our learning process. If we read thoroughly we learn better and are able to retain it for a longer period. Whatever may be the view of researchers, you can enhance your retention by practice and repeated learning.

Recalling the learnt knowledge at the appropriate time is the third stage of memory. Though it is also an innate quality, constant practice can strengthen it. An important factor in recall is the keenness and frequency of observing a thing or the situation. A review of what we have observed or seen makes recall easy. Recall can be improved if we avoid emotional conditions like fear. It is sometimes possible to control it by finding an outlet for your nervous tensions. It is particularly important if you are going for an interview. The fear or tension may not permit you to recall simple facts.

Distracting thoughts can also act as a mental block. You should train your mind not to be disturbed by distracting thought or events. Some people have the tendency to stray thinking. While reading they would often think of other things and persons. This not only hampers the speed of reading but also slows the retention of information and facts.

Lastly, build up a confident attitude. No one can help you if you suffer from a poor-memory phobia. Much can be achieved if you have the confidence of carrying through with the project and remembering what you are reading. A high level of confidence leads to a high level of concentration and focus on the work you are doing. A high degree of energy is released when accompanied by a high level of confidence. The energy gets divided if you are not confident.

These are some of the tested ways of sharpening and improving one's memory. But one must not be disheartened if one forgets a part of the read material. Forgetting is an important element of remembering; your mind is trained to retain necessary and relevant information and forget what might not be needed. You should attempt to learn what is essential and necessary.

Maintaining deadlines

The shrill incessant ring of the telephone woke me up with a jerk just as I was drowsily about to turn over and resume my sleep. I picked up the receiver with an indignant feeling of disgruntle. It was an old contributor of mine, Tarun. He was calling up to say that he was sorry and that he would not be able to submit his article that he had promised. The deadline was just a week away. An intelligent writer with a good command on the English language, Tarun would often request for assignments to write articles. But he was a frequent defaulter and missed deadlines. He would come with all types of excuses. He repeated his excuses many times and so was losing his credibility.

I was fully awake by then and decided to rack my brains for someone who would be able to write at such a short notice. After going through the list mentally, I decided on Rajan. Two hours later I was on the phone explaining the situation to him. Rajan listened carefully, asked relevant questions, and accepted the assignment. I offered to extend the deadline but Rajan was sure that he would be able to finish it within the stipulated time. He gave the article to me a day before the deadline expired.

I wondered how Rajan could finish the task in less than a week whereas Tarun failed to do so even in three weeks. There must be something in their styles of working that made Rajan a go-getter and Tarun a shirker. I decided to talk to both of them and find out their style of working. I realised three golden rules for maintaining deadlines.

Rule One: *Do not postpone work.* Do the work as scheduled and do not keep on postponing till the deadline arrives. Rajan always fixes a deadline to finish the work and never postpones work except in an emergency, which is very seldom. He keeps several files, one for each assignment with its deadline written on it. Then he draws a work schedule in which he mentions the date on which he would work on it. He works according to the schedule. In fact, for his own convenience he advances the deadline by a day so that he can send the copy well in time.

Tarun fails to do the work on time because he gets overwhelmed by problems and tends to postpone them. On the other hand Rajan believes that as there will never be problem-free days, the only way to success is to deal with them as they come. Postponement only means accumulation and the higher the pile the harder it becomes to work according to schedule.

Rule two: *Keep in mind alternative lines of action.* Rajan told me about a Brigadier who was being considered for promotion to the rank of Major General. A part of the test was a simulation exercise. He was given a situation in which he was to attack the enemy and capture the territory. The position and the resources of the enemy were given to him. He was told that the attack would be from the north. He was given a day to prepare the operational plan. Next day he was given the signal to attack the enemy. The Brigadier deployed his forces and went into action. Within a few hours of the start of the operation a message came from the Army Headquarters that the enemy was not in the north but in the south and was ready to attack any moment. Rather than panicking the Brigadier just gave one order: "Change to plan two." His commanders redeployed their forces with no confusion.

Like the brigadier Rajan also thinks of several alternatives well in advance. If one of them fails he tries the second one, and if even that does not work he uses the third one. "What if the third one also fails," I interjected. He told me another story.

Once a sailor was being considered for his promotion. In the interview the officer asked: "What would you do if there were a storm?"

"I would use the anchor," the sailor answered.

"What if there were another storm?"

"I would use one more anchor."

The officer asked the same question two more times. The sailor gave the same reply.

Frustrated the officer asked the sailor: "From where would you bring so many anchors?"

"From the same place from where you will bring so many storms, Sir."

The reality is that failures cannot be infinite. And you can think of either one or at the most two back-ups and not more. The basic idea behind backups are that one should not be restricted to only one alternative. One should always have alternatives ready for use in case there is a need. Rajan gave another example of his: "I plan to do some writing at night. Suppose there is a power cut. I have got an inverter installed. But suppose that also breaks down, I have lamps and candles in the house and use them if the need arises."

Rule three: *Maintain good public relations*. Rajan is a good conversationalist and remembers names and is always willing to help others. As a result he is remembered even by casual acquaintances. His strategy is to maintain contact with at least one important person in every organisation. This helps him in getting information without any problem.

Learn from Rajan and not Tarun. Maintain deadlines and establish your credibility.

Manage time

Everyone has the same amount of time – 24 hours a day and seven days a week. The unique thing about time is that it can only be spent; it cannot be saved and stored. But different people spend it in different ways – some intelligently, some foolishly. The Prime Minister of India can attend to all the matters of the state during a single day. While in eight hours a clerk in most of the government offices in India cannot dispose of even one file. Most of us are at wits end wondering how to get everything done and still have a life. Here the concept of time management arises.

Time management is about managing your day affectively so that you can do an activity in one hour what others do in two hours or may be in a day. It also implies maximum use of the time today, so that you can do much more work in the future. Better management of time will develop a feeling of accomplishment and satisfaction because you are not only doing more work but are putting your time to good use. As such, time management can be seen as making the best use of your time, so that you can handle all your responsibilities, without giving in to the misery of procrastination.

1. Developing time management is a journey

The best way to learn the importance of time management is to watch a horse race. This was cited by a successful management guru who in one of his lectures said that the winning horse wins twice the money than the runner up. Interestingly, the winner horse does not run twice as fast to earn twice the money. It only has to be a "nose ahead" of the competition to reap twice the rewards. Time management is much like the horse race metaphor. If one wants to win the race of life, doubling the efforts is not required. The only need is to be a "nose ahead" of others to get better results

Five steps were adopted by Rajan to get a "nose ahead." First, every night he *prepared a schedule for the next day* so that there was an action plan to guide him without wasting time on thinking what to do next. He had learnt by experience that whenever he had tried working without a schedule, he would start the day with the least important work leaving other useful tasks for the remaining part of the day. At the end of the day he found that many of the important listed items were left undone because no time was left for them.

The work schedule contained all the items he wanted to finish during the next day. He prioritised items in order of their importance (#1 for most important, #2 for next most important, and so on) and began the day with the most important item and then went to the next most important item. He followed it up till he reached the end of the schedule. There were days when he could not finish all the items on the list. But that never discouraged him. How much was left undone at the end of the day was not important. What was actually accomplished was all that mattered.

Second, he *planned more than what he thought he would be able to finish* during the day. The Parkinson's Law that: "A project tends to take the time allocated for it," was always at the back of his mind. He realised early on in his career that planning to finish just one job during the day meant doing that job only. If he decided to finish two jobs during the day he completed both. When he placed six things on the list for the day, he would not get all six done, but he was able to complete three or four items. Planning more than what he could chew created a healthy sense of pressure on Rajan and he naturally became a better time manager. When he had a plateful, he was more focused, suffered less interruptions, and delegated better.

Third, he always *kept his desk clean* as it created a better work environment. The saying: "Out of sight; out of mind," was no more relevant for him. What he believed in was: "In sight; in mind." An overcrowded desk full of papers and files distracted him and pulled him in the negative direction and he failed to accomplish any work of significance.

Fourth, he *would not encourage unnecessary meetings*. He knows that an average business executive spends long hours in meetings. During every business day, hundreds and thousands of meetings are conducted in our country. Studies in developed countries like the United States and the United Kingdom have shown that an average manager spends about 17 hours a week in meetings and about 6 hours in planning and preparing for those meetings and untold hours in the followup. Rajan remembers that as a middle level manager he attended 250 meetings in three months. Though meetings are an essential part of any business, as much as one-third of the time spent in meetings is wasted. In fact, most of the meetings are institutional time wasters. Before agreeing to attend any meeting he always asks himself two questions: "Do I contribute anything to that meeting?" and "Do I get anything of value from this meeting?" If the answer to both questions is "no," he tries to find a way to avoid that meeting.

Finally, he *reads a paper only once to take a decision*. He does not keep it to read it again on some other day and then take a decision. He handles every paper just once. Rajiv always avoids the widely followed normal practice of "shuffling blues" when the paper is looked at again and again while deadline knocks at the door step and the person gets buried under a blizzard of paperwork. When a paper is presented to him, he responds then and there. If it requires serious attention and advice from other persons, he sends it for opinions and schedules it for a time when he will consider it and take a decision.

Proper time management skills benefit a person in several ways. One, he can plan activities and schedule time for completing them. He can know in advance when he will be busier. One can plan the activities so that those things get done well in time. Two, one can remember meetings, appointments, and deadlines so that there are no delays and misses. The person becomes more efficient in work.

Time management skills enable a person to implement the work plan in the most effective and efficient way. And the best part is that it does not take much to prepare a plan. For example, a time management plan for a project can be prepared in just less than half a day and the weekly grid in only one hour. It only takes about 20 minutes each week to keep schedules up to date, making additions and revisions.

We can continuously improve our time management skills and experience fewer stressful situations resulting from procrastination or overextending (trying to do too many activities). It gives us a sense of control over our lives.

Five tips to manage your time better

One: Learn to **have patience** *with yourself. It takes time to do things you want to complete. Understand that time management is an amazing skill.*

Two: **Stay calm**. *Being in a relaxed and calm state of mind is more productive than being hysterical. Practice being and remaining calm.*

Three: Learn to **prioritise**. *Know which out of all the work the most important one is. Attend to the most important first. Do not do the easy and simple tasks first.*

Four: Making a **list**. *Those who manage their time well are those who have a list of things that need to be done. You will be able to see in black and white what it is you need to do. Only include what you really feel you can accomplish within a specific block of time.*

Five: Buy a planner and **plan your workday**. *It may seem odd in the beginning but it will take a little time to adjust to using it. Once you develop the habit of implementing a planner it will become second nature for you. You need to schedule time to accomplish your goals and your tasks.*

These five tips will make you an excellent time manager.

Learn to say "no"

We live in an interdependent world where dependence on friends and neighbours is essential. It, however, does not mean that anybody or everyone has a claim on your time or energy, whatever may be the reason. If someone asks for assistance it must be done willingly and not reluctantly. Unfortunately a large number of people are not able to muster sufficient courage to say "no". They are always ready, many a times unwillingly, to help anyone who approaches them. Later they feel guilty for themselves and their family, and realise that they were used and exploited with no appreciation expressed for their help.

Important to look at is, "Why can't you say no". It is because most of you want approval and acceptance. You want to be admired and you think that if you say "no" you would become unpopular. You may not like to say "no" out of consideration for people who are close to you. You may also think that others will feel indebted to you when you say "yes". Unfortunately, saying "yes" often yields the opposite results. For example, you might accept a dinner invitation from a close friend, though you know that he always invites persons you cannot stand. During your stay at the dinner you will be uncomfortable and your host will definitely sense the unease on you. So by agreeing to join the dinner you end up doing exactly what you wanted to avoid, hurting the feelings of your friend. It is, therefore, very important that you should not say "yes" if you want to say "no".

Why is it important to learn to say "no"?

The first reason is that every time you acquiesce against your will, you build up a certain amount of resentment within yourself. And if you are constantly giving in, the backlog of unreleased anger may cause several complications like depression, skin rashes, headaches, ulcers, or other psychosomatic complaints.

You have a right to be you. So nothing is wrong if you say "no", especially if it is a well considered one. After all, there are limits to your being generous and tolerant. No doubt friends and relatives have a claim on you, but to be truly unselfish means to love yourself as well as others. As an eminent psychologist has put it: "It must be a virtue and not a vice, to love myself, since I am a human being too".

However, not saying "yes" always does not mean indiscriminately saying "no". A generous person tries to help others but there would always be certain situations when it would be necessary to say "no". The question is when does one say "no"? Here are some guidelines.

Thoughtless and inappropriate requests can always be turned down. If someone asks you to drop him at the railway station 40 kilometres away, when cheap regular transport is available, you can understand the request to be thoughtless. On the other hand, if you were requested to take someone seriously ill to the hospital it would be inhuman to say "no."

"No" can definitely be said to those who want you to speak lies on their behalf. It is not necessary for you to say "yes" to a person who wants you to tell his boss that he was sick when he was not. You can also refuse to do what others can and should do by themselves. If a person can do anything himself, why should you do it for him? If he is in a difficult situation you can always come forward to help him.

You should not say "yes" if the request made to you conflicts with your own priorities. Also you should be careful not to commit others against your will. If your friend asks to bring the whole family for dinner, you may say "no" if your children are preparing for a competitive examination.

Now comes the most important aspect of the whole situation—how to say "no"? It must be said promptly. If you delay or postpone, unnecessary hopes would be raised. If someone asks you to help his son in doing his homework, it would be tempting to delay saying "no" so as to soften the blow of refusal. But this may create some sour feelings. It will be better to politely say sorry, that you are occupied for the time being and that you would definitely help him when you are free.

It is not necessary to justify every "no". You have a right to make a decision keeping in view your own priorities or requirements. This is particularly true when people make unreasonable demands.

Refusals must be firm yet uttered without any expression of bitterness, anger, and impatience. If you softly express your inability, you would find that your refusal has been taken well. You should always decline with serenity and assurance.

> *Once selected for a job, a long journey begins. The first essential is to develop an institutional approach because organisations do not change their culture to accommodate individual likes and dislikes. The second essential is to market your personality by understanding yourself, your competitors, and your customers and by acquiring USPs and communicating them to the right people. A sound and organised memory system helps to achieve it. Finally, you must manage your time efficiently and effectively.*

Chapter 6

For a Better Tomorrow

All truly great thoughts are conceived while walking.

FRIEDRICH NIETZCHE

Preparing yourself for the fast lane is like preparing for the battleground. You have to be in good shape, possess a thinking mind, and an effective communication system. These three traits are absolutely indispensable for an effective success system. Develop the trio and move fast as the years roll on.

A fit body

A gerontologist will tell you that the biological clock ticks non-stop in all living beings from the time of birth to death. We all know the hard fact of life that ultimately we will all grow old and die. But, we still want to halt the process of ageing. Old people are increasing in numbers in all countries, particularly the developed ones. Two reasons are responsible for the new trend: the falling birth rate and the increase in the life span of human beings. In 1990, in the United States only four percent of the total population was over 65. Now the percentage is around 20. In India in 1911 only one per cent of the population was over 60 years of age. Now their number is touching eight per cent. The increase is due to the fact that many fatal diseases have been controlled. Now, as more and more people survive in their 60s and 70s, old age has become a major medical preoccupation. We have gerontologists and geriatricians who study the various aspects of ageing.

Why does a human being age? Scientists have reasoned it out in different ways. One opinion is that "ageing is simply a part of the genetic master plan imprinted into the cells, much the same way puberty is". Dr. Leonard Hayflick, an American gerontologist believes that: "There may be a specific gene carrying a specific program for ageing, or a sequence of genes at the end of the DNA strain that stays in effect. That's enough; let's start closing things down now".

The second view is that the genetic programme like a completed computer tape simply runs out, depriving cells of necessary instructions, and leading to greater and greater disorganisation in the body—and finally complete disintegration. The view is propagated by those who believe that nature wants organisms to survive long enough to reproduce themselves and thereafter loses interest in them. The process of converting a body from young to old age is short in animals, only two weeks in the Pacific salmons and several decades in human beings. However, the basic character of growth essentially remains the same.

The third view is a modification of the second one. The genetic programme may not run out, but the blueprint of the DNA molecules may become smudged with an accumulation of errors. These may result from mutation. It may be that either the cosmic radiation that reaches every nook and corner of the earth or factors like pollution that damage the environment cause mutation. Man lives longer because his cells can cope with these kinds of errors. However, even this system is far from perfect.

Though ageing in human beings normally starts in the late fifties, three places in the world have successfully delayed this process. These are Vilcabama, a village in a lush green valley in the Andes Mountains of Ecuador; Hunza, in the mountains of Pak occupied Kashmir; and Abkhasia in Georgia. People living in these places, situated in different parts of the world, enjoy longevity of 130 to 140 years.

> Yoga—a complete way of life—considers the body, mind, and spirit as inseparable.

Gerontologists visited these areas to find out the reasons for the inhabitants of these areas to have combated ageing. They found some interesting similarities. People of all ages were involved in a very high level of physical activity. Even people at the age of 130 years worked at least a few hours each day. In fact, exercise and diet were the two secrets of their long lives.

Exercise is a real rejuvenator. Psychologists and doctors worldwide have found that regular exercise keeps men and women in good shape. It improves the functioning of the heart and lungs and the flow of oxygen through the body; exercise also causes the blood pressure to drop. When done correctly and under expert guidance, people can control their heartbeats and blood pressure and tone up other functions of the body. Exercise also helps in reducing the body temperature that increases the life span of a human being from 25 to 40 years.

Diet also plays an important role in checking the ageing process. Dr. Clive M. McCay experimented on rats in the 1930s. He found that many years could be added to their lives by reducing the intake of calories in their diet. However, it cannot be said with certainly that extreme dieting will greatly enhance human life expectancy. Yet, the people of Hunza, Abkhasia, and Vilcabama take an extremely low-calorie diet. The intake of animal fat and proteins formed only one per cent of the diet of the Hunza natives. Vegetables, coarse grains, and fruits were the main ingredients of their daily food.

Besides physical factors, the attitude of the younger members of the society towards the older generation also influences ageing. In all the three regions known for longevity, the aged persons, like in the old times in India, were held in high esteem by the younger generation. They had deep faith in their wisdom and experience. This made the older generation feel wanted and they didn't dread old age. Rather they were able to function effectively in very active roles. In societies which have a youth-loving culture, like the US and, to an increasing extent now in India too, the old feel themselves to be a neglected part of society, something like over-ripe oranges. This takes its toll on the average older person's mental and physical well being.

In a nutshell, a person stays and feels young for a longer period if the right lifestyle is adopted at the appropriate time.

Physical fitness

We were a gang of four students — Balbir, Bipin, Mani, and I known as the four musketeers. Balbir was a methodical boy. He regularly participated in outdoor activities and spent not more than four to five hours in studies. He was well read and could discuss a variety of subjects with ease. He retired as a senior diplomat who even at the age of 60 walks erect and does not need glasses. He is working in an international research organization working on Indo-Sino relations. He often advises the Indian Government on diplomatic issues.

Bipin was a different type of a student — studious and more of a bookworm. He spent most of his time either in the classroom and his study room or in the library. He had no interest in games, music, or films. He studied eight to ten hours a day and hardly went for a morning walk. At the age of 20, he started wearing thick glasses and retired as a Section Officer in one of the ministries of the Government of India.

Mani was deep into sports and spent most of his time in bodybuilding and tennis. He was left with no time to study and had no interest in books, as he wanted to become a national champion. He could not achieve his dream goal and the lack of academic excellence gave him no opportunity to get a good job. He retired as a physical training instructor in a government school in Delhi.

These three examples of three promising boys, two of them who could not get their efforts rewarded show that one should focus on all aspects of one's personality instead of only one particular feature that one has more interest in. What is needed in today's fast and dynamic life is a holistic personality, a balance between physical fitness and academic excellence. Physical fitness is essential because mental fitness can only exist in a fit body. It is foolish to believe that a lethargic body can have a brilliant mind. The developed countries did realise it long back, and made physical fitness an essential aspect of education. Even today, from the beginning, boys and girls are encouraged to participate in a variety of games and sports. Consequently they develop a deep interest in sports and games. Everyone may not be included in the school or college team, but no one misses physical activity during the day to keep him fit. They also continue to play games and taking part in sports even in their old age. No doubt, they are more alert and active than an average Indian.

In India, there is an erroneous feeling that any time spent in the filed to play games is a wastage of time. Parents, in particular, goad their children to spend more time on studies. They rebuke them if they spend time in playing games or sports. Parents fail to understand that regular physical activity rejuvenates the entire body and freshens up the mind. Whatever tensions and mental lethargy one develops at work or at home is released if one is involved in games and sports. It helps in developing better concentration at work and in studies.

There are several ways of acquiring physical fitness. A few can be mentioned here. These are physical training, *yoga* exercises, playing games, jogging, running, or walking. Swami Ram Dev is doing great work in making yoga popular among the young and the old because of which apathy towards physical fitness is vanishing. If this continues we could soon see a fit India in the years to come.

Yoga for concentration

The greatest problem of today's youth is a lack of concentration. The flow of knowledge and information is so rapid and voluminous that an average person finds it difficult to absorb it. He, therefore, has to be better equipped so that he can absorb and use knowledge to his maximum advantage. And to make this possible he needs to develop better concentration.

A number of problems of our daily life and of our own personalities can be adequately dealt with if we learn to concentrate. Better concentration enables us to become less prone to be influenced by other people, or to be bullied or worried by them and become our own personal property. This happens because concentration puts our minds in order and enables us to deal constructively with specific problems. It becomes possible to apply concentration for a few minutes and to wait for the answer to a problem or for a new idea which we have vainly been seeking simply to come into our mind by the exclusion of all extraneous thought.

Concentration is basic to any serious work. In fact, all those who have achieved greatness have done so because of intense concentration in their work. When you concentrate you put your thoughts in order, excluding those that are irrelevant. It would not help you achieve one simple clear solution which otherwise could get lost in the crowded hurly-burly of a disordered mind. If you concentrate you are in control of yourself and of the situation. You will also not be dominated by others against your better judgement.

So well marshaled would your thoughts be that you would know why another person's judgement was faulty. You, in fact, would be totally clear headed.

Of all the devises to train and control your mind, yoga has proved to be the most effective. Yoga, a complete way of life, considers the body, mind, and spirit as inseparable. It is not exactly an artistic or spiritual exercise, but more a series of healthy exercises. If you are looking for success, you should practice yoga. It would help you in relaxing, increasing self-awareness, and improving concentration. Here are a few ways to train your mind for better concentration.

The first concentration exercise is "sense-withdrawal". When you do this exercise you become unaware of the world. Select a place where the senses are unaware of the surroundings as far as possible (quiet and dark), a seat neither too hard nor too soft, and sit cross-legged. Consciously and deliberately withdraw your senses of hearing, sight, and smell. Breathe deeply and control your senses. It may take some time. This exercise gives mental passivity, and the consciousness of the external world decreases.

The second exercise is the focusing of the mind on a single point. Simply let your thoughts have full control of you. Allow them to roam through your mind unchecked. Do not make any attempt to control them. Detach yourself from your own identity. Monitor the whole proceeding as if you were watching a chaotic movie. The thoughts that flow through your mind will surprise or even shock you. However, after a few sittings you will find that the chaotic rush of thoughts smoothens out to become an orderly chain, with one thought following another. Soon you will be able to separate each succeeding thought from the preceding one and will be able to achieve a fractional pause — the ability to suppress arousing of the next thought for a fraction of a second. This signals the beginning of a controlled and orderly mind.

The quality of concentration can be further improved with the help of the visual method — you concentrate on an object chosen entirely to your own taste. It can be a flower or a tree in the outdoor surroundings or a picture or a cup inside a room. Never concentrate upon the sun. Seat yourself comfortably 45 cm away from the object. Focus your gaze on to and consider it further in minute detail. Ask yourself what, where, when, why, and how about the object. Follow each thought smoothly and easily to its logical conclusion. Soon the object will fill up your mind so completely that you will identify yourself with it. At that moment, you will have crossed the line between concentration and meditation.

The third exercise is *Shamatha* or focused attention. It involves learning how to observe what is going on in a person's mind and body without judgment and keeping focused on breathing or chanted mantra. It is one that specifically aims to strengthen the mind's stability and to counterbalance the symptoms of an agitated or depressed mind. There are two aspects to shamatha practice—formal and post formal. Formal involves selecting a specific period of time and suitable place to practice. The post formal practice is how you incorporate shamatha practice into your everyday life.

Steps

1. For a formal sitting pick a length of time to sit. Five minutes is a great time to introduce yourself to this formal practice. It's recommended to formally sit around ten minutes a day.
2. In the formal sitting: assume a relaxed and upright posture. Sitting in a chair is best for a beginner. Sit so that your feet are flat on the floor with your spine upright without overly slouching or sitting too rigid. If possible do not rest on back of chair. Knees should be at the level of the hips or lower.
3. Initially select a place to sit where you will not be interrupted for your selected time period. In a city there

is rarely a sound-free place to sit. Quiet isn't necessary for shamatha, but you would not like to play music either.

When you sit down, rest your hands on your thighs, so that your fingers come right up to your knees. In an upright posture your shoulder will rest naturally down, but if you pull your hands too far back it raises your shoulders. Work to find a relaxed place to put your hands where you won't develop back pain.

Complete relaxation is critical. Continuous monitoring of relaxation by introspection is the sine qua non. Any time your mind wanders or you lose complete relaxation, relax more deeply. A wandering mind is agitated.

Rest your gaze directly in front of you. Because this meditation is about being present, you can keep your eyes open. You will see three things in front of you, and you will blink and your eyes will move. You do not focus on a spot, but simply rest your gaze. Naturally you will focus and unfocus. Come back to a resting gaze.

Once you have settled into your posture, you then begin the practice by resting your attention on your breath. The breath will be the primary point of attention which you come back to for the selected length of time. You are not going to focus on the breath, but rest your attention on it. There are many ways, you will find, to understand when you are resting on the breath and when you are focusing on the breath. That comes later. For now, your attention should notice the breath going in and going out.

As you sit with your attention resting on the breath, your mind will wander. Thoughts and ideas and feelings will come up. Most noticeably will be a narrative of what you are doing. When you notice this you can say to yourself "thinking" and then return your attention back to the breath.

"Thinking" is just a neutral label. You might just say "Ding!" It is a way to signify to yourself that you have wandered from your object of attention.

It helps to have a pattern you can follow from your "Ding!" to getting back to the breath. For example, you see you are off your point and you say to yourself "Ding!" Then you check your posture—is it still upright? Then you can come to your gaze—am I staring at a hole into a speck of lint on the floor? Then you come back to the breath. To start, rest the attention on the breath as it comes in and out of the mouth and nostrils. Then more specifically rest your attention on the exhaled breath as it goes out from you in a whoosh. Then relax and wait for another outward whoosh. Without concentration, without focus, just being present and aware of how the breath goes out.

In between the exhaled breaths, you can explore all the other ways you are resting in the formal meditation setting. Do a sweep of gaze and body and environment, all seeking to relax into resting rather than focusing or spacing out.

End significantly. At the end of five minutes you can bow to yourself or ring a bell or take a deep breath—something to signify the end of your formal setting. You can personalise a code: "By this may everyone be happy."

Yoga as a method to achieve concentration is an overwhelmingly optimistic promise, something from the realms of magic. Those who regularly practice yoga claim that they are able to concentrate on a problem in a much better way because they have trained their minds that are under their complete control

Walking

Walking is the simplest and most inexpensive way to fitness. It is a complete exercise in itself. The Greeks were the first to believe in the superiority of walking as an exercise over the other ways of fitness. They could observe that walking made their thought process more lucid and helped them in tackling intricate problems of logic and philosophy. They discovered that their minds remained clear whenever they were walking as it helped increase blood circulation from head to toe. It decreased obesity and cholesterol levels, controlled blood pressure and diabetes, and improved muscular fitness and overall well-being. It also de-stressed you, keeping your heart in shape.

Gandhiji firmly believed in the importance of walking. He walked almost across the Indian subcontinent. Thomas Jefferson, the legendary President of the U.S. once said, "Walking is the best possible exercise. Habituate yourself to walk very fast". Franklin D. Roosevelt, the incapacitated President of the United States, walked about 13 kilometres every day to improve his physique. He had several ailments right from childhood and became a victim of polio later. It was only because of walking as his main physical exercise that he managed to enjoy the longest duration of presidency.

An eminent American heart specialist, Dr. Paul Dudley White, believed that walking had a stimulating effect on the body as well as on the mind. "It is the easiest exercise for most individuals and can be done without any equipment except good shoes, in almost any terrain and weather, and into a very old age," he said. For health addicts, walking is a health package in itself. "It is the best form of de-stressing. It releases negative energy. You feel better and more mentally stabilised," says fashion designer Manav Gangwani. Indrani Dasgupta, a known model, finds walking "something that you can do anywhere, anytime and it's good for all age groups." It is the best and the most cost-effective way of keeping your health in order. You do not need any fancy treadmills, convoluted steppers, or trendy gyms. All you need to do is to take a walk.

The benefits of walking are several. The most feasible and immediate effect is that the oxygen intake is increased. As the entire muscular structure of the body is at work, muscles get more oxygen. The increased oxygen intake causes a high rate of pumping by the heart that increases the blood circulation throughout the body. The most important effect is on the human capillary system. We have 95,000 km of blood vessels in our body. Most of them are capillaries. These are tiny vessels distributing blood to the flesh. In the body of an ordinary person who does not indulge in exercise, most of the capillaries remain dormant. A Swedish physiologist, Lange Anderson, proved in 1961 that regular walking not only awakened the dormant capillaries but also increased their number.

Walking needs only a few essentials. First, all you need is a pair of good and comfortable pair of walking shoes and a pair of cozy socks. The shoes, preferably canvas or sneakers, should have a flat sole. Jogging shoes with thick soles are ideal. But as these might not be available everywhere, you can use ordinary canvas shoes which are comfortable for your feet. The socks should be either in cotton or in towel material. Some companies make sports socks that are specifically made for walking shoes.

Second, walking must be for the purpose of walking. Running for errands or catching a bus cannot be counted as an exercise. You should have no pressure on your mind so that you are relaxed and can walk without any mental tension and pressure.

Third, the walk must be brisk and without rest. A leisurely walk is of no use. A short brisk walk is better than a long leisurely walk. Dr. Upendra Kaul of Fortis wants walking to be at the right speed. One way of finding out if your walking right is, "if you are sweating slightly in good weather." Dr. Ashok Sen of Max Hospital says that if "you can't even speak two words, you're too fast. If you can easily hold a conversation, you're slow. The happy medium is if you can handle single short sentences while being slightly breathless".

Fourth, walking is enjoyable when carried out in a group. In the company of four or five friends you can take a longer enjoyable walk that would be less tiresome. But a walk it must be.

Waste no time and start your day with a good brisk walk in the neighbourhood park. The general system of blood circulation, breathing, and muscular control would work in a coordinated way giving shape and balance to your body. Also, before you begin your evening studies, spend some time walking in fresh air preferably walking before sun set. This would reduce the fatigue of the day and would make the body active and efficient. And your body would thank you.

> **Walk the walk**
>
> *A 60-kg person walking for 40 minutes at about 3 km/hr on a firm surface burns 139 calories.*
>
> *Start at a pace at which you get slightly breathless in good weather, but can talk a short sentence.*
>
> *Walking uphill burns more calories than walking on a plain surface.*
>
> *Always remember to warm up for five minutes before your walk, and take five minutes at the end to cool down.*

Overcome stress

Most of the young managers feel stress in their jobs because they had never worked so hard in their life. Why does this happen? Probably unfulfilled ambitions, job conflicts, and may be other related pressures. Whatever may be the reason, stress greatly hampers the efficiency and productivity of a young manager. Those who develop a system to bear stress move fast in the career. But those who do not do that are left behind. Let us find out how you can cope with stress.

Primitive man had an easy way to relieve stress. He would scream, tear off his hair, bash his opponent—man or beast—with a club, and thereby let off steam. This activated a chain of activities within his body. His blood was flashed with adrenal secretions that mustered strength in the form of both sugar and stored fats to his muscles and brain. It instantly mobilised full energy and stimulated pulse, respiration, and blood pressure. His digestive processes turned off at once so that no energy was diverted from meeting the threat.

His coagulation chemistry immediately prepared to resist wounds with quick clotting. Red cells poured from the spleen into the steeped-up blood circulation to help the respiratory system take in oxygen and cast off carbon dioxide as he bludgeoned the marauding opponent.

But the young manager cannot do this today. He has no option but silently fume in his black suit. It does not mean that he does not react. He does but within his skin, in much the same chemical way. He finds other ways to repress his rage by pushing too hard, smoking too many cigarettes, gulping down cups of coffee, and becoming a prime target for ulcers, heart attacks, and nervous breakdowns.

1. Work-related stress

As early as 1972, Walter Mcquade in an article *What Stress Can Do to You* pointed out the reasons for stress. He said, "Perhaps the answer, or at least part of the answer is that modern societies have to a great extent lost the support that helped people in earlier times endure toil, hardship, and suffering—religious faith, sustaining frame-works of tradition and custom, a sense of place in the social order, a sense of worth derived from the exercise of craftsmanship and awareness that toil, hardship, and suffering were likewise endured by the other members of the same community and the same social class..."

Particularly destructive of the individual's sense of security have been the side-effects of one of the industrial world's most precious products—social mobility. This bright trophy of our times has its deeply etched dark side. Social mobility has weakened the sense of belonging to a class, the sense of having a place in the social ladder. More importantly, social mobility implies that success depends on merit alone and to the extent that society believes in such a correlation, individual bread-winners are thrust into an endless competition where lagging behind or losing can be interpreted as a sign of personal inadequacy.

In today's corporate world, managers are increasingly draining themselves out, inviting emotional and physical illnesses. Unfulfilled ambitions, job-conflicts, and other pressures are constantly taking their toll on young managers' health until they approach a complete breakdown. Stress is not only a killer, but also a vicious force. Nevertheless, stress should not and cannot be avoided. The secret is not to live less intensely but more intelligently. Each manager must find his innate stress level and live accordingly.

The warning signs of stress are irritability, chronic fatigue, cynicism, frustration, boredom, avoidance of personal contacts (isolation), depression, loss of sexual desire, emotional instability (for example, the over-powering urge to cry), inability to concentrate, constant anxiety, insomnia, nightmares, and increased use of alcohol or drugs.

2. How to cope

Work-related stress is a universal malady that causes excess tension and produces confusion. You don't think straight and often cannot organise yourself properly; you jump to the wrong conclusions; you dwell on negative, unproductive factors. All this is true, but how do you cope with stress? Rule number one is, don't sweat the small stuff. Rule number two is, it's all small stuff. If you can't fight and you can't flee, flow.

Take a break: To prevent executive stress from affecting your personal life, discover relaxing activities outside the scope of your work. Spend more time with your family and friends. Take a vacation. Take a break between new projects. Re-define your goals in life and assess your work pattern. Remember, there's no such thing as a perfect job or a perfect company. As most of us have to spend our entire working lives as someone's employee, it's important to assess whether you are suited to work for a corporation. If you think you are instead of being frustrated, look objectively at the company you are working for and adjust your expectations realistically. Learn the art of being emotionally detached and resist the feeling of victimisation to overcome stress resulting from office politics, differences, and tensions with colleagues. You have to understand that if you handle your work situation skillfully, the company will offer you ample opportunities to develop your potential. Or, it can give you ulcers. The choice is yours.

Learn to relax: Anger can be a serious strategic error — you are displaying your weaknesses and inviting exploitation. Learn to make your anger an asset and channelise the energy otherwise uselessly spent in doing something constructive.

Next time something or someone attempts to give you another ulcer, try this. Tense each of your major muscles starting from your neck, shoulders, and arms and down to your legs for about five seconds. Take a deep breath to help pump oxygen into the blood vessels and body tissues and send refreshing blood to the brain. Drink a glass of water and close your eyes for a while. After about 10 minutes, think of pleasant things that happened in the past or those that are coming up in the future. You'll find your body feeling more comfortable and your breathing will become even and normal. Now, isn't that better than, say, reaching for and lighting up a cigarette or drowning your sorrows at a bar?

Power nap

Scientists from the United States have claimed that a nap (a brief snooze) during the day improves the brain's ability to absorb new facts. Volunteers who slept for 90 minutes during the day did better at cognitive tests than those who were kept awake. The latest study, from the University of California at Berkeley, has suggested that the brain may need sleep to process short-term memories, creating space for learning new facts. In their experiment, 39 healthy adults were given a hard learning task in the morning, with broadly similar results, before half of them were sent for their siesta.

According to a BBC report when the tests were repeated, those who had taken a nap outperformed those who had carried on without sleep.

> *Checks on brain electrical activity suggested that this process might be happening in a sleep phase between deep sleep and dreaming sleep, called stage-2 non-rapid eye movement sleep, when fact-based memories are moved from temporary storage in the brain's hippocampus to another area called the pre-frontal cortex.*
>
> *Dr Matthew Walker, who led the study, said: "Sleep not only rights the wrong of prolonged wakefulness, but, at a neurocognitive level, it moves you beyond where you were before you took a nap."*
>
> *However, Professor Derk-Jan Dijk, the director of the Surrey Sleep Research Centre, said that there was no clear evidence that daytime napping offered a distinct advantage over sleeping just once over 24 hours.*

Thinking—make it effective

Skilful thinking is sine quo non to success. Yet most of the time our thinking is confused, inappropriate, and ineffective. The reason is that our education does not train the mind to think independently and creatively. It hampers the quality of the brain. A person is not able to think broadly and deeply. He becomes a recluse with no ambition. But if you are ambitious and want to achieve something better in life, you have to develop your quality of thinking.

Thinking is at the root of everything you do. Yet not many try to develop a thinking process of their own, let alone analysing the thinking of those with whom they deal. It may be due to the widespread myth that thinking is abstract, having no real bearing on ordinary life. To bust this myth and give a new approach to thinking, Jerry Rhodes and Sue Thame, specialists in creative thinking have suggested in their book *The Colours of Your Mind* a colour code for recognising and improving the thinking style of a person. Making comprehensive use of questionnaires, exercises, examples, and illustrations, Jerry and Sue have shown that by using three colours—red for facts and realities, blue for judgements and opinions, and green for ingenuity and imagination—you can help yourself in penetrating the very working of your mind, behaviour, emotions, and intellect. If you can find out the colours of your mind, you can have access to the inner working of your mind and even the minds of other people.

The basic premise of Jerry and Sue is that blue, red, and green are the three colours that represent the basic dimension of your thinking process. When you are thinking, you are always operating from one of these three colours, each of which covers a different aspect of your deep thinking intentions. In a way your mind is divided into these three colour zones. When you are thinking, you use the colour zones that are relevant to that thinking category. For example, if you want to speak or ask for the truth, you go to the red part of the mind. When you either judge something or persuade someone else to accept your judgement and change his or her own, the blue part of the mind is being used. When you actively search for ideas and are willing to accept insights for others, you are in the green zone. Therefore, all your thoughts spring from these three colours. These, in fact, are your fundamental intentions, the basic drives of your thinking. They, sometimes, operate consciously but more often go beyond your consciousness, affecting the direction your mind will take.

Though one has a dominant colour, the remaining two colours operate to create a different mixture of these colours. They cause everyone to think differently. Colours can be looked at as separate entities, but they always exist together in your mind. As none of these colours is ever missing, there is always a kaleidoscope effect, as one shade finely merges into another or as one level of colour overlays or is woven into another.

Once you have identified the colour, you have to find out the two sides of your thinking, called "modes". Each colour can be used either of the two modes. The one you adopt when using a particular colour makes a profound difference to the outcome. It is because the two operate in opposing ways. If you are not aware of the dynamics between the two modes, you will not be able to get the better of the two. "But when you handle them well, harmonising the potential conflict, they help you to match up to the realistic complexities of life". Jerry and Sue call the two modes "hard" and "soft".

This combination of colours and their modes have been called the two sides of your thinking. The two modes have been called the two sides of your thinking which must he brought together for effective action in all spheres of endeavour. An understanding of the hard and soft modes "gives you access to every corner, every nook and cranny of you thinking" so that you can go beyond the extreme limits of thinking. The hard mode is objective; it is the scientific world of reality. The soft mode is the artistic world of beliefs and values. We all want to be both, a scientist and an artist, and so everyone has to live in the hard world of objective reality as well as in the soft world of our own beliefs, dreams, and values.

This technique helps you to find out your own personal style of dealing with others and understand why people deal with you the way they do, The new language of colours may help you to maximise your strength, improve work satisfaction, and build successful relations with colleagues, friends, and family members. You can interpret the chief characteristics of your own thinking style. Increased knowledge of the colours and modes could improve the accuracy of your responses. You can understand yourself and others better. The colour and mode combination enables you to manage better relationships with people with whom you work and live — colleagues, seniors, juniors, friends, relations, and clients. You can coordinate your style with others. Knowledge of the working of your mind and of those around you can give you an idea about the range of differences in the thinking styles. It helps you to avoid conflicts. Creative coordination is possible with others, and you can analyse the causes of conflicts and avoid head-on collisions. You can go to the root of the conflict by analysing various thinking styles.

Regular exercises can boost the colours with which you have the least facility and enrich the ones for which you have the greatest affinity.

Skilful thinking is comparable to mastering a musical instrument or conducting an orchestra. Excellence in these skills is only achieved through repeated practice, coupled with live performances in front of critical and appreciative audiences. Several creative specialists have developed concepts and exercises to train the human mind. Edward de Bono's concept of lateral thinking talks about the creative part of the mind. Hudson's convergent and divergent problem solving, and the left brain and right brain work of Ornstein have opened up people's consciousness to their own thinking process. However, Jerry and Sue's colour coding is a more practiced and easy way to train your mind and better thinking.

Train your mind and think well.

Creative thinking

Creativity, the quality of employing a playfully exploratory rather than a mechanical process of problem solving, is an essential requirement to be successful in life. Unfortunately many persons are unaware of this and make no efforts to develop these characteristics in their personality. They are, therefore, unable to find solutions that are both novel and useful.

Creativity is not just one but a cluster of abilities. The various abilities are:
- *Identical fluency,* which measures the ability of a person to come up with a large number of brief solutions to any one given problem.
- *Flexibility,* the ability to provide a large variety of viewpoints and to use a variety of approaches in solving problems.
- *Originality,* the ability to come up with unusual but appropriates responses (a related ability being capable of coming up with novel relationships between ideas).

- *Problem sensitivity*, the ability to sense problems, to notice the unexplained, the unsatisfactory, or the incongruent.
- The *ability to grasp on a theme*, which is indispensable in putting a creative idea to work.
- The *ability to restrictive problems* to see beyond the superficial features of problems and identify what the real problem is.

These abilities are not all found in an equal measure in the same individual.

Creativity in many individuals is inborn. However, those who are serious and diligent can develop this quality of the brain. It needs a high degree of motivation, appropriate training, and an encouraging environment. A high degree of success can be achieved through the creation of a cultural environment. This can be done by taking up some creative hobby or activity by finding creative friends and, if possible, by getting into a more creative job or occupation.

There are several ways of promoting and planning creative thinking. Pradip N. Khandwala, former Director of Indian Institute of Management, Ahmedabad, has suggested certain techniques. These are:

- *Structure the problem* so that it is well understood.
- *Separate the phase of idea production from idea evaluation*. Do not evaluate or criticise ideas, whether one's own or another's, during the time of their articulation.
- *Storm your brain.* Churn out a large number of ideas. It heightens the possibility of coming up with some really good ones. Also one idea leads to another and still another and so on like a chain reaction.
- *Create a constructive psychological strength* by continuously moving from the known to the unknown situations and back to the former.
- *Shake your perspectives* by asking such questions as what would be the opposite of the current solution; how could you magnify or unify the solution, or is there

a radically different way of looking at the problem? Choose the ones with the greatest potential by some assessment or selection procedure.

Several techniques can be used for creative thinking that De Bono calls "lateral thinking." Brainstorming is the most important of them. It is based on the principle that quantity begets quality, so to get many ideas it is necessary to suspend evaluation of ideas during the idea generation phase. However, brainstorming is useful as a technique where the problem has a unique solution that can be reached by analysis. Although brainstorming is done in groups, it can also be done by individuals. Brainstorming is not just a technique, it is a culture. It is a clear message that for divergent thinking at least, democratic and collaborative culture works. Brainstorming increases self-confidence.

The significant technique of creative thinking is attribute-listening. It is useful for designing and redesigning a specific activity. In attribute-listening, the attempt is first made to list the basic attributes or properties or specifications of a particular object or activity. Then an attempt is made to generate alternatives to the current attributes or specifications.

The third technique is synectics that has been adapted from the Greek word *synectico* meaning "fitting together diverse elements." It is a remarkable technique of solving problems at the group level, and to a first-timer, it looks like a crazy method of finding solutions.

Creativity can be improved with the help of several tools. These are:

- *Effective listening:* Listening carefully and patiently to others.
- *Empathy:* Suspend your critical faculties while the other person is struggling to express himself.
- *Classificatory questions*: If the problem being discussed is not very clear, try to bring the problem into sharper focus by asking questions, such as how do you look at

the problem or what do you think will be the impact of the problem on the present situation?
- *Feedback:* Find out the feelings and opinions of different people, for this you must be in a receptive frame of mind. Share your feelings and views with others in a factual non-evasive manner.
- *Evocative questions*: Do not ask hostile questions. Ask questions that will make the other person come out with her/his own ideas and expressions that can lead to creative solutions.
- *Analogies:* A problem can be seen from a fresh perspective with the help of analogies. For example, if the problem is concerning engineering, analogies from biology can be sought. When talking to others for feedback, try to find out parallel situations.
- *Converging* of a solution or conclusion.

Step one to four will help you to articulate the problem more clearly. Steps five and six can help in handling any divergent and creative thinking. It is often useful to help the other person get a sense of closeness or conclusion by helping him move to a satisfactory choice. Helping with frank feedback and information, and evolving criteria for evaluating alternatives, applying these criteria when there is a conflict, planning actions that will increase the probability of a successful execution of the chosen alternative will help in this phase of interpersonal interaction.

Be an avid reader

Eighteen years back I was in Richmond, a small university town in Kentucky (USA) as a visiting Fulbright Professor. Being not accustomed to the severe winter of the United States, I developed a minor health problem as the winter set in. A friend of mine took me to the hospital. After some waiting my turn came and I went into the chamber of the doctor and occupied the examining stool beside the doctor.

To my utter bewilderment and annoyance, the doctor was looking at my face rather examining me. Before I could say anything the doctor asked me hesitatingly, "You are Yogi. Aren't you?"

I could not believe my eyes. It was Rajiv, my childhood friend. We had studied in the same school, same classes, and sat on the same bench for more than a decade. Our ways parted when we cleared the tenth standard. I joined social sciences and he went to pursue biology with the intention of becoming a doctor. He was not a brilliant student, just a mediocre. Despite several attempts he could not enter any medical college. Disgusted he left India after completing his graduation in science as an escort to an elderly lady to West Germany. I lost touch after that. Now we were meeting after decades.

"Wake up, Yogi," Rajiv's words woke me up from the trance in which I had entered recollecting the past. "Let me examine you first and then we will catch up with the past," he said. After a thorough check-up he said that there was nothing serious, just a minor cold due to exposure. He gave me a few tablets and not the prescription with a promise that I would shift to his home in the evening. The same evening he came with his wife and two children and took me to his house.

In the days that followed we had long discussions whenever we could find time. We went into the past and he narrated his experiences and I mine. One question echoed in my mind always: "How could a person who had failed totally in his own country, become a professional in the U.S.?" Several discussions over the weekend gave me the answer. The reason for his success was the western education system that developed three qualities in a person. These were wide reading, an efficient recall system, and an effective communication mechanism. All the three are essential for success in life. I thought I must share with my readers how Rajiv developed these qualities.

Wide reading lays the foundation for a strong knowledge base. It is essential for developing a complete personality of a person. That was the reason the British while training officers for the Indian Civil Service taught them a little bit of every discipline—sports, science, economics, politics, and even classical music and painting. The idea was that they should feel comfortable in whatever company they were in and could leave a lasting impression on others. It helped in creating an impression on others that they knew about everything.

Rajiv read widely when he was in medical school in Germany. He read even subjects like art and culture that were remotely connected with medicine and surgery. He read current journals to acquaint him with the latest trends in the medical profession. He not only gained additional information but also was motivated to improve his professional competence. The habit that he developed during his student days continues till today. This is what makes him a thorough person even now.

Only reading is not enough. There are persons who read a lot but are not able to *recall the information* when they need it. Most of us do not possess the remarkable recall system of persons like Lala Hardyal of undivided Punjab who after reading a book would throw it away as he could repeat the entire book verbatim. We must learn efficient and effective ways of acquiring knowledge and retaining it. Rajiv was taught several steps to develop a good recall system.

He was trained to read a book in a day and prepare its summary and review. The objective was to understand the main theme and the various ideas it discussed. He would then consult book reviews published in magazines and newspapers. He was asked to read and review about 12 books in a year.

Besides wide reading and a good recall system, he was trained in *efficient communications* that is sine qua non for acquiring higher positions in one's career. He was taught to use proper words and expressions to convey his ideas to avoid a communication gap. An effective communication system can be developed by improving both the spoken and written expressions. Rajiv believes that there is no substitute to writing. The only way to improve is to write and write more—letters, articles, papers, and essays. It is an art that takes time to develop, but if you are determined you can develop the skill in four to five years. Once learnt, it grows on you. There is no short cut to that.

Better conversational ability requires better coordination between the mind and the tongue. You should indulge in conversation whenever you get an opportunity. Rajiv would never miss an opportunity and would participate in seminars, conferences, discussions, and lectures. He always participated actively and in a positive way. After constant and prolonged practice he acquired the art of developing a theme, providing his point of view, and disproving another person's argument and thesis.

Those who want to become a strong personality and be a success story should follow Rajiv's three-step strategy. If you do that you will find yourself to be an entirely different personality. Fame and money may be at your doorstep.

1. Read comprehensively

Suresh, an old colleague of mine, conducts interviews for recruiting junior and senior level managers for a large multinational corporation. He also works as an expert at various other recruitment boards including the UPSC. I have been after him for many months to give me details of the selection process. My pointed question to him has been what is the cutting edge that determines the final selection? He was evading the issue for a long time but I was after him. At last he gave in and decided to enlighten me on this subject. He gave me two case studies.

The first was of Ram Lal who came from a small village that had no good school or library. After finishing his graduation from a nearby college in the city, he went back to his village. Ram appeared in the civil service examination and because of his serious, comprehensive, and diligent studies qualified for the interview. His next task was to prepare for the personality test and interview with a determination to get a high ranking as he had done well in the written test. The task was not easy because there were no facilities for reading books, newspapers, and magazines in the village. Because of the weak financial condition of the family he could not afford to stay in the city again and prepare. He, however, was not disheartened. Every day he would cycle down to the town library that was five kilometres away and read whatever newspapers and magazines were available. He would go to the city library once or twice a week and spend the entire day in the college library to read the latest books. By the time his turn for interview came he was well read and prepared to talk on national and international affairs. During the interview he was able to impress the board members on the various issues by his up-to-date knowledge and intelligent analyses. No doubt, when the results appeared, he was among the merit holders.

Another case study was of Sanjay. He came from a metropolitan city and an affluent family. He had graduated from one of the good colleges but was over confident. He thought he possessed knowledge on every subject and his views were the best. However, during the interview he was not able to impress the board members because his knowledge was not up to date and his analyses were mediocre. The poor fellow failed to appear in the list of the selected candidates. He blamed the selectors saying they were biased and could not understand his answers and analyses.

These are two typical categories of students who prepare for and appear in interviews. The number of Ram Lals is small and Sanjays is large. Suresh's comments were that the reading habits among the students are declining and therefore many were not able to perform well in the interviews. Most of the candidates do not read the latest books by good writers. If they read, their choice is confined to cheap books of inferior quality. It leaves a poor impression on the board as they always try to find out the reading range of a candidate to assess her/his knowledge base and finer qualities. Newspaper and magazine reading is also not comprehensive and serious. Therefore, the candidates do not know much about what was happening around them. Many are even ignorant of the environment in which they have grown up. In an interview for the position of rural marketing manager, the boys from rural background did not know the problems in their own areas and the changing social and family behaviours in villages.

Suresh gave me several examples of how knowledge acquired by some candidates was entirely wrong. A student of economics was not able to name the top three businessmen in India. He could not tell the difference between gross national product and gross domestic product. An MA in political science from a state university could not distinguish between parliamentary and presidential forms of government. The fate of geography and history students was worst. Only a few candidates had a clear idea about chronology and important dates. When it came to cultural characteristics of different periods and kings, most of them knew nothing. It was painful that geography students were ignorant about elementary geographical data. It was agonising that these candidates didn't even know about the southern or northeastern states in their own country.

Suresh's experience was that students coming from English medium school were better informed than those from the Hindi medium schools. The former students were able to provide information on subjects that were not part of their syllabus. Non-science students were able to explain simple scientific facts and those coming from the science stream knew about the government, music, films, and different countries. The reasons were many. These schools, from the elementary stage, prepared students to have a diversified personality. The schools also held varied programmes and contests like quizzes, debates, group discussions, and essay writing to develop the creative, speaking, and writing skills of the children. The students had to read and think widely to prepare for these contests and, therefore, were better informed.

The time has come when a person who wants to move upwards fast cannot ignore reading, discussions, or public speaking. The reason is that competition is becoming more intense day by day. The selection boards and commissions are inundated by applications running in to several thousands. They have to eliminate large number of candidates and therefore ask difficult questions. The concept of division and merit has become obsolete. A student getting 90 per cent, or even more, may fail in the objective type tests if he has not been able to understand the concepts and follow the questions clearly. Most of the students securing high marks cram solutions to a large number of questions without understanding the concepts or situations. This type of knowledge does not help in an objective-type testing.

When Suresh had finished, I asked him a question. How could the boys and girls studying in schools strengthen their knowledge base, creative speaking, and writing skills? His suggestion was that the students should read comprehensively during their student days. Their reading should not be confined to their discipline. They should read on all subjects. What they read should be discussed with teachers, relatives, and friends in school and home. They should also form their views and should be articulated in a convincing way. This would help them in any group discussion and interview.

2. Effective reading

If I am asked to name one single factor that revolutionized the civilization and modernised the society my answer would be in two words—"The Book". It was a book that became the invaluable repository of thought and knowledge. It provided and continues to provide a means of collating a considerable store of information in a small space and in a durable form.

Certain books were so influential that they influenced the intellectual equipment of many and their availability was a stimulus to literacy. It was books that changed the social process and structures and brought to an end the long era in which the ignorance of the majority of population was excluded from political life. People in towns and villages scattered around the globe became better informed than ever before, and could form their own opinions on issues that directly affected their lives and livelihood. In brief, books changed the relationship between the authorities and the majority of people, and conserved and stabilised societies. Books, in reality, are the strongest institution for the diffusion of great ideas. Goods books enrich a person's intellect, help him cultivate a better personality, and are essential for self-development. Reading books opens doors for self-development.

The number of published books is increasing every year. Therefore, it becomes difficult to choose good books for reading. Unplanned and unorganised reading is not very useful. It is a time wastage. If you want to read comprehensively and wish to improve your knowledge base, you must read with a purpose and enjoy what you read. It is necessary to select books carefully because it is humanly impossible to read all books that have been published.

The best way to reading is to plan the book selection and then read the selected books. It involves three steps. One, you must select books that could provide useful knowledge. Second, the book reading should not be occasional. It should be a regular habit. Third, you should be able to recollect what you have read as and when the information and knowledge gathered from the book is required.

Book selection: It is not an easy process. Millions of books are printed and published all over the world in a large number of languages. Every writer claims that every book written by him is great. You can't believe and buy every book. First there is no need for it, and second you do not have enough resources to buy all books. Therefore, you adopt either of the two ways suggested to select books for reading. The first way is to go through book reviews in various newspapers and magazines. You can form your opinion by reading reviews of the same book in a number of newspapers and magazines. It is required because many reviewers are not balanced in their critique and they have certain biases. Many libraries keep clippings of book reviews. You can also take the help of the Internet. A second way is to quickly go through the book at some bookshop. Glance through the index. It would give you an idea about the coverage in the book. It may not be covered in contents of the book. Read certain parts of the book. Make your selection from the index. Read parts without any definite plan. This will help you determine its worth.

Regular reading: You should not read on an *ad hoc* basis. It is essential that you read regularly on a weekly basis. You should have a reading schedule. Regularity in reading needs determination and effort. The minimum target should be to read at least one book every fortnight. If you want to be better read, your minimum reading should be one book every month. If you do not do that, you surrender yourself to self-chosen ignorance.

Comprehending a book: If you do not register what you have read, reading a book is of no value or use. You would be wasting your time and energy if you just read and do not comprehend and understand what you were reading. Foremost is to understand the basic focus and thrust of the book, and then try and retain it. Your effort to retain the knowledge should include making brief notes on the book that you are reading. Also it would help to maintain a list of books you have read and, if possible, try and maintain the database on a computer. If that is not possible, use catalogue cards and arrange them alphabetically.

3. Speed-reading

If you want to read more books in less time, you should develop a good reading speed. Norman Lewis suggests six principles to "transfer your potential speed under pressure into a normal, comfortable and habitual speed."

First, your reading plan should have a *reading schedule*. Allocate time for reading books in your weekly schedule of activities. Assign at least three evenings every week and two full continuous hours for reading. You cannot think of becoming a good or a fast reader if you do not develop the habit of reading for at least two hours at a stretch, twice or thrice every week.

Second, *read broadly*. Do not waste time on minor details unless it is a text or technical book. Try to understand the main focus, the theme, and the overall view of the book. Follow the development. Find out the framework on which the author has developed the book and carefully keep it in mind when analysing it.

Third, *read seriously*. Do not indulge in easy reading. It means you should not read in a leisurely way. You must read seriously and widely if you want to develop the ability to understand the book even while reading it fast.

Fourth, *fix a deadline* by which you must finish the reading of the book. This will make you an avid reader. If you decide that you will finish the book in two days your reading will be fast. If you are determined to finish it in four hours, you would be able to do that too. With concentrated reading your comprehension would be faster. You would scan the book and understand it fully in the allotted time of two hours. The human mind is highly productive under pressure. It is amazing what people can do if they really want to do something.

Fifth, *pace your reading*. In the first 15 minutes the entire book should be read for quick understanding. Then you find out your per hour required speed—the number of pages that you must finish in one hour. Find out the total number of pages in the book and divide it by four. You get your per hour potential speed for reading this book. This must be practised regularly. Only then can you become a fast reader who can read fast both comfortably and naturally.

Six, develop *better concentration*. This is essential for fast reading. If you read slowly, your mind does not operate at full capacity. It is likely to wander, and you will not be able to comprehend the material you would be reading. Slow reading is wastage of time. If you are reading fast, you are constantly challenging your understanding, stimulating your mind, and getting involved in the book.

If you follow these six steps, eventually you would become a fast reader. Faithful implementation is necessary. The important thing is to believe that you can do it.

Try this and reading will become more interesting, enjoyable, and illuminating.

4. Systematic reading

"All the business of war, and indeed all the business of life is to endeavour to find out what you don't know from what you know," said Arthur Wellesley, the first Duke of Wellington. Arthur served in India from 1799 to 1805 and later became the Tory Prime Minister in 1828. The only way to find out what you do not know is to read, read, and keep on reading regularly. It is only reading that "maketh a full man" said Francis Bacon, a 17th century British philosopher. Rev. Sydney Smith, a 19th century British journalist, was not wrong when he commented that those who read "live always in the best company". No doubt "a good book is the best of friends, the same today, and forever".

Unfortunately, we are neglecting our "best friends," and the habit of reading books is confined to certain category of persons. No doubt an average young student is not well read and well informed — an indication of an ill-balanced personality. It is indeed disgraceful not to know about contemporary authors and recently published books. While interviewing candidates for the post of public relations manager, I asked a candidate to name two recently published books read by him. He could not mention even one. This lamentable state of affairs is not isolated but widespread.

Why shouldn't the habit that did contribute to the growth of many achievers be revived? Those who want to move to the fast lane in their career must particularly develop this valuable habit.

The important question is how can you develop and improve your reading habit and capacity? It is not a difficult process, but a simple one if you adopt a three-step formula consisting of quick reading, reading for registration, and reading for recapitulation. The three steps may seem time-consuming, but if practiced seriously, simultaneously, habitually, and with determination, you can become an impulsive reader.

Quick reading: The method of reading quickly to get an overview of the material you have at hand is called quick reading (QR). You need not go into details about the material you are reading. You should only try to find out what the author wants to prove or disprove. You only read to get a general idea of how the book has been organised and what is the major theme of the book. The following steps should help you in your QR:

- Read carefully the chapter titles to know what is likely to be written under those headings. Try to recapitulate what you already know about the subject that you elicit from the chapter title.
- Glance through a couple of paragraphs of each chapter so that you can get to know the major themes. Make yourself conversant with the writing style.
- While scanning through the chapter, move from heading to heading to get a feel of the main ideas of the author. While you are progressing from heading to heading, scan the text and absorb the key words. They might be given in **bold face** or *italics*.
- Give special attention to pictures, diagrams, tables, graphs, and maps. These may be central to the theme developed in the book.

- Read the last paragraph of every chapter carefully as it may summarise the entire chapter.
- Once you have finished the book, close your eyes and think for a few minutes about what you have read. Try to recall the sequence of ideas and ask yourself what the main idea or theme was.

Reading for registration: Quick reading should be followed by reading for registration (RR). This is done with a view to thoroughly understand each theme, idea, or concept discussed in the book. Adopt the following procedure:

- Differentiate between the main theme and the supporting themes. Look for the central argument and the central idea in each section or paragraph, and understand the terms the writer tries to explain or highlight.
- Read the chapter structures as if it were a map of the author's ideas. The introduction to the chapter is important because it outlines the ideas that follow. Look for step-by-step explanations of main ideas in various paragraphs, and go through the summaries or conclusions at the end of the chapter. This may condense the text to its main concepts.
- After finishing a few paragraphs, test your comprehension by summarising the material in your own words. Go through the material quickly to check your understanding. Re-read the parts you have forgotten or misunderstood until you are sure of your comprehension. Once you feel you have understood the entire chapter, go back and underline important phrases or write notes in the margin if you have anything to add to the arguments given in the book.

Reading for recapitulation: The final reading is for recapitulation (Recap). This, in fact, is the revision of what you have read. In this stage you should re-read headings, summaries, and key words and terms as well as the passages you have underlined. Concentrate on how various ideas fit together. Read again carefully any passage that does not seem familiar or clear. You must recite aloud or write the main ideas before putting the book aside. This would store the various ideas and main themes developed in the book in your mental computer.

Try it once; you may like it to make it a routine reading practice.

Humour helps

Good communication leading to a lasting friendship is the real key to success. Only those who know it become popular and are able to influence people. A touch of humour adds strength to communication. If used properly and judiciously, it can be an effective management tool, a superb communication device, and an excellent stress-relieving agent. In short, it is a powerful booster to productivity in every walk of life. In fact, humour motivates, relaxes, and inspires.

A sense of humour or an ability to laugh and make others laugh is one trait that distinguishes human beings from other animals. Humour does not mean just a smile or a laugh; rather it is one way to put a person at ease. Effective humour can disarm the opponent, confound a noisy speaker, and promote happy friendship. In fact, there is no substitute to humour and there is no situation in this world where a little humour cannot help.

Humour, the elixir of life, emanates a fragrance that attracts people. Unfortunately, the scholars in ancient civilization did not realise the significance of humour. Plato considered laughter as an evil-minded behaviour accompanied by jealousy, hatred, and an aggressive force designed to hit at the enemy. Aristotle saw in humour some form of distortion, an ignoble behaviour that disgraced morals, art, and religion. His advice to all civilised men was to shun humour.

The importance of laughter was realised at the turn of the 15th century. At that time it was agreed that comedy functioned as a social corrective to the follies of mankind. Later, Jean Baptiste Poquelin, a French dramatist of the 17th century (who wrote under the pseudonym of Moliere) and Jonathan Swift, the British satirist of the 18th century lampooned the social idiosyncrasy and hypocrisy of the Western society of their time. In the modern society, humour is an accepted and respected human behaviour. In fact, a comedian is accorded high recognition in the contemporary society. The amount of recognition and respect that stand-up comedians like Navjot Singh Siddhu, Shekhar Suman, and Raju Srivastava get is an indication of this.

Over the past 60 years, scholars from all over the world have researched on the relevance of humour in management and administration. Though it is difficult to establish a correlation between humour and efficiency and productivity, it has been proved that it positively impacts the problem-solving efficiency of a person. "Research has provided empirical backing to the advice, "use humour in your presentation," says S. Ramani, the former Director of the Mumbai-based National Institute for Training in Industrial Engineering (NITIE). "Wit in conversation is, in the midwives' phrase, 'a quick conception and an easy delivery'," said Swift.

Humour, however, is like a surgeon's scalpel. If used properly it does wonders but a wrong use may prove fatal. Likewise, a poor sense of humour may kill a warm friendship. It is a powerful tool like fire, but can also backfire. Humour is a good servant but a bad master. So acquire better control over it and follow certain precautions to get the best results. When in doubt, it is better not to crack a joke rather than spoiling it. Given below are some precautions to be kept in mind:

- *Never joke about a person's name.* The name of a person should not be distorted in jokes as there is nothing more personal than one's name. Therefore, do not distort the name of a person or associate it with something bad or unsociable.

- *Don't narrate jokes about one's race,* religion, and ethnicity. It, however, can be done in private talks between friends who are close friends. But be sure that it should not injure anyone's sensitivity. Sometimes friendships come to an end because of a bad joke.
- The *technique of narrating a joke* should match with your style, mannerism, personality, and thinking. Do not narrate a joke if you feel you would not be able to present it as effectively as someone else would.
- The humour *should always be relevant*. It must suit the subject and the occasion. A joke that does not fit into a discussion will be counter-productive. The right kind of humour is a must.
- *Do not go into unnecessary details.* Briefer the joke, the more effective it would be.
- The *uniqueness of a joke* makes it memorable. People not only hear what is said with humour, but also remember it better and longer, if the anecdote is new and interesting.
- An *environment of reciprocal humour* should be developed. You can crack jokes only if you accept them from others. Such an environment can be created through well-conceived jocularity regarding you.

"Most of the humour must have a motive behind it. We are communicating (in any form) with humour for a purpose and objective. Sometimes our communication style may be funny, but not necessarily the reasons behind it," says Ramani.

Mr. K. Raghunath, the former Foreign Secretary is a person who has successfully been able to achieve his objectives with an appropriate sense of humour to suit occasions and people. "With humour and charm, he can mix as easily with kings as with the *hoi polloi* and can make good friends even among hostile people," says one of his close friends. It was through his sense of humour that he coped with the trauma in Beijing (where in 1968, he along with another India diplomat was held up and beaten up by the Chinese) and the burning of the Indian High Commission in Dhaka years later.

We should develop a good sense of humour and a good-humoured approach to life. Wit costs nothing but pays in abundance. It is one of the free and abundant resources for improving the quality of life and success in work.

Communication shrinks the world

We have already entered into a global village type of living, much different from the isolated mode of living of the 20th century. The importance of communication has become topmost in this setup. It now is so central to all social, economic, and political activities at the community, national, and international levels that Sean MacBridge, an Irish journalist and Nobel Laureate said: "Human history becomes more and more a race between communication and catastrophe. Full use of communication in all its varied standards is vital to assure that humanity has more than a history ... that our children are ensured a future."

Throughout history, the human effort has been to acquire knowledge through communication. The first concrete step towards effective communication was the development of language. It gave scope and depth to the content of communication as well as for the precision and details of expression it allowed. Writing was man's second major achievement. It gave permanence to the spoken word. It gave birth, around 500 B.C., to a book that became an invaluable repository of thought and knowledge.

The publication of newspapers in the 17th century was the next important development that changed the communication scenario completely. Newspapers, unlike books, give diversified information on everything on earth. Growth in literacy and income, and the low price of the newspaper soon made it popular. Quick and cheap means of transportation made newspapers readily available.

Information that took months to reach a distance of 1,000 kilometres, reached the next day. Now with the development of the electronic media it reaches instantly.

In India, however, the fullest use of the newspaper, especially by the students, is not made. It is neither a part of the study material nor is it used for acquiring and storing knowledge. A regular study of the newspaper could be a major asset in making one's career. With the job market becoming increasingly competitive day by day, it becomes imperative for you to be well informed.

Information and communication are primary requirements for an effective personality. These have no substitutes and cannot be developed in a short period of a few weeks or months. It takes a couple of years to become well informed and articulate. Those who try to take shortcuts are bound to "trip up" sooner or later. Wouldn't it be better, therefore, to work systematically towards acquiring these two qualities with the help of newspapers?

Let's take information first. An enlightened person should be well informed about political, economic, and social affairs, international and local events, and contemporary problems. Besides being aware of happenings around him, he must be acquainted with the background and what led to the present situation. A historical perspective will help him to understand the nature, complexity, and the gravity of any problem.

A newspaper is the storehouse of information. A person who regularly and intelligently reads a newspaper knows all about contemporary issues and problems, not only around him but also all around the world. And those who read more than one newspaper are conversant with different viewpoints. A few years back, the Newspaper Advertising Bureau conducted a survey in San Francisco (California, USA) for its Newspaper Readership Project. Two groups were selected. One was of those students who used newspapers in the classroom, and the other of those who did not read newspapers as part of their classroom education. After a few weeks' observation it was found that the students who read newspapers were better informed and knew much more about contemporary problems and issues than the students of the second group.

Unfortunately, we in India do not realise the importance of newspaper in educating students. Right from nursery to the post-graduate level, the whole emphasis is on textbook reading. In the United States, the Newspaper in Education (NIE) programme is sponsored even in kindergarten classes. Cecil Smith, NIE coordinator for two newspapers in Lawton (Oklahoma, USA) accompanied as a representative from sponsors on a trip with the kindergarten class to a wildlife sanctuary. Smith noticed that all the kids were carrying their newspapers with them on the bus. When she asked one little girl why she was carrying a newspaper, she replied, "We read newspapers to learn things about the world. That's how we know about Premier Gorbachov." Smith's comments were: "Here was a kindergarten girl and she was saying words I couldn't even pronounce."

Equally, if not more, important is verbal and written communication. It is at the heart of all social interactions because people cannot live in isolation. It is through communication that a person explains his views to others, or can benefit from the knowledge of others. A good communicator is always able to enlarge the impact, diversity, and intelligibility of his views.

Communication is possible in two ways: through speaking and by writing. Language and expression are important whether you speak or write. Confucius, about 2,600 years ago, worried about the correct use of words, wrote a long treatise to warn his disciples about serious misunderstandings that could arise if proper care was not taken with the use of words, as also about spellings and punctuation.

More important than spelling is effective writing. To be effective, whatever comes from your pen should not be unstructured, verbose, or unedited. If you want your writings to create an impact, you should give a brief introduction, a lightly written main report, and a clear well-presented and well-substantiated conclusion. Your work should give an impression of being well researched, well presented and well written. You should differentiate between facts and opinions, between conclusions and recommendations, between assumptions and assertions. Writing skill, essential for success, has become a neglected art in present India.

Presenting your views at interviews, meetings, and seminars is verbal communication. It is an art and technique that any person with average intelligence can develop. One only needs to acquire the ability to communicate clearly and persuasively.

Effective speaking is a shortcut to social recognition. To command influence, popularity, and success, develop the art of speaking clearly, concisely, and persuasively.

1. English—world's lingua franca

Language is the most effective medium of communication among people. It not only has cultural dimensions, but in the shrunken contemporary world, the knowledge of a widely spoken language is absolutely essential for modernisation and interaction, both within the society and with the international community. Societies that have failed to select and master their language have suffered in various ways.

India was fortunate to adopt English as a language to link various regions of the country. Though it was learnt under pressure, the people of India accepted it. It was instrumental in not only bringing about national unity but in achieving independence. A sound knowledge of English enabled the Indians to become world citizens. Today you can find an Indian (about ten million) almost all over the globe. It is partly because of their competence and mastery of the English language. It today is the language of international business; Indians, therefore, are getting high-income jobs in countries like Hong Kong and Singapore, even in the U.K. and the United States. English has made technology transfers easy, trade negotiations comfortable, and diplomacy more successful. No doubt, India has become a significant country. No country of the world can ignore it, not even China.

The journey has not been smooth for English to acquire an important place in the contemporary Indian education system. A few years after independence, the Hindi-speaking states, particularly Uttar Pradesh started a campaign against English as a language of education and communication. There was an immediate reaction in South India. Tamil Nadu refused to accept Hindi as a link language. The reaction of other non-Hindi speaking states was also the same. As a compromise formula, English was allowed to continue as a link language after the 10-year embargo on it by the Indian Constitution. However, Hindi-speaking states were given the freedom to discontinue teaching in English and perform their administrative work in Hindi. English was made optional in schools, particularly government schools. This led to a growing feeling of regionalism and non-Hindi speaking states also started using their mother tongue as the medium of education. The total impact was that there was a marked deterioration in the knowledge of spoken and written English.

But the private schools (known as public schools) realised that English would remain important in the national and international context. They continued to teach through the English-medium. This caused a social divide.

The importance of English cannot be undermined because of some chauvinistic and shortsighted thinking and reasoning. Just 400 years ago, English was the mother tongue of only seven million people. Today it is the mother tongue of more than 600 million persons. Besides, an equal number of people can communicate in English as fluently as in their mother tongue. Therefore, almost one-fourth of the total world population communicates in English. It is spoken in 40 countries, is one of the two working languages of the United Nations, and is the language of international business, diplomacy, culture, and science. Diplomats throughout the world use English widely, and major trade negotiations are conducted in English.

When we were busy belittling English, many other countries in the world were spending large sums of money teaching it to their citizens. The late Shah of Iran in the late 1960s realised the significance of English and hired the British and American teachers at fabulous salaries to teach English to Iranians. Currently, the Chinese are most enthusiastic about learning English. About a quarter of China's 1300 million population is learning English. Certain schools have made it compulsory to speak only in English.

English has several advantages over other foreign languages like French, Russian, and Spanish. It is easy to pronounce. The basic syntax is fairly straightforward, the words can be readily isolated, and the structure is relatively stable. The Roman alphabets are supple and economical. Further, English is easy to speak and can be understood in whichever manner it is spoken. In fact, English has as many variations as the countries where it is spoken. The only problem is the spelling, which, for historical reasons, is out of kilter with pronunciation.

English today is truly a world language. Many attempts to replace it with other languages have failed. The two serious rivals of English, Esperanto, for example, though 100 years old, has only 100,000 fluent speakers in some 85 countries. Basic English devised in the 1930s had an even shorter life. The question asked is, why should one devote time and resources to learning Esperanto when English can be learnt easily?

India by now has developed a huge infrastructure to teach English. We have the largest number of English teachers. It is taught even in the remotest villages of the country. Why then should we not learn this language and acquire the benefits of modern science, technology, and education? This, however, does not mean that we should ignore our mother tongue. We can learn a lesson from Gujratis residing in virtually all parts of the world. The first thing they learn is the local language. However, in their homes, they speak only Gujrati. Even fourth and fifth generation Gujratis in Africa and the United States go to a Gujrati school in the evening to remain in touch with their roots and culture. But they also learn English for their business purposes and can speak and write fluently.

Unfortunately, some politicians in our country are motivating people not to learn and use English, for their vested interests. Interestingly, their own children get their education in the best English-medium schools. Many of them are either settled or working abroad, earning huge salaries.

In the modern world those who want to be successful cannot ignore English as a language of international communication.

2. Mind your words

As we were moving out of the marriage *pandal*, thanking the hosts for the excellent food and the well-brewed hot coffee, a gentleman butted in and said: "The coffee was good, Mrs. Batra." The lady smiled and retorted: "I hope the food was also good, Mr. Sharma."

"Yes, yes, of course," said Mr. Sharma rather sheepishly and walked out of the *pandal* not realising the full implication of what Mrs. Batra had said.

Not many people talk realising the impression made of what they are saying. They do not remember that every spoken word has an impact. In this particular case, what Mr. Sharma conveyed to Mrs. Batra was that only the coffee was good. Actually he wanted to say that the food including the coffee was good. If he had said, "Coffee was also good," he would have effectively conveyed his feeling to Mrs. Batra.

Language, in reality, is the vehicle to communicate with each other. You have to use different kinds of words with different people to communicate the same idea. Suppose your friend has been given an extension of service. You can safely say to him: "I am happy that you have got an extension of two years." But if your boss has been given the same two years extension, you cannot say the same words to him. If you do, you would be offending him, to your peril. An appropriate expression would be: "Sir, I have heard that you have agreed to work for another two years. We are happy as it would be good for the company and for us too."

Churchill, it is said, attached great importance to the correct usage of words. Once at a dinner table he told his wife: "You ought not to say very delicious. Delicious alone expresses everything you wish to say. You would not say very unique." In this connection, Lord Moran (the famous physician) says that Churchill once thought of including the following in a speech at a university. "A man called Thompson went to a surgeon and asked him to castrate him. The surgeon demurred. But when the man persisted and argued, he eventually agreed and took him into the operation theatre. The morning after the operation, Thompson woke up in great discomfort. He noticed that the man in the next bed was in great pain and was groaning. He leaned towards him over the side of the bed. "What did they do to you?" he asked. The man replied, "I have been circumcised."

"Good lord!" Thompson exclaimed. "That is the word I couldn't remember when the surgeon asked me what I wanted done."

One evening Churchill was sitting on his bed and shouting for his hot water bottle. The valet appeared. Churchill asked him where the hot water bottle was. The valet replied, "You are sitting on it, sir, not a good idea."

"It is not an idea but a coincidence," replied Churchill.

Words change their meaning in different times and societies. If one is not careful, one can suffer a great deal of embarrassment. B. Chandramouleeswaran, a project director in a Chennai-based software company says that he had to carefully choose his words while working in a cosmopolitan ambiance. "In India, while the word "no" could mean "maybe". The same word is taken as a flat refusal in America or Singapore.

I visited America about 30 years back. An American friend invited me for dinner on a Sunday. I asked him, "When should I reach?"

He said, "Come anytime. Earlier the better as we would have more time to chat."

He had also invited a few more Indian friends who were in the United States for a long time. Foolishly I did not inquire the exact time, thinking that, like India, here too one could reach for dinner around 7 p.m.

I reached at 7 p.m. and found no one there. The host welcomed me and offered a drink. I was a little confused as there was no sign of a party. I thought I may be early and persons would come later. But there was no sign of anyone joining. Then after some time I asked him: "What is the matter. Is no else coming?"

"Oh they all came in the noon. We had a good time and great fun. As there was no way to get in touch with you, we thought you had forgotten, as many Indians do."

My pride was hurt and in an annoyed tone I retorted: "Didn't you invite me for dinner. I have come for that. Haven't I?"

"Dinner on Sunday means the noon meal. On other days we invite persons for supper in the evening. Dinner is a formal affair and is only on special occasions."

I learnt a lesson to ask for the precise time, particularly in a foreign land. I have never suffered, neither food, nor pride since then.

The Chinese have become crazy about learning English, as the language is now the sure road to success, particularly if you want to operate at the global level. Apparently, the Chinese have also realised that knowledge of an international language like English is most essential for getting jobs in foreign countries and promoting business in the international market. Though the Chinese have the option to learn other languages, like Japanese, Russian, French, and Spanish, the majority prefer to learn English. The learning of English has gained prestige among intellectuals, and those who do not know the language feel envious of those who know it. Subsequently, the prestige of an English teacher has soared high. Keeping in view the importance of the language, the Chinese government has made teaching of English compulsory from class eight onwards.

As the Chinese are far behind as far as the knowledge of English is concerned, they devised imaginative ways of teaching the language. Many magazines have come up to help the Chinese in learning English clearly and systematically.

The Chinese authorities are afraid that the manner in which English language is gaining importance in China it may replace the Chinese language itself. Therefore, great care is being taken to protect it. The Chinese are not encouraged to have day-to-day conversations in English, and it is considered preposterous to speak English wherever it is not desired.

We, on the other hand, have discouraged the learning of English since the early 60s. Though we have a well-developed infrastructure to teach English and a strong desire on the part of an average Indian to learn it, teaching of English has become sub-standard due to the myopic vision of our politicians.

We need a pragmatic approach towards the English language. There is no doubt that it is an international language and knowledge of it is a definite advantage. Why then should it not be taught scientifically and widely in India? We have a large number of English teachers; the only problem is that English is not taught at the right stage and in the right way.

3. Right use of words

You are in the middle of an interview and answering questions with ease and intelligence. The board is impressed by your personality. Suddenly, while discussing the Constitution of India, you are questioned about the presidential powers. The question is: "What are the President's powers in relation to a minister?"

"Sir, the President has the power to appoint and disappoint ministers," you answer.

The interviewers break into a smile. Your answer has "disappointed" them enough to dismiss your application in favour of a smart person who walked after you and answered: "The President has the power to appoint and dismiss ministers."

Right expressions and correct usage are essential for success.

Word usage implies two things—using the appropriate word to match the expression or situation, and using words economically. For the former, it is essential to be familiar with the words you are using. Its connotation must be clearly understood and you must know its various meanings and usage. I have come across several people who say they were "going for marketing." In fact, they want to say "going shopping." Marketing means "selling the produced goods" while shopping means "going to the market to buy the desired stuff".

In the absence of appropriate words you may land yourself in a serious situation or may suffer grave loss. You may end up conveying what you do not want. I have seen persons using wrong expressions and facing embarrassing situations. A few years back I attended a public function where an important minister was the chief guest. The speaker was eulogising the minister. At one point he wanted to say, "Your speech has really "inspired" us." Instead of "inspired" he used the word "expired" to the sheer amusement of the audience.

One way to avoid such situations is to pay attention to the usage while reading or listening. Understand the whole sentence and observe the way the word is being used. The second important aspect, economy of words, means using a word in place of a sentence and a sentence instead of a paragraph.

The need for brevity has increased because of the changed nature of tests. In the good old days, an essay was a long treatise. Now an essay can be written in 500 words. There is no need to waste words unnecessarily. The secret to exactness and brevity is an extensive vocabulary. English is a language that provides a variety of words for similar situations, making it possible to find the exact word for a given situation. For instance, burglar, filcher, highwayman, and swindler are different words for different types of thieves. By using the appropriate word the nature of theft can be expressed in one word only.

Vocabulary can be expanded in several ways. Two good ways of doing so are using a dictionary, and reading it regularly and widely. Flipping through the pages of a dictionary in leisure hours is interesting as well as instructive. I prefer those dictionaries that give the usage, synonyms, and antonyms. One useful dictionary is the *Oxford Advanced Learner's Dictionary of Current English*.

Reading books, newspapers, and magazines for fishing out new words is engrossing. When engaged in the exercise, try to find out new words and their usage. Half an hour's reading twice a week yields a good harvest of words.

The system works efficiently in the initial stages. But when the number of words becomes large you start forgetting more words than you are learning. This can be prevented if you use the library catalogue system. You can start a "vocabulary record". Buy a packet of one 13 cm x 8 cm index cards that are used in libraries for maintaining catalogues manually. Write the new words you have learnt and their meaning and usage. It would be better if you include their synonyms and antonyms too. Write the pronunciation in your mother tongue. These cards should be arranged alphabetically. If you are comfortable doing this on a computer or a laptop, use them for making a record of new words learnt by you. A periodic reference to these cards would help you recap the words you have learnt.

Knowing the correct meaning of a word and its exact usage are the twin concomitants of exactness and brevity. Wide reading, discussions, and conversations are also good exercises to learn new words.

The choice of words and their usage go a long way in the success or failure of a person. Choose the right word and use it with care, and you will definitely be on the forward march to success.

4. Write appropriate letters

"Just read this letter", said Narayan, an executive director of a big business house and placed a paper in my hand. The letter read like that:

> *"Last evening when we met at the dinner at Mr. Mathur's place, you told me that you were looking for a marketing manager. I would like you to consider me as I have exceptional CV. I am definite your Group would really be performing better if I join you. I can be called at this telephone number...."*

"File" he just wrote on the letter and threw it in the "out" tray. He was visibly annoyed and unhappy. He kept on looking at various papers in the file and also chatting with me. After an hour we went to have our lunch at a club. He had cooled down by now and his mood had become better. Finding him in a relaxed mood, I asked him "Why did the letter offend you?"

He got an opportunity to steam off. "What! that son-of-a-gun was trying to impress me. If he thought he was a rare phenomenon, he would not have been rotting in that God-forsaken company. By now he should have been the managing director of some multinational. His desire is to serve my company. Who cares for his desire? I am interested in what I desire. And he has not written a word about that", Narayan said.

"Narayan, you must be receiving hundreds of letters every week — some bad, some good, some excellent. Tell me the difference between the three. Tell me what you expect in a good letter that impresses you. I wanted to know what in a letter leaves a lasting impression on the reader of the letter like Narayan.

With a twinkle in his eyes, he looked at me from the corner of his specs and said: "That is difficult to say. Still let me tell you what I would expect in an impressive letter." After that I was a listener and he the speaker.

Remember that a letter is a means of communication. It is written with a definite objective — to get some work done or to seek some favour. You are, in a way, asking for a favour and obligation. Therefore, your letter must arouse in the receiver of the letter an interest in you. Remember that the person is worried about his own problems and has many other things to do. Your letter is not the only one paper he has to deal with. So if you want a favourable response you must care to write in a way that the person is impressed by you. There must be warmth towards the receiver. The writer must present himself in a modest way. It does not mean humiliating or supplicating a position. This becomes all the more important if you do not know the other person too well.

Why should a person be interested in you unless you are first interested in her/him? Therefore, your letter must show your interest in him. Think of the many things for which you can congratulate, thank, or compliment him. The person may have gone through some personal tragedy, illness, or mishap. Express your sympathies with him. By doing so you may be able to win the attention and cooperation of even the most difficult people.

The letter should not portray you as a grabbing, self-seeking person. Do not show that your only purpose is to get maximum benefit. Instead, show that you are a highly intelligent person, belonging to a cultured family. Come out as an unselfish, thoughtful, warm, affectionate, courteous, and modest person. Dale Carnegie in his book *How to Win Friends and Influence People* has mentioned that by writing simple and sincere letters glowing with kindness and admiration, he was able to persuade eminent people, even American Presidents, to come and talk to his students.

Let your letter make pleasant reading, be well worded, brief, and to the point. Effectively articulate your arguments to make your point. Even if you don't like the person, be appreciative instead of satirical.

Express your thanks and send your regards. Remember that he is sparing his precious time to read your letter.

Read the letter as if you have received it. Put yourself in his place. Change those portions that annoy or irritate you or where the right impression has not been created. Fold the letter properly and put it in an envelope.

I asked Narayan how he would have written the letter that he had received. His reply was that he would send the reply to me the next day. The letter that I received said the following:

> *I am writing this letter to tell you that I really enjoyed every moment I spent with you last evening. Your views on the present management crisis were imaginative. I hope you will find time to develop them into an article for wider interaction.*
>
> *What motivated me to take the liberty of writing you was a feeling that you were searching for a marketing manager. I do not know if I fit into your corporate profile. If I do I would like to be considered for that position. The enclosed bio data of mine will help you in forming an idea about me and my work.*
>
> *May I tell you that if I were privileged to have an opportunity to work with you, the interests of the company would be foremost in my mind. I can be contacted on the following telephone numbers.*
>
> *Looking forward to meeting you again; meanwhile I send my warm regards.*

Decide to write warm and sincere letters to get a favourable response.

5. Diplomatic words

As soon as they reached Rashtrapati Bhawan, the two Presidents sat down to coffee in the Morning Room. After a few pleasantries, Leonod Illich Brezhnev remarked through an interpreter: "Mr. President, you have been an Ambassador in the USSR and you said you like the country. Why have you not come again in spite on the many invitations extended to you?"

President Radhakrishnan replied: "I am sorry, Mr. President. I have been too busy. You know after I left Moscow, my wife expired and therefore, I have not been able to come."

President Brezhnev replied: "It was quite some time back and now you may be having time to come to come to our country. I am sure we shall not have to reprimand you for not accepting our invitation."

Perhaps the interpreter had translated President Brezhnev wrongly, but the word "reprimand" seemed to have nettled President Radhakrishnan. Contracting his eyebrows and with a hint of tartness in his voice he replied: "I will come to Russia when I am sick. You have nice hospitals there."

There was no further conversation about a visit to Russia during the rest of Brezhnev's stay in India.

On March 1 in 1961, President Rajendra Prasad had gone to see off Queen Elizabeth II. As the two were standing side by side, General Beig, Military Secretary to the President of India mentioned to the Queen that Dr. Rajendra Prasad was writing his autobiography. Turning to the Queen he added: "After Your Majesty's visit is over the President is adding another chapter to his autobiography."

"Really?" said the bewildered Queen, looking at the President.

"Yes. I have been able to write a few chapters already," replied the President.

"How many have you written?" the Duke butted in.

"About 1,200 pages."

"Oh! Where did you get all that time?" the Queen interjected.

"Your Majesty, I have been writing for a very long time. Don't you forget, I was in your father's jails for 16 years. There was plenty of time to write in jail," the President quietly said.

The silence that followed was of the graveyard. The listeners were struck dumb. Their minds were numbed.

These are real life stories indicating the type of damage words can do. If Brezhnev and Radhakrishnan would have been more discreet in selecting their words and expressions used by them, the personal relationships between the two would have been more cordial and warm. Brezhnev could have said: "Mr. President, we miss you very much in Russia, the country and the people are a great fan of yours. We have requests, pressures and even entreaties to invite you and follow the invitation. They want to see and listen to you. Mr. President, I would request you not to disappoint our people."

When President Radhakrishnan told him about the death of his wife, Brezhnev should have offered his condolences and profound sorrow. He could have said: "Mr. President we are very sorry to know about that. However, time is a great healer. Our people reprimand us and hold us guilty for not being persuasive in our invitation. On behalf of our people I would like you to accept our longstanding request to visit our country."

If he had spoken like that President Radhakrishnan would never have declined the invitation and would have visited USSR.

It was a folly and discourtesy on the part of Dr. Rajendra Prasad to have emphasised that he was in the jail of the Queen's father for 16 years. Many a times you have to forget the past. Even if one wants to be straightforward, harsh words can be camouflaged in softer expressions. Much better results can be achieved by being diplomatic.

Here is another situation in which carefully selected words and expressions saved a difficult situation. This happened in a small city in Rajasthan in the early 1950s. Students in a government college were on a prolonged strike and local authorities were unable to handle the situation. Ultimately the Director of Education had to come to the town to settle the dispute. He sent a message to the students through the Principal of the college to meet him at the Circuit House where he was staying. The students felt insulted as they did not receive any letter from him and refused to go and meet him. The Director's secretary, when he came to know about it, offered to bring students to the Circuit House.

The same evening, a smartly dressed middle-aged person was talking to the students who were sitting at a *dharna* (sit out) outside the college. He asked one of them, "What is the matter. Why are you people on strike?"

"We have certain problems and nobody cares to attend to them. We had to resort to strike, though we did not want to."

"I understand the Director is in town. Why don't you tell him your problems?"

"Why should we go? He sends oral messages through the Principal and does not officially invite us by writing a letter. We will meet him only when we receive a letter from his office."

"Are you fools? You are not accepting the invitation conveyed to you through a highly respectable person like the Principal of your college. You would accept a letter sent by a lowly clerk from his office."

Next morning the students were in the Circuit House and all the grievances of the students were solved within a few hours.

Several examples can be given to show the havoc words can play and also the wonders they can achieve. In real life, you have to establish a long-term relationship and get your work done not once, but time and again. Your strategy should be to create a warm and friendly relationship. Whatever you want to write, can be written in a friendly style. The words used will induce a person to do your work. It is necessary to prepare a background and not use any unnecessary expression to offend the other person. If you think that the person may feel offended and might refuse to oblige you, you may put forth the idea in such a way that the person does not immediately say "no". For example, you can say: "I know it is difficult to do this work. However, I will appreciate if you could help me out because if it is not done, I may be doomed. If it is not possible to do it immediately, consider it some time later."

Never close the door by using direct and rude words. Words can be used as bouquets as well as bullets.

Tips

- Choose words carefully and appropriate to the occasion.
- Select words that do not offend the person.
- Do not use words that undermine the authority of the person such as, "See to it that it is done by tomorrow." A better way of saying it would be: "I will appreciate if it can be done by tomorrow."
- Do not offend any person in any way.
- Do not use strong words.
- Do not come to the subject immediately.
- Do not insist on getting a firm commitment from the person.

To prepare to drive in the fast lane in your career, it is essential to develop a fit body. Creativity is another skill that needs to be developed. A good sense of humour and a good-humoured approach to life also helps. Proficiency in the English language has also become an essential condition for success in the contemporary world.

Chapter 7

Be a Leader

"Don't be afraid of enemies who attack you. Be afraid of friends who flatter you".

GENERAL ALVARO OBREGON,
President of Mexico

Now you are in the fast track, galloping and leaving others behind. Your ultimate objective is to become "numero uno" in your organisation. This is possible only if you become a team leader. If you are not a born leader, and most of us are not, do not lose heart. You can acquire leadership traits if you have a vision, can understand people, and are action-oriented. You have to develop all the three qualities, besides many others. Only then can you reach the apex in your organisation.

Who is a leader?

The terms leader and manager are usually used interchangeably in the corporate world to describe those who manage a group of persons. But the two terms are not synonymous; in a way they are complementary to each other.

BE A LEADER

If one wants to be a successful manager he has to know and acquire the traits required for becoming a great leader.

A leader is a person who motivates his followers and provides leadership through strategic thinking. He should be able to set examples for others, build trust and support his followers, and build a team. A manager, on the other hand, is a person who is task-oriented and gets things done from his team.

All organisations, whether public or private, simple or complex, need an effective leader to lead various teams to achieve the organisational goals. The success of an organisation is reflected when the leader is efficient and enterprising. It is indicated by flourishing performance and the company not only achieves its targets but overshoots them. However, if the manager is a status quoits or conventionalist and does not change with time, the company may stagnate.

A manager, invariably, holds a formal position in the company. His authority is well defined and it provides him power to operate and administer. A leader has no such formal power and position. He becomes known on the basis of his personality and develops his own style of functioning for achieving goals. The main function of a manager is to explain to his team how to do the job. On the other hand a leader describes what and why the work is to be done. A leader has to have a vision and has to realise that he operates in his own way. The manager, however, implements a plan to achieve the set targets. He motivates his team to achieve those targets.

A leader has to have vision, creativity, intellectual drive, and knowledge. All this enables him to foresee and understand issues and handle them by adopting proper strategy. The managerial position, on the contrary, has five functions—planning, organising, recruitment, directing, coordinating and budgeting, and administration.

A leader and manager are complementary

According to an old adage: *We lead people and manage things.* The implication of this saying is that an organisation requires two types of persons leaders who do the right thing and managers who do things right. This indicates that both the sets of skills are needed to run an organisation efficiently and productively. Though, leaders and managers have their own place in the organisation, managers need to have both managerial, as well as leadership qualities to run the organisation successfully. This is necessary because a manager without the leadership quality will be functioning only to maintain the status quo and that would bring only stability and no growth to the organisation. Such a situation may be boring and unproductive for the team members. Therefore, a mix of both the skills will bring about a great difference to the organisation. An appropriate example would be the manner in which India's military unit functions.

When an army unit moves towards a battle field it has to be commanded by a person who possesses both the qualities of a leader and a manager. As a leader he must have the ability to take immediate decisions during operations, motivate the soldiers, and always be ready to face challenges; and as a manager he must have the capacity to maintain discipline and be able to make the soldiers follow the rules in the battle field.

Leadership does not require one to be in any managerial position to act as a leader, but a successful manager needs to have leadership qualities, because sometimes the situation demands a manager to act as a leader for his subordinates. So, a successful manager has to have the stability of a manager and the creativity of a leader to make an organisation successful. An efficient organisation is not born automatically; it is created under the guidance of an effective leadership and an efficient management.

> **Mahatma Gandhi had a unique personality. Reading his biography one comes across his amazing leadership qualities in the management of a nation's mindset.**
>
> *The Dandi Yatra of 1929 epitomises the flawless human management skills of Mahatma Gandhi. It was the first of its kind when Gandhi took a long-walk to protest against the salt tax that was imposed by the British. In those days, walking for a political protest was totally unheard of. This innovation of Mahatma Gandhi clicked with the Indian masses. For the first time, a leader reached villages and involved them in a greater mission. People used to walk for getting firewood, for getting water, and for their daily chores but now they were walking for freedom. While narrating the above instance, Chetan Shah, MD, Synygy India adds, "Gandhi was not a theoretician; he was a man of action. Gandhi made no distinction in man and woman; both were equal in his eyes. He favoured decentralisation and his idea of trusteeship was based on the humanitarian ground of "bread for all before cakes for some'."*

Learn to be effective

The real world of a manager is quite different from the perception developed in business schools as managing is "being responsible for the work of others." To some extent it is true but not sufficiently inclusive. Managing is about people—how to develop skills and competencies that meet the needs of the organisation and provide opportunities for personal growth. Managers are paid not for the effort of activity, but for getting results, usually for the performance of other people who work for them.

In today's workplace the newly appointed manager faces a daunting range of challenges. Success can come only through radical and rapid adjustments to the way you work, especially in relation to your team. As a newly appointed manager you need to develop some operational philosophy that will guide you through the maze of the decision-making process.

1. Talk to each team member individually

Donning the cap of a new manager is painful and stressful because you are now responsible and accountable for your entire team. Your performance will not be judged on your work alone. You are going to be judged on your team's achievements and failures. Therefore, you need to develop better communication skills. You also have to ensure that your team is in the right spirit and mindset. Each member should work such that the work is completed on time and in the best form. Therefore, you have to understand the personality of each team member. Do not begin with a biased mindset or what others have briefed you about them. Make your own opinion and view about each team member. Give everyone a clean slate, no matter what you've heard. Remember, you represent a fresh start and they want to be seen in the best light. So meet each of them personally and individually, and give them plenty of one-on-one time. Find out about their history and aspirations while talking to them. Watch them in action to see who is with you or who is not.

2. Fix targets and objectives to achieve

From the very beginning you should fix the goals and targets to be achieved within the time schedule. This will help you in getting their attention. Capitalise on it and set ground rules in the first meeting. In this meeting delineate your short-term and long-term vision. Identify what is critical; make everyone understand that why and how everyone's work will contribute to the final result. The goals that you fix should be relatively short, unambiguous, and achievable. Establish time limits and benchmarks to measure progress. The team must be made to understand that they are working toward something larger, and how their careers, lives, and world will profit from their performance.

3. Find a mentor

When you join a new company and accept the new role or challenge, you would do well if you find out someone who has handled that department or work before and who is willing to give you advice. Some people look to their predecessor to mentor them. But it has two problems. First, the person may not be a good mentor. He might have been more interested in results or getting things done than guiding or giving advice. Second, he may be your boss now and having the boss as the mentor is not a good idea. The reason is that if the mentor is not your boss, he can advice you on your boss' behavior. Select someone whom you respect and who is an experienced manager. Friends can also be your mentor, but the further removed your mentor is from your current inner circle the better perspective he will be able to give you on your work.

4. Make a mark for yourself

You must make an impact of your personality from day one. Make everything clear. In American slang: "Strip everything down and simplify." Make sure that you present a picture of a person who believes in dynamism and change. Take a dramatic action to send the message that times have changed. This will help you in getting the best possible work from the team and contribute as much as possible to making the organisation successful. Adopt the attitude of "best possible things" from the team by getting their best work. For that you need the best people, and to get the best people you need to provide interesting work to your team; and to provide interesting work you need to create clear but challenging goals, delegate responsibility, and back them up when they need help.

5. Have a plan

If you do not prepare a plan to work, your entire performance is doomed to fail. After meeting your team members individually, draft the short- and long-term plans. Set targets, replete with start and end points (and the steps in between). Hold yourself accountable by evaluating progress weekly and making adjustments as circumstances evolve. Your effort has to be to get your team members on the same mental level as yours and foster an environment where they can excel. Without a plan and a dedication to executing it, your team will without doubt drift, gradually losing sight of their potential and value.

6. Develop every team member

Your objective has to be: "How can the team be taken to the next stage of excellence?" It requires planning, attention, and commitment. Before you begin work, understand each person's strengths, goals, and areas for improvement.

Working as a manager is a balancing act. It requires taking tough decisions. Therefore, a manager has to be a mix of both—a close friend and buddy as well as a demanding boss.

Essentials in an effective manager

01. *Achieving higher levels of energy and drive*
02. *Self-confidence so that intelligently calculated risks are possible*
03. *Return-oriented approach—every expenditure should earn profit for the company*
04. *Ambitious but achievable goals*
05. *Capability to get work done by the team*
06. *Should be able to monitor his development, path, and destiny*
07. *Should be able to learn from their failures and mistakes*
08. *A long-term vision*
09. *A competitive urge*
10. *Should be able to develop applicable, fruitful two-way relationships*

To be an effective leader

Leaders are not commonplace persons. They are the top-ranking functionaries who take their organisations to the maximum heights of performance that might not have been imagined earlier. Such persons like Indra Nooyi, Vikram Pundit, Jack Welch, Lakshmi Narayan Mittal, late Aditya Birla, and late Dhirubhai Ambani, must have possessed certain unique qualities that made them great leaders. What were those qualities? Leadership analysts have identified some leader-like qualities for effective leadership.

Change

A leader has to be a harbinger of change that is always resisted by those working in the organisation. Yet it is an essential element to rejuvenating the organisation.

An organisation is an everchanging entity. It has to change with the changing times at the global level. But many do not. Such a situation makes the functioning of the organisation aberrant and imperfect. The skill of a leader is in exposing such dullness and changing the functioning of the organisation in such a manner so that it yields maximum profit. Indeed it is difficult to find out dysfunctioning or abnormal functioning in an organisation. Despite that a leader has to know how to locate dysfunction and check it by improving systems, inter-personal relationships, conflict management, and existing corporate culture.

Change is widely resisted by dysfunctional managers and workers. Forward-looking persons, though, look at change as an opportunity to learn something new, to pick up additional skills, and to become a better person; they are those who believe in maintaining status quo and do not feel that change will ruin the company. One such situation happened in the Bennett Coleman & Company Limited, the leading newspaper house, during the mid eighties when the owner's young son wanted to bring a 360-degree change in the corporate functioning and decision-making. The old guards resisted to their full strength. The determined young boy dismissed all of them and introduced a new corporate culture that was performance oriented. Within 10 years, the Rs. 60-crore company became a Rs. 2,000-crore corporate entity. Today it is one of the top ranking global companies. Thus the success of a business leader lies in converting dysfunctional energy into functional and positive energy, or removing such negativity to bring in a fresh and new life in the organisation.

Three critical areas: Three crucial areas of systematising change are — What needs to be changed? What is the present state of affairs? How would it look after the change is implemented?

These three areas have to be addressed systematically and effectively in a planned manner by the leader to bring about productive change. Such change would be instantaneously accepted if the leader is able to convince the seniors in the organisation that the change would accrue benefits across the company and not harm anyone.

Reaction to change falls in three categories — proactive and assertive; reactive and aggressive; and inactive and submissive. The first category of persons are innovative and respond positively to negative comments, difficult challenges, collective concerns, and personal criticisms. They are the ones who solve problems and make things happen. The second category of people have a negative approach about most things and tend to openly resist change in counter-productive ways. Such people avoid responsibility and even indulge in sabotage in thwarting change. The third group of people go along with change without enthusiasm and accept it when they see it being functional. The challenge of a leader is in handling the second category of persons who have a negative attitude and resist change.

How to smoothen change

William Bridges, an American author, orator, and organisational consultant, in his book Managing Transitions: Making the Most of Change *suggests that a leader should follow the following process:*

Identify dysfunctional behaviours and understand their impact in the workplace.

Outline and detail the terms of changes that are to be brought about.

Identify individuals and groups to be severely affected by the changes.

Analyse willingness to change on the following criteria:

How is the change being perceived?

How well is the change understood and accepted?

What is each workunit's openness to the change?

Do people, by and large, support change?

How much of it is understood and absorbed by the grass-root level worker?

Is the current behaviour and attitude of the peer groups consonant with the change being envisioned?

Finally:

Analyse the political implications of change.

Fix a time-bound schedule for each phase of change.

Form a team to monitor change implementation.

Identify new skills required and develop training programmes for re-tooling — training them in new skills.

Re-train dysfunctional workers to develop a positive attitude towards change.

Guide workunits that are resistive to change.

Monitor communication within each workunit and make adjustments to keep people informed.

Deal with conflict

Conflict is a normal element of the work process, and with growing competition the importance of conflict management is also increasing. The American Management Association (AMA) has rated it "as a topic of equal or slightly higher importance than planning, communication, motivation, and decision-making," and suggested that conflict management ability will increasingly become important in the years to come.

Some leaders have negative perceptions of conflict and want to avoid it. But it destroys the creative aspects of blending different perspectives. In fact, a well-managed conflict-resolution process uncovers buried issues, opens up new ideas, and inspires innovation. Therefore, a viable conflict-resolution process needs to be developed. It should follow a four-step strategy.

Step one is to track the crisis down as soon as you come to know of it. An emerging conflict can be sensed if there are raised eyebrows, caustic comments, unanswered requests, or over-reactions to minor issues. The leaders should find out the viewpoint of the different groups.

Step two is identifying key players in the conflict. Discuss the causes of the conflict with them and encourage antagonists to share the basis for their views. Give and take is necessary in the final resolution of conflict.

Step three is to involve various groups connected with the conflict in discussions. The rules of the game should be set such that everyone should follow. Each one should listen to others, understand their point of view, and voices should not be raised. Focus on what needs to change rather than on who needs to change. If the conflict is not likely to be resolved, try to get an acceptable arbitrator appointed.

Step four is finding a lasting solution. Ensure that hurt feelings are pacified and differing groups understand each other's sensitivities.

Managing conflict needs selecting an appropriate resolution process, building a strategy that meets the organisational needs, blending individual expectations, setting the stage for negotiations, and searching for permanent solutions. It is not easy, but there is no escape from it. If the leader does not manage the conflict, conflict will manage him.

Problem solving

Leader is a problem solver so that the team can advance towards its goal. Those who depend only on their understanding the problem, fail to get the right solutions. Therefore, the entire team should be involved in problem solving as collective wisdom is better than individual wisdom. A successful leader will create an atmosphere of understanding by involving the whole team in the problem-solving process.

It is basic to problem solving that the problem should be precisely described and information concerning the causes of the problem should be collected. The second step is to decide the solution. The third is to determine the implementation plan of the solution. Evaluation of the result is the fourth step. At the end of the whole exercise, an evaluation should be done. The questions to be asked are: "Did the solution work?" and "If it failed, then what went wrong?" The entire experience should be recorded.

Be the role model

The leader is the role model for his team. He is sort of a support system as the team looks to him in moments of crisis to solve the problems. Therefore, he has to play different roles for his team members. The following are the most common expectations from a leader.

Confidence builder: The leader has to provide encouragement when the team members need it. The leader, who is respected by his team members should sense when the spirits of the members are low and when they need a boost.

Challenger: They want someone to question them and suggest a course correction. They need a sturdy sounding board to test their notions, thoughts, and ideas.

Motivator: Leaders need to stimulate their thinking and prompt them when they need a reality check. The leader is a starter on an engine. He is particularly useful when, after a period of idleness, they need a quick burst of energy to get moving again. People should be inspired and built up. Leaders should provide a positive influence as a motivator.

Compassionate: The leader should be concerned for the welfare and well being of his team members. When the mental health of members sags, they need the leader's help not just a prop-up, but a lift-up. A leader should be a person who should be known as one who cares what happens to his team members.

Friend: The leader should be a friend who cares for his team members. They should feel free to discuss their personal problems and concerns, and easily express their frank opinions.

Reflector: Team members should aspire to be like their leader. The leader should serve as a "mirror" reflecting the thought and feelings of his team members. They should feel comfortable bouncing ideas around in his presence without fear.

Strategist

The art of planning, which involves a sense of strategic direction, is essential for effective leadership. Good strategies are necessary; however, they are not sufficient for good planning. Detailed action plans based on those strategies are critically important. The key to effective leadership is how the team members are involved in the development of these action plans. Input should be accepted from all. Everyone should be listened to with an open mind. A consensus should be negotiated, and an action plan finalised. Once an action plan is adopted, the leader should ensure that the team has the resources (e.g., funds, equipment, and human power) to execute those plans.

Keen listener

A leader should listen more and talk less. The benefits of good listening are numerous. Relationships improve, productivity and work performance are enhanced, team spirit is fostered, morale increases, and the team gains better perspective and understanding of the team's mission.

When the team members are talking or giving their views, the leader should listen effectively. Towards the end, the leader should ask short and simple questions to clarify and identify the areas that have been left out.

Accept responsibility

The most fear-provoking aspect of leadership is that he becomes responsible for other's performance. People do things their own way, and sometimes they make mistakes. While team members are responsible to the leader for their mistakes, he is responsible to the top leader for those mistakes. The blame should not be passed down to the team members. It is the leader's responsibility that the members do not commit any mistake; the buck stops with the leader.

The abstract of leadership is to have big aims. If he has low aims he would remain a small-time player. Compare Indra Nooyi and Jack Welch with millions of other leaders. "Not failure, but low aim is a crime," said the former President of India, A. P. J. Abdul Kalam.

Nurture the right attitude

Leaders have to develop the right attitude. It implies that the way they think about themselves, others, and life in general has to be positive and creative. A leader does not have the right attitude if his answer to any of the following questions is a NO:

Do you make efforts to make yourself presentable?
Do you maintain a pleasant temperament?
How do you remain calm in a crisis?
Are you able to control yourself when angry?
Do you maintain eye contact while talking to others?
Do you expect respect from others without giving it?
Are you modest in front of others?
Do you avoid rebuking your subordinates openly?
Do you care for your family?
If the answer to any of these questions is a NO, then change your attitude to improve your personality.

How can you develop the right attitude

Make sure that you have a good appearance and are presentable.
It will develop self-confidence in your personality.
Do not lose self-control even in anger.
Be polite always and do not become rude or abusive.
Maintain a calm temperament as it generates the power of understanding.
Develop clarity in your thoughts.
Your thinking should always be positive.
Appreciate the efforts of others by saying, "Thank you."
Feel sorry and say it if you are wrong.
Be firm and assertive, not aggressive.
Do not have a dictatorial and self-righteous attitude towards your juniors.
Be polite and humane as these virtues create a comfort zone to develop better relations.
Always find out solutions and do not get irritated over problems. When talking to others maintain eye contact.
Always wear a smile. It creates a comfort zone and automatically draws people towards you.

Strategise to come first

This is an old story but is still relevant in the light of the Indian cricket team's mortifying defeat in the ICC T20 World Cup at St. Lucia, an island country in the eastern Caribbean Sea. It was 25 June 1983 when India, for the first time, won the Prudential World Cup against all hopes. It could not win it again till 2011. In the 2007 World Cup, India was eliminated in the first round, being defeated by teams like Bangladesh.

Naturally in 1983 there were jubilations all over India. At the Coffee Shop of the Taj Mahal Hotel, Mumbai, the large crowd that had gathered to watch the game stood up and sang the national anthem. This unusual burst of patriotism made me ask: "What was so exceptional about this victory that motivated the elite of Mumbai to act so uncharacteristically?" I realised that when nothing great was happening Kapil Dev, the captain of the Indian team, gave us an occasion to be proud of being an Indian. I further thought how this unprecedented achievement was made by the same Indian team that was unsuccessful in the past and remained so in the following 28 years. It, in fact, was the strategy designed by Kapil and its meticulous implementation.

The core of Kapi's strategy was, be a good leader and not a boss; assess the strengths and weaknesses of each team member; select appropriate tactics at the right opportunity; seize every occasion that can lead and help you in the achievement of your objective; and do not lose your heart during moments of crises.

The first step to be a successful leader is not to boss around but involve all team members to put up a combined effort. Every member of the team must participate in one activity or the other. West Indies captain Clive Lloyd's comment was, "He's been able to rally the entire team behind him." No doubt Kapil acted authoritatively but he was always "one of them," giving due respect to senior payers and guiding the younger ones. He gave a place of pride to Sunil Gavaskar, the former skipper, and Mohinder Amanath, the man of the match of the 1983 World Cup Championship. On the field, he was an amiable and modest colleague ever ready to advise and console failures. This helped in smoothening out personal rivalries, inner tensions, regional loyalties, and commercialism. The net result was that India won because every player threw everything he had and Kapil led from the front. And they turned their rivals upside down.

Kapil as a leader carefully assessed the weak points of his team. He realised that their greatest weakness, particularly in the one-day matches, had been fielding. So his first priority was fielding and he bluntly told that "anyone who does not give his all in the field" would not be condoned. He made his boys go through intensive fielding practice sessions, keeping them in the field for six hours a day.

The success of a leader depends on the tactics he adopts during operations. Kapil carefully selected his tactics for each game and changed them at appropriate moments. He maneuvered the bowling cleverly. Each time India looked to be in trouble, Kapil's shrewd bowling changes swung the game back in their favour. It was his intelligent use of tactics that made our medium pace bowlers, often ridiculed by critics, the major reason for winning the 1983 World Cup.

Accepting the challenge and not losing heart during moments of crises was important to his strategy. No one hoped for a victory. In fact, the London bookies had offered 50:1 odds against India winning the World Cup. Kapil took up the challenge and was determined that he and his boys would prove the pundits wrong. It was this confidence and determination that saw the Indians through their crises and helped them reach the top.

We too can achieve what Kapil achieved at Lord's, provided we lead our team from the front.

The team wins

As an individual, an Indian excels in all walks of life but fails when he works in a team. On the contrary, the Japanese perform better when they work as a team. Why so?

This is so because the Indian society is individual-based where an individual feels not just important but powerful. In Japan, a man is important too but as a member of the team. An ingenious management expert has evolved the following equation:

- One Indian equals three Japanese.
- Two Indians equal two Japanese.
- Three Indians equal one Japanese.

It means that when an Indian works individually, his efficiency and output is at the peak. It is equal to three Japanese. When two Indians work together, their output is reduced from 300 per cent of the Japanese to 100 per cent of the Japanese. But as you add more Indians to the team, the productivity and efficiency of each member declines. Three Indians working in a team produce equivalent to a single Japanese—one Indian producing only one-third of what a Japanese is producing.

The "individualistic culture" scenario developed during the British regime when the Englishmen were at the helm of affairs. As they belonged to the ruling class and did not understand the language of the masses, it was neither feasible nor necessary for them to work as a team. Power was concentrated in the hands of an individual, an Englishman, and since nobody could afford to disobey him, whatever he wanted was achieved. They did not work in a team as power was concentrated in their hands. Their whims prevailed. This system continued even after they left in 1947. Today too the bureaucracy and political leadership does not work in a team. The bosses do not share their work experience and working strategies with the team members.

The individual-based working system is not good for the contemporary India as its success depends on one single person who thinks that he is indispensable to the institution. The indispensability tag carried by an individual helps him assume substantial power. Because "power begets power" and "power corrupts, and absolute power corrupts absolutely", even the most balanced person gets power-drunk. The downfall of the former U.S. President, Richard M. Nixon can be quoted as a classic example of absolute power causing the fall of a team leader. Even our political leaders have never allowed a second-in-command to emerge and take over responsibilities when the occasion arises. Therefore, the institutional system of functioning has not come into operation in India.

An individual-based system also develops an army of sycophants and flatterers who stoop to any level to achieve their objectives. This is not peculiar to India but has happened in almost every country where the functioning is centered in an individual. In India this system has developed during the last 60 years, giving rise to a chain of power brokers.

With the expansion of the information technology India is going through the third revolution. Moreover, India is also no more a developing country. It is now known as an "emerging economy" ready to become the leading economy of the world by 2020. It, therefore, is high time for us to think and develop team-oriented functioning in the corporate and government sectors. The advent of the IT revolution should help us in developing such a system. The advantage of a team-oriented workforce is that the same mistake is not repeated again and again. Picking up the second-in-command at an appropriate time, as practiced in the Indian Army, would make succession of heads of departments, corporate, and institutions smooth. The second-in-command would be familiar with the functioning of the entire organisation, and the question of indispensability would never arise. After all, no one should ever become indispensable to a system.

Studies have proved that the modern business and governmental system is best suited for a task-oriented management where the leader gives directions that the team members follow instructions. There is not much need for the sharing-management system where all the members of the team are expected to play an active role in decision-making and implementing policies. No wonder many departments that follow this system have failed to deliver the results.

The individualised working pattern is not the healthy way of organising work. Those who want to perform have to work as a team member first before assuming the team leader's role.

> Strive to be a leader who has vision, creativity, intellectual drive, and knowledge.

Lead to win

"A commander needs an army and the army needs a commander", is an old affirmation. A commander, a leader in fact, does not go to the battlefield without soldiers; and soldiers would run away the moment their commander is killed. In the 1971 war with Pakistan, the Indian Army killed the Pakistani commander, a Brigadier, in a fierce battle. Soon the whole brigade retreated and ran away from the battlefield. The bottom line is that leaders are indispensable for any organised work. In fact, the development and growth of a company, like that of a nation, depends on the quality of the person who is leading the team. Leaders like Franklin D. Roosevelt, Winston Churchill, and Jawaharlal Nehru pulled their nations out of crises while leaders like Adolf Hitler and Benito Mussolini led their people to great disaster. Similarly, corporate leaders like Jack Walch, Indira Nooyi, Lee Iacocca, Vikram Pandit, Vinita Bali changed the direction of their companies to convert them from loss-bearing to profit-making units and then further from profit-making to super-profit earners.

You definitely would like to be a dynamic, proactive, and effective leader, and would like to lead your team to achieve the targets and goals, won't you?

Leaders are not in abundance; they are hard to find because they possess a unique combination of magnetism, vision, and personality traits that pull people to join them and work with them. If Indira Nooyi invites a person to join her team, the person would not think twice. Therefore, first understand who a leader is?

Leadership is all about getting along with others—juniors, seniors, colleagues, and people from various spheres of life. It is the greatest challenge and the most difficult quality to acquire. To some, it comes naturally. But others have to acquire and develop it by understanding the reasons to earn the trust and support from their team members. Here are a few tips:

Have a **positive attitude** towards your team members and colleagues. It helps to deal more easily with the assigned work at office. It brings optimism into your daily routine, and makes it easier to avoid worry and negative thinking. If you adopt it as a way of life, it will bring constructive changes into the work pattern and process, and would make you and your team happier, brighter, and more successful. With a positive attitude you would always visualise the brighter side of life, become optimistic, and expect the best to happen. It is certainly a state of mind that is well worth developing and strengthening.

You must understand that no human being is perfect. You have to accept a person as he is and not as you want him to be. You must understand all of your team members and work by establishing harmony with people around you, as suggested by Napoleon Hill (1883–1970), an American author who is widely considered to be one of the greatest writers on success, in his book, *Law of Success*. If you can do that, you will have a large circle of friends and followers to assist and work for you in your assignments.

Understand the psychology of people around you. Each person wants to be recognised and accepted. He should be treated as an individual and not as an insignificant part of the large group. Everyone's emotions and sensitivities have to be respected. You can do that, as the Americans widely do, by calling people by their first names.

Ninety-five per cent of people have negative feelings. In reality, they suffer from fear of criticism, of being ridiculed before others, of failure, and a whole lot of other things, though most of them believe they have no fears. To win them over, make them feel comfortable by appreciating their needs and contributions. Listen to what they have to say. This creates confidence in them and they feel important.

Do not enter into unnecessary and long arguments. They lead to nowhere. It is always better to say what you need to say, then disengage and move on to something or somebody else. You can never win friends by scoring brownie points. You will lose the confidence of a person if you try to win an argument by the force of your authority. Your arguments should be logical, neither authoritarian nor imposing. Your views should be accepted voluntarily and not out of fear.

Learn to **keep your problems to yourself**. Moody and grumbling people can never become popular. Nobody likes brooding and sulky leaders. Smile and get a smile in return. If you brood or sulk, you will soon find yourself alone. Everyone would leave you. If you are smiling and friendly, the number of your followers will keep on increasing.

You should try to **become popular** with your colleagues and bosses. Almost one-third of your life is spent in the office where you work. To make yourself successful and happy, it is essential that you become popular with your colleagues. Juniors are your best ambassadors; they are the ones who talk about you in public in your absence. They can really boost or damage your image. Keep them contented and satisfied. Lift their morale so high that they look upon you as someone in whom they can put their confidence. You should be their friend, philosopher, and guide and not the boss. You should show your full confidence in them and gradually pass on a part of your responsibilities on to them. If they commit mistakes, don't expose them to the higher authorities. Do support their actions and protect them. You must know that only those who work and operate make mistakes. Therefore, do not let them down. You should demand respect from them; win it over through your deeds and actions.

Colleagues are the next with whom you have to maintain a good rapport. It is not something easily done as they are in the same position in which you are. They can neither be treated like your juniors nor like bosses. You work with them professionally and your success, to a great extent, will depend on their cooperation. You have to be cordial, friendly, and helpful to them. Losing your temper and giving orders will worsen matters. You will have to understand their point of view and explain yours to them to keep a balance.

Seniors are very important for horizontal progress. You have to understand what exactly they expect from you and why. They all are responsible people who have made certain commitments to the management that they want to accomplish through you. If you do not fit into their framework, they will sideline you and pick up someone else to deliver the goods.

Besides these three types of persons in your office, you also come across a large number of persons in your daily life. Don't look down upon those who are in inferior positions. In a democratic setup, you never know who will become important. When Mayawati was a simple school teacher no one in her institution could think that she would be the Chief Minister and a powerful political leader with an ambition to become the Prime Minister. It would help to develop a long-term perspective and be gracious to all.

The ability to get along well with all with whom you come in contact with is a personal challenge. Accept it and develop a wide circle of friends and followers if you want to get along with all if you want to become a leader.

Develop entrepreneurial skills

Economic development and technological diversification do not happen unexpectedly. Neither do they adopt a zigzag path. In an environment charged with cut-throat competition, the upward movement of an organisation depends on its ability to take care of the critical factors required for development. Raymond W. Smilor of the University of Texas at Austin in the USA, is a strong believer of the above view. However, more important than an organisation's ability is the entrepreneur (from the French word *entreprendra*, meaning the one who undertakes risks). He is the person who takes risks by introducing both new ways of making old products and developing new products. He assumes responsibility for the accompanying financial, psychological, and social risks, and receives the resulting rewards of monetary and personal satisfaction. If you want to succeed in life you have to have some entrepreneurial element, creativity, and innovative skills in your personality. What type of a personality should you have to show a high element of entrepreneurship?

First of all you must understand the business environment. Second, you should be a visionary, be flexible, and have the skill of arriving at alternative solutions and creating management or administrative systems. Third, you should have the ability to encourage teamwork and initiate discussions. Fourth, you should have the capacity to build up a wide circle of friends, followers, and supporters. Finally you should have tolerance and be able to display patience and persistence. The stronger are these traits in your personality, the more successful an entrepreneur you would be.

A person by nature is creative if he understands the business environment, national as well as international, and shows originality in thinking and inventiveness. Such a person is also able to stimulate the imagination of others who work with him. Unfortunately, creativity declines with age, faster in some than others, and may lessen rapidly when it is not being used regularly. Children have it in them in the maximum amount. But it declines as they grow in age. It, however, can be kept high if the person keeps his mind open, applies it in solving problems, and changes himself with changing times.

An entrepreneur is a person with a long-term vision; he has dreams for which he works intelligently and diligently. It is difficult to define a visionary. In simple language, a visionary is like a gardener. When you want a tomato, you take a seed, put it in fertile soil, and carefully water it with tender care. "You don't manufacture tomatoes, you grow them", is how Robert G. Hisrich, Professor of Marketing at the University of Tulsa, Oklahoma in the USA explains a visionary. A successful visionary must have a dream and the ability and willingness to work against all odds to achieve it.

As an entrepreneur you have to develop flexibility in your actions and behaviour. You should also be able to provide alternative solutions so that the best solution can be chosen to acquire success. The best solution is that which provides the best result with minimum cost and inconvenience. It is necessary to assess the situation seriously and comprehensively, keeping in view the wide-ranging implications. You should also think of different options. Being stubborn and rigid in thought and action gives bad results. You should challenge the beliefs and assumptions of the existing setup and find opportunities to create something original and new.

An entrepreneur has to form a good team with a multi-dimensional approach. The established departmental structure and reporting system may be obsolete and unable to provide the best and maximum results. A new approach should be developed to use the various skills of production, engineering, marketing, and finance in an integrated way so that the objectives are achieved within the stipulated time. Tact and diplomacy is needed for the success of a multi-disciplinary approach.

An entrepreneur always encourages open discussions. This must be encouraged at all levels—junior, middle, and senior. Many entrepreneurs do not allow frank and open discussions, frown at disagreements, and build protective walls to safeguard their power or empire. The need of the contemporary society is contrary to it. A successful entrepreneur must form a team that has the freedom to disagree. Free discussions should be allowed till the best solution is arrived at.

Openness is essential to develop a strong group of followers and supporters. A good entrepreneur learns a lot by listening to his teammates because he knows that, after all, wisdom is not the exclusive domain of one person alone. Openness develops a system in which the door for change and improvement is never closed. Anyone who tries to shut the door becomes mentally indolent. An entrepreneur must encourage each team member to express his views, particularly during critical moments. This is essential because good career promotions and job security are not sufficient motivations to provide encouragement. A successful entrepreneur should work to make every member of the team a champion.

The Japanese, in fact, have developed all these traits and are the best entrepreneurs in the world. This is despite the fact that they live their lives on volcanic islands with the constant threat not only of major earthquakes, but also of typhoons, tidal waves, savage snowstorms, and spring deluges. Their islands provide them with almost no raw material except water, and less than a quarter of their land is livable or arable. Can there be any comparison between the Indians and the Japanese?

Patience and persistence is the last, though not the least important trait needed in an entrepreneur. It is universal that frustrations and obstacles appear in plenty whenever a new venture is instituted. The entrepreneur can achieve success only when he does not lose patience and continues to try till the objective is achieved.

Attitude

An American tourist travelling in a bus in Sweden began to converse with his fellow passenger. He began glorifying the democratic system of his country and said: "The reality of democracy in the United States is that one fine morning you may get a call from the President himself." The Swede looked at the American in bewilderment and retorted: "Well in our country you might be travelling in a bus and talking to a person who might be our king." The passenger got down at the next stop. Other passengers told the American that the person was the King of Sweden.

In contrast is the story of an Indian minister who visited the Netherlands. The Indian ambassador received him at the airport and both were waiting for the minister's baggage. The minister, declaring how important he was in the Government of India, went on to lament about being made to wait for his baggage. The ambassador, instead of reacting to his grumbling, took him to a tall fellow at the other end of the baggage belt and said: "Let me introduce you to His Majesty, the King of Netherlands." The King was also waiting for his baggage.

These two real-life incidents indicate two different attitudes in two different civilizations — modesty in one and arrogance in the other. Unfortunately, more and more people are forgetting the virtue of modesty and are becoming increasingly arrogant. I remember a friend who was preparing for the IAS examinations. The moment he filled in the form he began to behave as if he were already an IAS officer. He would boast about what he would be doing when he would become the District Magistrate. He even picked up a tiff with the police constable and bragged: "Don't you know to whom you are speaking to? You will salute me after a few months." The poor fellow could not qualify even for the main examinations shattering his dream to get a salute from the policeman. An assistant in the ministry of Home Affairs, he is still called Mr. IAS.

It always pays to be modest. Such a person is a down-to-earth realist in his relationships. He is friendly, warm, and possesses an open mind and a rational outlook. A believer in the goodness of human beings, he is not moved by selfish and crude instincts. He does not try to downgrade people around him. In fact, he gives more importance to them than himself.

An immodest person is directly opposite of a modest one. Braggart, boastful, trumpeter, and bravado-lover, he always finds an opportunity to put others down. He is constantly busy talking about his importance in the setup. He is always ready to take credit whenever the results are excellent, claiming that all went off well as it was done as per his advice. However, if things go wrong, he will pass the buck on, saying it all happened because his advice was not followed.

It is usually believed that a person who talks high about himself becomes popular because people believe what he says. But this is an erroneous notion because when you highlight your own achievements, good qualities, and importance, you do not create any positive impression on others. It is possible that most of them know about your past. Out of modesty they may not contradict you, but they definitely do not believe all what you say. If you are modest about yourself, you are likely to get much more acceptance than a braggart.

Being modest, however, does not mean that you become subservient to others and obey them like a minion. In fact, you can be firm and convey your point effectively if you are humble. Here is an example: Referring to an incident in the Working Committee, Gandhiji wrote to Sardar Vallabhbhai Patel on July 01, 1945: "I did not like our conversation today. It is nobody's fault. You know that I have been at a loss to understand a number of things which you have done.... You speak in the Committee with much heat."

To this Patel replied: "What can I say after your letter? I must be at fault. Only I cannot see it, and that makes me very unhappy. I do betray some heat when I speak in the Committee... that is a temperamental defect... but there is nothing in it."

Modesty has certain virtues. Apart from inspiring more respect than a braggart, you are talked about respectfully even when you are not present. Another advantage is that if you fail to achieve the expected results, you do not have to give explanations to save your face. If you have been telling your friends that you definitely will be getting the promotion, you will be laughed at when you fail to get promoted. On the other hand, if you keep quiet about the possibility of your promotion, you will receive high commendations when you get it. A braggart has to concoct stories when he fails. Sometimes he narrates different stories to different people and when he is exposed he faces a humiliating situation.

A bigheaded person develops an attitude of self-righteousness, believing that he can never be wrong. This attitude makes him resistant to learning and his learning process stops. A modest person is always open to learning more and improving his personality.

So why not be modest and win the world.

Humility pays

More than two hundred years ago, the Americans in their need to expand markets, sent their ambassador to the court of the Chinese Emperor. The ambassador presented his credentials to the Emperor and offered several gifts to him. After the ceremony was over the ambassador left for his residence. On his way home he saw a big chariot with all the gifts he had presented to the Emperor and banners fluttering all around them. Since they were in Chinese, the ambassador could not understand them. He asked his interpreter as to what was written all over. He was told that the slogans read: "The American Government surrenders to the Chinese Emperor and has sent gifts."

The story demonstrates the relation between power and arrogance. No doubt everyone aspires and works for authority as it confers power. However, you should remember the old assertion that "power corrupts and absolute power corrupts absolutely." When one is holding a position of power, one thinks that it would be always with him. He forgets that power is transitory. Since times immemorial power has never stayed with one person. Therefore, it should be used in such a way that when it is not there, the successor does not become vindictive. It has been happening in Tamil Nadu where Jayalalithaa and Karunanidhi took vengeance with each other soon after becoming Chief Ministers.

Those who acquire towering success, like Lal Bahadur Shastri, do not allow power to convert them into an egocentric person. An egocentric is a self-centred, self-righteous, self-satisfied, and smug person. A self-centred person is concerned in the fulfillment of his own interests only. He only cares for his desires, requirements, and benefits. He would not have any consideration for the interests of others. Such a person wants others, of course those who are weaker than him, to dance to his tunes. He shows his power off and others tolerate him because of the powerful position he holds and the harm he can cause to them if displeased. He may reward them, if happy. However, when such persons are out of power they feel like fish out of the water and face miserable situations.

An egocentric person is firmly convinced of his righteousness, especially in relation to the actions and beliefs of others. He is obsessed with his righteousness and feels no need for improvement in his behaviour and actions. He can move only in one direction. Whenever there are obstructions, he stops and cannot go further. He can never think that obstructions can block the way. He never admits to his mistakes and finds excuses to explain his failures. He will hold others responsible for his omissions.

The main drawback of the egocentric person is that he stops to learn. As he suffers from acute self-satisfaction, he thinks that no one is more capable than him. This insulates him from new breakthroughs in knowledge, information technology, and techniques.

Humility and modesty, on the contrary, open the mind of a person who is always willing to learn. He, like Einstein, believes that he is picking up shells at the ocean of knowledge. It is this feeling that motivates him to keep his mind open and the learning process alive. A person with humility is willing to learn from everyone, even from juniors, because he acknowledges that he does not have all the answers to all the questions. Remember humility is the process of recognising your own weaknesses and respecting the other person's strengths.

Humility and modesty never lead to a weak personality. In fact, a modest person will always be stronger than an egocentric because his discretion and proper use of authority will give him wide acceptability and respectability. Such a person is sure to reach the victory pole. It has happened in the past and will happen in future too.

Appreciate support

Dale Carnegie in his best-selling book *How to Win Friends and Influence People* observes: "You want recognition of your true worth. You want your friends and associates to be hearty in their appreciation and lavish their praise on you." True he was. You definitely can work magic if you adopt the prescription of sincere appreciation as opposed to blatant insincere selfishness. The obvious corollary of this rule is that a person who does not appreciate the efforts of others tends to fall out of their favour.

I will narrate the experience of a fellow editor, Narendra, to illustrate this truth. One day he came to my office visibly annoyed. I tried to calm him down and enquired what had happened. "I will never help anyone in future," was his reply.

"Don't raise your blood pressure, Narendra. Tell me, what has happened," I asked him offering a glass of water. A thoroughly indignant Narendra told me what had happened that made him unhappy.

A young boy Ajay came to his residence one evening. He made a good impression with his pleasing personality and disposition. He told him that he was a graduate from a small town in Rajasthan and had come to Delhi to take admission in a good college. But his father was a person of modest means and, therefore, unable to finance his studies and expenditure of the education in Delhi University and hostel. Ajay further told him that he did not want to put any financial burden on his father, as he was already worried about his sister's marriage. He was reading a magazine that was being edited by Narendra and came to him for help thinking that he was a member of the wider family of the magazine. He sought Narendra's help in finding tuitions so that he could finance his study in college and also prepare for the civil services examinations. Impressed by the intention of not being a burden on his parents Narendra appreciated his initiative and decided to help him. He asked Ajay to come next day to his office.

Narendra spoke to a few friends about Ajay's predicament. Hari, a friend of his, agreed to engage Ajay for his son's tuition. Narendra asked Ajay, when he came to see him next day, to meet Hari.

A few days later, Narendra happened to go to Hari's clinic, a dental surgeon, and was surprised that Ajay had started teaching the boy. He had also taken a loan of Rs. 500 saying he needed the money for depositing the fee in the college. The careless Ajay did not care to inform Narendra about getting the tuition and loan from Hari, not to talk of thanking him. He should have done it because Hari gave tuition and money to Ajay because Narendra recommended him. It was an obligation on Narendra and not on Ajay.

Ajay visited Narendra twice during the next one month. But did not mention the loan he had taken from Hari. First he came for another favour of a fresh loan, as he wanted to migrate to a better college. The second time he wanted more tuition. Both the times Narendra helped him out thinking that he was helping a student from a needy family in building up his career. He thought it was an act of charity, better then offering money in a temple. But Ajay neither thanked Narendra nor informed him when he got the money or tuition.

"Tell me, Yog, was it not expected from Ajay to inform and thank me when he got favours on my recommendations? I had taken obligations of my very close friends. What were they thinking about me? How ungrateful I am that I did not acknowledge their favours," said Narendra indignantly. He was rightly feeling embittered that he was used by a stranger.

Amused by what had happened to Narendra, I thought I must know the story from Ajay to find out the reasons for him acting so irresponsibly. I called Ajay to my office. He came the next day on the appointed time. I was surprised to find him a pleasing person. He did not seem to be guileful, devious, or selfish. After talking to him for thirty minutes I realised that the fault was primarily in his inability to realise the implications of his actions and his ignorance of human psychology. Living in a small town in a backward region he did not learn elementary etiquette. Obviously, he could not visualise the backlash of the *faux pas* that was because of his innocence and not by design.

Narendra was also not wrong and was justified in feeling hurt. Ajay did not observe the common courtesy and decency to thank him when his work was done on Narendra's recommendation. This put Narendra in a poor light because his friends took him to be rude. As Carnegie said: "There is one all-important law of human conduct and that law is: Always make the other person feel important. The deepest principle in human nature is the craving to be appreciated."

> **Remember the following while seeking help from anyone:**
>
> *If you want someone to put a word of recommendation for you, you are indebted to the former and not the person who obliged you.*
>
> *Always keep your mentor informed about the latest developments that have taken place between you and the person who will finally do your work. If you do not do that your mentor will cut a sorry figure before the person whom he recommended your case.*
>
> *"Everyone likes a compliment," was Abraham Lincoln's belief. Appreciate the efforts of the person who recommended your case. It was, in fact, the secret of the success of Rockefeller's success and might be yours too.*
>
> *Always return loans on time and as promptly as possible. For, as Carnegie said, "If we are so contemptibly selfish that we can't radiate a little happiness and pass on a bit of honest appreciation without trying to screw something out of the other person in return — if our souls are no bigger than sour crab apples — we shall meet the failure we so richly deserve."*
>
> *You definitely do not deserve failure.*

Avoid criticism to outshine

Seldom comes a time in the history of a nation when everyone discusses the same issue across the country. In the first half of 1987, India passed through that time. Eighty per cent of discussions invariably centered on regretful relations between President Giani Zail Singh and Prime Minister Rajiv Gandhi. The problem in the relationship was due to lack of communication and misunderstanding. The two heads of the Government and the State stood on false ego. If we look into the problem, it was a behavioural problem. The two did not like the conduct of each other and thought the entire mistake was of the other person. Defined broadly it was the problem of relationship between the two heads of the nation. Problem of similar nature does arise every where and with every one.

I discussed this problem with persons of two different mindsets. They approached the problem in a logical way from two different angles. First I discussed it with a senior diplomat. His feeling was that important and responsible persons should refrain from publicly reflecting their differences. They should not indulge in mud-slinging particularly where the media is present. He cited the example of Abraham Lincoln, an American President, who as a young man in Pigeon Creek Valley of Indiana used to criticise people and write letters ridiculing them. He would drop these letters on busy roads for wider circulation. Even as a practicing lawyer in Springfield, Illinois, Lincoln wrote open letters against opponents in newspapers. The matter became serious when Lincoln published an anonymous letter deriding James Shields, an Irish politician. Shields took up cudgels and found out that Lincoln wrote the letter. He challenged him to a duel. Unwilling Lincoln had to accept the challenge. However, good luck favourd him and the duel was shelved at the last minute. Lincoln was sure to lose the fight. He learnt his lesson for life in the art of dealing with people, and never again did he offend people publicly. This was one of the reasons for him becoming an icon President of the United Sates. He became a turning point in the American history by abolishing the slavery system.

"Criticism," argues Dale Carnegie, "is a dangerous sport—a spark that is liable to cause an explosion in the power magazine of pride; an explosion that hastens death". Benjamin Franklin's huge success as an American Ambassador to France at the most crucial period of history was due to the dictum he followed: "I will speak ill of no man... and speak all the good I know of everybody". Adds Carnegie: "Any fool can criticise, condemn, and complain and most fools do. But it takes character and self-control to be understanding and forgiving."

The second person I spoke to was a Supreme Court retired Judge. He wanted the person enjoying substantial power and prestige to understand the difference between appreciation and flattery. Carnegie's differentiation is that "One is sincere and the other insincere. One comes from the heart out; the other from the teeth out. One is universally admired; the other is universally condemned".

Kaiser William II of Germany is an excellent example of a person who rode a tiger and could not jump off to safety because he lived in a world of sycophants. He could not stand persons who stood up to him. When pushed to war, he not only lost the battle but his life also. To know something about him would be interesting.

"There is only one master in this country and I am he," he said when in June 1888 he became the Emperor of Germany at the age of 31. Rather than sharing power with Otto Von Bismarck, known as the "Iron Chancellor" and the builder of the modern powerful Germany, the Kaiser dismissed him in 1890. By doing this he converted a powerful supporter into a devastating opponent. The new autocrat did have some admirable qualities—a bold and comprehensive outlook, a powerful and exact memory, and an eye for detail, piety, and patriotism. But there was another side of him too. The famous British historian H.A.L. Fisher wrote about him: "But with these shining qualities were mingled others of a baser alloy, an egregious vanity, an ungovernable temper. There was no flattery so base that he would not accept it. A nervous excitability and impulsiveness always made him dangerous as a ruler, so that, after experience of many alarms and excursions, his ministers began to ask themselves in trepidation whether the headstrong and loquacious master of Germany was not in fact deranging in mind".

On the other side of the scale is the popular British monarch, King George V, who displayed a set of six maxims on the walls of his study at Buckingham Palace. One of the six maxims was:

"Teach me neither to proffer nor receive cheap praise"

Equally sagacious was Queen Victoria's Prime Minister Benjamin Disraeli who believed that flattery did you more harm than good. He compared it to counterfeit money that would eventually get you into trouble.

Perhaps General Alvaro Obregon, a famous Mexican President was right when he said: "Don't be afraid of enemies who attack you. Be afraid of friends who flatter you."

When we know so much about the reasons behind the successes and failures of so many powerful people, why then can't we learn from them?

Networking

"In today's world you need two things to move up in life and career: merit and contacts," said Rajan revealing his secret of developing a large network of contacts.

"Why need merit, if you have contacts? There are several mediocre people occupying important positions. I can give you as many examples as you want," I argued.

"You may be right. However, these are exceptions that do not prove the rule. A few people may acquire important positions because of their contacts. But an ordinary person needs both," said Rajan.

"But you have not answered my first question: Why need merit to move up?"

"Because if you want someone to push you up, you must give him some base to support you. As you move up towards the top of the pyramid the competition changes from tough to tougher and toughest at the end point. Remember that there is only one position at the top."

I agreed with Rajan who gave me tips on how to develop a network of contacts.

Developing a network of contacts, known as networking, is a delicate art, more akin to diplomacy. Certain people are born with this art. On analysing their *modus operandi*, certain tips can be formed that can be practiced by those who also want to develop a network of contacts. However, these have to be used with great care, like a surgeon's scalpel. Rajan follows a four-step strategy.

1. Meet people

The core of networking is to know as many people as possible in different walks of life. You should try to meet new persons whenever you get an opportunity to do so. Attend parties, join club meetings, go to lectures, and attend seminars. Introduce yourself to different persons wherever you go, talk to them finding out their interests and get to know them. Show interest in their work and hobbies, and appreciate their achievements. Do not be critical of them and do not dominate the conversation. Talk as little as possible in the first meeting. The first meeting is just to know each other and not to get close.

2. Create an impact

You should be able to break the ice in the first meeting. Find an opportunity to meet the person again if you have been successful in creating an impression on him. The second meeting should be as close as possible to the first one. It is always better to write a letter or make a phone call. Whichever of the two you do, be polite and courteous. You can start with the conversation you had in the first meeting and pick up some point from there to go further. Try to meet again within a short time and if it is possible fix the appointment on phone. But you should not try to force yourself upon the person. If you do that he may feel that you had some purpose and he may try to avoid you.

Grabbing the second opportunity to meet depends on the individual. If you find the person willing, invite him for coffee or lunch. You can suggest meeting him in his office with some agenda or for seeking advice if he is not willing to accept your invitation. The latter option is always better. Do not try to insist a meeting as shown in many films!

3. Develop friendship

Once you develop some friendship and the other person becomes interested in you, the process of developing it can be pushed further. How you go about it is important. You have to be cautious so that there is no misunderstanding. Do not give the impression that you are developing the friendship with some ulterior motive or selfish purpose. If you do that the person will drop you like a hot potato.

Develop healthy relationships. You should remain in touch with the person so that the contact is not lost. You can send your good wishes on birthdays and marriage anniversaries. If the person needs help at critical moments, extend a helping hand. Friendships are fastened in days of need and crisis. Appreciate the actions of the person whenever he helps you. However, do not indulge in excessive praise leading to flattery. It is important to maintain your self-respect and dignity while developing friendship.

4. Get going

Once you have established a firm friendship, you are in a position to ask for favours. Follow one golden rule:

Do not ask for favours frequently, ask only when it is required.

Do not ask favours for all your friends and relatives.

Developing contacts is a long-term investment. Maintain contacts with successful and important persons to ensure a high social standing. Enrich your life in the process.

Doing the homework

"Hon'ble Governor Sharma and extinguished guests". This is how a superstar's wife, herself a superstar, addressed a meeting in Mumbai a decade back. She, it seems, was delivering her speech without knowing what she was speaking. You should never commit such a mistake. It will only put you in a precarious position and weaken your confidence and keenness to continue speaking in public.

You, in fact, will become a laughing stock, a butt of jokes. It is better to decline an invitation if you can't find time to understand the topic and the audience.

If you accept an invitation to speak you should carefully note down the date and time of the meeting. Then inquire certain basic details—venue of the meeting, specific topic on which you are being invited to talk, duration of the talk, if there would be any one else speaking on the same topic in the meeting, find out the name, profession, and status of the person who would be speaking besides you, who would be presiding over the meeting, and the likely size of the audience.

Another piece of important information that you must ask, besides the above one, is about the nature of the audience. It would help you to plan the level of your talk. If you are not aware of the level of intelligence of those who would gather to listen to you, your address may not interest them. It may be too elementary if they are enlightened listeners, or may go over their heads if they are less educated. Also you may use the facts or information that may not interest them. For example, those born after 1950 would not be aware of the sufferings by those who fought for the independence of India. Any elaborate mention of the sufferings by the people who fought against the British will be of no relevance to them.

Begin preparing for your talk about three weeks before the day it is to be delivered. Keep a notebook to write down the ideas, good phrases, illustrations, quotations, and facts on the subject as and when they occur to you. Also discuss the subject with your friends and colleagues. However, do not let them influence you too much. The ideas and expressions should be entirely yours, though you may consider using their views if they fit well in the broad outline of your talk.

1. Organise your speech

Most talks can be divided into three main parts: the introduction or the approach, the main body of the talk, and the conclusion.

Introduction: It is how you present the topic to the audience. The introduction allows you to explain how you propose to tackle the subject. It builds up the interest of the audience about the theme of your talk. They become eager to know what you would be saying. It would also develop their interest in the rest of the talk.

The introduction should be short, simple, and straightforward. If possible include points of widespread interest and something of local interest to generate an interest in your talk.

Main body: It is the main part of your talk. It, in fact, is the most vital part of your whole address and, therefore, needs maximum attention and planning. You should select two or three most interesting aspects of the topic. Then select a few clearly expressed ideas to develop the main theme of your talk. These should be arranged in a logical way to give your talk a natural flow. A chronological approach, going from the past, via the present, to the future or going from the familiar to the wider implications of the subject are some ways of arranging your talk logically. Keep your audience interested throughout the talk. Deal with minor points first. Build up the main and the most interesting point at the end. The main body of your talk should have an integral logic with one idea flowing naturally on the next.

Conclusion: It is the concluding part of your talk. The conclusion gives the audience a chance to recapitulate the main aspects of the subject. It also gives you a chance to stimulate them into action, if your talk is intended to motivate the audience to do something.

Once you have planned your talk, you will become aware of the gaps in your information and knowledge. Check and double-check your facts so that you are not proved wrong. Even one wrong fact will affect your credibility. Prepare your notes accurately and carefully. Take photocopies or clippings of the material that you want to refer to during the talk. Make sure that you note down the sources of your facts in case you want to consult them at a later stage.

Now is the final preparation. Write down the whole talk in full. However, you should not read it like a research paper at a seminar. It is to give you confidence that you have good material to talk about. It also gives you an opportunity to crystallise your ideas and expressions. Now prepare note cards. For note cards compress each point to a single word or short phrase. Leave sufficient spaces between the lines and on the margin. You should write on one side of the card only. To identify different points without problems it is better to use different coloured inks. Number all the cards so that there is no mix up.

2. What to speak

When you are speaking to the audience you should bear in mind certain tips. Consider the arguments you want to prove and the nature of the audience. Imagine what they would like to know and the information they would find interesting and what quality of information they would be able to absorb. Do not tire them with mere facts. Talk "with" your audience and not "at" them. Use examples linked with everyone's experience. Do not act superior to your audience or try too hard to be "one of the crowd". Use simple and straightforward words and phrases.

Use humour sparingly and remember three important points—first, it should be relevant; second, it should suit your style; and third, it should suit the particular audience. Humour should not be dragged too much to lose its punch.

The expressions should be apt with witty phrases. These should be short, easily remembered, and should be popular with the audience. Quotations should not be used frequently. Your audience wants to hear you and your views and not those of others that they might already know. Metaphors, similes, and analogies can be used but their use should be moderate.

You should guide your audience through your talk. They should understand the link when you change from one idea or set of issues to another aspect of the subject by providing suitable linking phrases.

Do not adopt irritating and unpleasant manners. You should not keep your hands in one position only. Rest your hands gently on either side of your body. Do not stand with crossed hands as it is considered being impertinent to the audience. You should move your hands to explain your points and should not be in contradiction to what you say. Movement of hands should not be irrelevant to what you speak.

3. At the meeting venue

Arrive at the venue fifteen minutes before the time of the lecture so that you can relax and absorb and get a feel of the place and the people. When you are taken to the lecture room, enter with a cool and calm temper. You should be looking and feeling comfortable and should not be feeling hostile or a stranger. Walk comfortably towards the rostrum, glancing in all directions, smiling and nodding to those who are wishing you. When the meeting begins, listen with concentration to every person who speaks before you. You should make brief comments of appreciation on them before you begin the lecture. Give special attention to the opening speech of the chairperson. Do not shuffle through your notes or papers or stare intently at the floor when others are speaking. You would not like them to do that when you speak. Extend the same courtesy to them. You should be looking frequently at the person who is speaking and the audience.

Do not jump up immediately when you are invited to speak. Rise from your seat, collect your papers, and walk comfortably and gracefully towards the podium. Slow and deliberate movements will make you look confident. Begin the lecture by addressing the chairperson and the audience. Look towards them when you mention them.

At the end of the talk you can ask the audience if they have any questions. When replying to their questions look courteous and reply without ridiculing the person who has asked the question. Many questions are frivolous or foolish, but do not react to them as if they are fools, even if they are. Do not pretend to be super-intelligent as the "Mr. or Ms. know-it-all." Note down the main points of the question if it is long and complex. Answer all the points in the order they were asked. If someone provides some information that you do not know, do not resent but thank him. If someone makes a valid criticism, do not be annoyed and try to prove that the person has not been able to understand the point. Accept if the point that has been made is correct.

Always remember that no talk is ever perfect. Learn from every lecture you deliver.

Effective public speaking

Public speaking is an integral part of professional life, one without which you cannot move into the fast lane. When you join a company as a junior manager you might not be required to speak publically or give presentations, but as you move ahead in your career you are required to do both. Most of us panic when asked to address top or senior managers or clients. Understanding the importance of public speaking and the difficulties young managers face in this art, the follwing text will discuss public speaking and presentation skills, dealing with public-speaking nerves and anxiety, skills, techniques, and how you can be an effective public speaker.

We all, at one point of time or another, have to speak to gatherings of professionals or a heterogeneous group of persons. Unfortunately most of us do not know the art of public speaking and shudder to think of giving a speech in public. Though a few are born orators and can speak on any topic under the sun, others have to learn this art.

How can one learn this art? A survey on what makes a successful and effective speech suggests that about 90 per cent depends on having something worthwhile to say and putting it across well. It is a skill that can be learnt if one works hard to read and think. The remaining 10 per cent depends on your personality which you can definitely improve. Therefore, it is a myth that certain persons cannot give a public speech. Most of the good and effective speakers were not that good in the beginning. But they learnt from their mistakes, worked hard, and mastered the art of speaking. You too can learn to give an effective and enjoyable speech.

The art of public speaking has acquired greater significance in the contemporary society. It has become an effective and proven method of knowing your communication skills. These skills are:

How you convey your ideas to others.

How you persuade them.

How you stimulate them into action.

So do not be surprised if when facing a selection board you are asked to give an extempore speech for one minute considering the board as the audience. Later when you join a company you may be required to give a presentation to your overseas buyers. Here are a few tips to effective public speaking.

1. Confidence is the core

The first prerequisite for effective public speaking is confidence. You can build it up if you do not have it in abundance. Most of you feel nervous when asked to speak in public. It may be because of the fear of making a fool of yourself, or the fear of losing the attention or support of the audience, or the fear of being inaudible, or it may be just a "fear of the unknown". The last fear has no reason. It is merely that you are fearful of speaking in the presence of a gathering, big or small and you do not know the reasons. Most people suffer from this fear. These fears can be overcome in two ways:

Prepare yourself thoroughly before you go to speak.
Present your views effectively and confidently.

2. Thorough preparation

It means collecting all the information on the topic on which you are asked to speak. You need to develop a broad background of general information that enables you to incorporate interesting facts and ideas into your speech. This requires you to be an avid reader and a keen observer of facts and ideas. Also you must develop a system of storing material and recalling it at appropriate moments because information is of no use if you are not able to retrieve it at the appropriate time. You should keep a notebook handy to jot down new facts and ideas. You cannot remember all the facts and information you come across. If you do not write down the points that can be useful to you in future, you won't be able to use them. Late Prem Bhatia, former Editor of *The Tribune* (Chandigarh) and a diplomat later, always used to keep a pen and notebook with him.

It is better to develop files on different topics. You can use key words to identify the main subject area before filing your notes, newspaper clippings, and articles from magazines. Jot down the source on all notes and clippings. Now all this is ready to be stored in your personal computer or laptop.

Wide and voracious reading not only enriches your knowledge, it also strengthens your vocabulary enabling you to choose the most apt word for the situation and expression. Frequent use of thesaurus and dictionary sharpens the existing armory of words and phrases and helps you to pick up new ones. Keep in mind that "The best word is often the shortest and the most commonly understood."

Develop your mental agility and practice thinking about everyday subjects from different angles. Try to develop a voice that is deep and clear to become an effective speaker. What you say must be clearly conveyed to those listening to you. Speak slowly and with modulation. Your speech should not be delivered in the same monotonous tone from the beginning to the end. Change the sound, tone and pitch according to the expression. Speaking in an expressionless voice means that your voice and mind are not in proper coordination. The audience may feel that you not really interested in what you are saying. Do not attempt to imitate an accent. Speak in your natural accent. Also do not speak in a way that the end of sentences fades away. This happens when you are jumping ahead, thinking about what you will say next and concentrating on what you want to say. Speak at a normal pitch and not very loudly. A loud voice is no compensation for poor articulation. Throw your voice in different directions and look into the direction you want to toss your voice.

Gesticulation and mannerisms are significant because while speaking your body and voice should be communicating with the audience. These two, however, can distract your listeners if your movements are unrelated to what you are saying. For example, a nervous twiddling of figures or a temporary shrug to shoulders at frequent intervals may distract the audience and may look funny too. However, appropriate gesticulations to what you are saying help to reinforce the message you want to convey to the audience. The nature and quality of gestures should be linked to your personal style and the size of the audience. When you go to lectures observe the gesticulation and mannerism of speakers. Later you should see your actions in the mirror to get an idea of how you look when gesticulating.

Always start the lecture with a formal style of addressing the audience. It is an easy-to-remember and ritualised way for you to get started. It also gives the audience a chance to "tune in" to your voice before you say anything particularly important.

Eleven skills of an effective public speaker

1. **Research** – *You should be well informed with the latest information on your topic. Therefore, you need to do thorough research on what you want to convey to your listeners.*
2. **Focus** – *You should help your audience to understand your focal points by concentrating on your view. You should take the help of stories, anecdotes, or other aids to connect to the core idea. Anything that is irrelevant should be taken away.*
3. **Organise ideas logically** – *A well-organised presentation can be absorbed with minimal mental strain.*
4. **Narrate a story** – *Everyone loves a story. Points wrapped up in a story are more memorable.*
5. **Start and close stronger** – *The beginning and the closing of your speech should be effective and strong. The body of the presentation should also be strong, but your audience will remember the first and the last part of your presentation.*
6. **Add in humour** – *Listeners do not want to hear a bore speech. You should add one or two humourous episodes and small jokes. However, you should know when to use humour.*
7. **Intonate** – *Speak slowly and with modulation. Do not speak in the same monotonous tone from the beginning to the end. So intonate the voice keeping in view the narration.*
8. **Use effective body language** – *You should intersperse words with gestures that should complement your words in harmony. If you want to tell how small the pigmy was, show them with the help of your hands.*
9. **Connect with the audience** – *Eye contact is the best way to hook up your listeners. Every listener should feel and say: "This speaker is just like me!" You should interact with the audience by asking questions and have a dialogue with them.*

10. **Show confidence and poise** – *Do not look nervous and confused. It may be difficult to remain confident and maintain poise, but listeners can easily understand if you are not. So let not your hands sweat and your mouth become dry. Your knees should not shake and do not let a quaver affect your voice. Your heart should not race and do not let the well-known butterflies invade your stomach.*
11. **Listen critically** – *Listen to the other speakers when they are giving their presentations. Study the strengths and weakness of other speakers.*

Managing conflict

Conflicts are a natural phenomena that, in fact, are essential for everyone. Those who face them, learn many lessons in problem solving. Many who have not faced conflicts would not be able to solve any problem when confronted with it. They would develop an escapist tendency, running away whenever a problem would arise. However, those who see them as challenges and fight them out are the ones who succeed. Who are such persons?

Those who believe in managing conflicts are known as "fighters." They know that conflicts are part of life and they take them as games. They believe that if there were no conflicts, there would be no challenges. In fact, every conflict helps the person to move forward. Conflict is always considered a painful, harmful, and sometime devastating appearance in a normal and easy-going life. More often than not it indicates that something has gone terribly wrong. It is a forewarning that a serious catastrophe is likely to develop if the present conflict is not handled properly and solved. Nations that suppress conflicts ultimately collapse but those that allow them to appear on the scene and handle them properly, prosper in the long run. The USSR always suppressed conflicts in its country. It ultimately collapsed. In India we have been moving from one conflict to another.

We have not only survived but have prospered to the benefit of the people. Therefore, conflicts should be accepted as a natural phenomenon, necessary for the betterment of the people and the nation.

Having accepted conflict as part of the game, the manager must seek effective cooperation from those who work with him. The cardinal principle to solve a conflict is to discuss it with the team rather than suppressing, postponing, or avoiding it. A business leader in the contemporary corporate world must be aware of conflicts and should be able to solve them through open discussions. Adequate and proper skills must be developed in the team to understand, handle, and solve every conflict.

The modern corporate sector respects those leaders who can manage conflicts. Those who suppress conflicts are not given responsible assignments. Conflicts are sometimes deliberately created to improve collaborations and understanding among the team members.

A conflict is difficult to define. It is often understood as clash of interests. A conflict appears when persons work in a group. It arises when the behaviour of one person obstructs, interferes with, or blocks the interest of another person. He then feels that his interests are being adversely affected. It also surfaces when people conclude that the actions of others are incompatible with their own and they begin to react to it. It is built in our system and is too basic to be ignored. The perspective should be to learn managing the conflict rather than running away from it.

1. Productive conflicts

It is being accepted that productive conflicts help individuals and organisations in more than one way. These are:

Conflict makes you more aware and capable to confront problems you face. A feeling that the work is obstructed or is being affected adversely because of certain problems makes you determined to solve the problem.

Conflicts strengthen relationships between you and others working with you. They heighten the morals of your colleagues. Those who work together realise that their relationships are strong enough to withstand the brunt of the conflict. Therefore, they need not avoid frustrations and problems. They can release their tensions through discussions and problem solving.

Conflicts promote awareness of self and others. Through conflicts, one can know the reasons that make others angry, frustrated, and frightened and also what is important to them. In solving conflicts we come to know what we are fighting for. It tells us a lot about our personalities. We also realise what makes our colleagues unhappy. It creates a harmonious understanding between the team members and helps them to accept each other better.

Conflicts enhance in the development of the personalities of those who are involved in solving conflicts. While solving a conflict you can find out how your style affects your team members. Your team members can also know what technical and interpersonal skills are required to upgrade their personalities.

Conflicts provide psychological strength to a personality. People become more focused and their perspective becomes clearer when they tackle conflicts. Through conflicts, they understand the perspectives of others in a much better way and become less egoistic.

A conflict can become exciting and interesting. People feel thrilled, involved, and animated in confronting conflicts that are a welcome break from an easy-going life.

Conflicts provide vents to steam off the frustrations and grievances against each other. Team members would feel more relaxed and closer to each other after they have expressed their annoyances during the conflict-solving process.

2. Handling conflicts

Conflicts can be handled in several ways. Some people begin shouting at others or some may cry and seek help from others. On the other hand, the real troubleshooters maintain their composure, serenity, and presence of mind. They analyse the conflict and think the ways in which that can be resolved. People who have the experience of handling conflicts successfully suggest three ways to manage such a crisis.

Cooperative dependence: It involves people who have to manage the crisis. All concerned persons are encouraged to share their views openly. They are motivated to explore and understand opposing views. Each one can understand the weaknesses in their perspectives and appreciate the desires and requirements of others. They can discuss the whole problem to integrate various ideas thrown at the time of discussion. A unanimous or widely acceptable solution can be arrived at in the end. It would be based on the ideas and views of all and would be workable on a joint basis. The focus of this method is cooperative dependence.

Competitive approach: It is contrary to the cooperative dependence method. This approach can be adopted when the first one fails. Various persons who represent different interests defend their own positions and try to win over others. Sometimes deadlocks are created because each one tries to assert his views. Many may use the influence of superior authority or a heavy weight in the society to get his views implemented. If such a situation arises, the team leader has to take his own decision and get it implemented with his authority.

Conflict avoidance: It is the most commonly preferred and used method of handling a problem. The team leader tries to postpone the conflict till such time it is not possible to do so. He does not expose the team with the arising crisis and hopes that it might not arise at all. He may also think that by the time the crisis becomes inevitable, he may not be there at the scene. In fact, avoiding conflict is not good management. It not only gives a false sense of confidence in the work relationships, but also undermines the capacity to identify and solve problems. It also shows poor and weak leadership.

> **Organisations prefer conflict managers**
>
> *The Indian organisations are no more interested in persons who function with an authoritative attitude. In the contemporary world, marketing has become the most difficult function as most of the first-rate companies are introducing quality products at lower prices. This requires homogeneous leaders who can work as a team with others. The organisations, therefore, look for persons who can handle persons of different temperaments, egos, and dispositions. In brief, they would appoint persons who can manage situations in which different members are in conflict with each other.*
>
> *Organisations are devising new techniques to find out how a person can mange conflicting personalities. One such method being used by forward-looking companies is asking candidates to participate in role play exercises. It can take various forms. One example is that the candidate is asked to manage an angry customer or colleagues who are fighting with each other. This, in fact, is to measure responses to various situations or testing the emotional intelligence of the person. Other methods being employed to understand the behavioural mechanisms of the person are psychometric and personality tests, case study sessions, simulation exercises, and behavioural-intensive interviews to find out whether the candidate can function with conflicting persons. These tests are able to give a fairly good idea of how the person handles other individuals who do not agree with him, and also tests his ability to work within a team that is functioning during conflicts.*

Whatever method is selected to solve the conflict, the essential requirement is a free and fair discussion. People should talk about the conflict, share their feelings and ideas freely, and keep communication channels open. The discussion should be used to let all team members know each other. It should be when the conflict arises and also after the conflict is handled successfully. The whole process of devising the strategy and its implementation should be critically analysed. Discussions and deliberations help people to understand the specific problems, how the conflict began, and how it was resolved. The key to making discussions constructive is to maintain, emphasise, and strengthen cooperative dependence. During the discussion, it should be emphasised that each one gained more by working together. Listening carefully and understanding issues and feelings through-and-through are critical. No one should try to dominate and control others. The effort should be to arrive at a consensus and reach an agreement. Once this is done all should cooperate to solve the crisis.

Fight a conflict to resolve it. Don't run away from it.

Executive stresses

Most young people feel stressed in their jobs because they are not accustomed to working long hours. Why does this happen? Probably unfulfilled ambitions, job conflicts, and may be other non-work-related pressures. Whatever may be the reason, stress greatly hampers the efficiency and productivity of a young person. Those who are able to develop a system to bear stress in their everyday lives, move ahead faster in their careers. But those who do not, get left behind. So how can you cope with stress?

Primitive man had strange ways to release his stress. He would shout, pull apart his hair, and hit his opponent with a bludgeon. This would get the stress out of him. This reaction would trigger off a chain of activities within his body. Adrenal secretions rushed into his blood. This helped him muster strength in the form of both sugar and stored fats in his muscles and brain. This instantly mobilised energy, and stimulated pulse, respiration, and blood pressure. His digestive processes turned off at once so that no energy was diverted from meeting the threat. His coagulation chemistry immediately prepared to resist wounds with quick clotting. Red cells poured from the spleen into the steeped-up blood circulation to help the respiratory system absorb oxygen and release carbon dioxide as he clubbed away at the prowling enemy.

But this is not possible now as the present high-profile business manager silently seethes in his black suit. He still reacts, but within his skin. His body's chemical reactions are the same—he suppresses his anger and remains calm and represses wrath within himself without targeting anyone. He pushes too hard, smokes too many cigarettes, drinks a large number of coffee cups, and as a result develops ulcers, faces cardiac arrests, and suffers from nervous breakdowns.

1. Work-related stress

As early as 1972, Walter Mcquade in an article *What Stress Can Do to You* pointed out the reasons for stress. He wrote: "Perhaps the answer, or at least part of the answer is that modern societies have to a great extent lost the supports that helped people in earlier times endure toil, hardship and suffering—religious faith, sustaining frame-works of tradition and custom, a sense of place in the social order, a sense of worth derived from the exercise of craftsmanship and awareness that toil, hardship and suffering were likewise endured by the other members of the same community and the same social class."

He further wrote that: "Particularly destructive of the individual's sense of security have been the side-effects of one of the industrial world's most precious products—social mobility. This bright trophy of our times has its deeply etched dark side. Social mobility has weakened the sense of belonging to a class—the sense of having a place in the social ladder. More importantly, social mobility implies that success depends on merit alone and to the extent that society believes in such a correlation, individual bread-winners are thrust into an endless competition where lagging behind or losing can be interpreted as a sign of personal inadequacy."

In today's corporate world, managers are increasingly draining themselves out, inviting emotional and physical illnesses. Unfulfilled ambitions, job-conflicts, and other pressures are constantly taking toll on the young managers' health until they face a complete breakdown. Stress is not only a killer, but also a drastic force. Nevertheless, stress should not and cannot be avoided. The secret is not to live less intensely but more intelligently. Each manager must find his innate stress level and live accordingly.

The warning signs of stress are irritability, chronic fatigue, cynicism, frustration, boredom, avoidance of personal contacts (isolation), depression, loss of sexual desire, emotional instability (for example, the over-powering urge to cry), inability to concentrate, constant anxiety, insomnia, nightmares, and increased use of alcohol or drugs.

2. How to cope

Work-related stress is a universal malady that causes excess tension and produces confusion. You don't think straight or organise yourself properly; you jump to the wrong conclusion; you dwell on negative, unproductive factors. All this is true, but how do you cope with stress?

Rule number one: Don't sweat the small stuff.

Rule number two: If you can't fight and you can't flee, flow.

Take a break: To prevent stress from affecting your personal life, discover relaxing activities outside the scope of your work. Spend more time with your family and friends. Take a short vacation. Take a break between new projects. Re-define your goals in life and assess your work pattern. Remember, there's no such thing as a perfect job or a perfect company. As most of us have to spend our entire working lives as someone's employee, it's important to assess whether you are suited to work for a corporate. And if you think you are, then instead of being frustrated, look objectively at the company you are working for and adjust your expectations realistically.

To overcome stress resulting from office politics, differences and tensions with colleagues, learn the art of being emotionally detached and resist the feeling of victimisation. You should know that if you handle your work situation adroitly, the company will offer you ample opportunities to develop your potential. Or, it can give you ulcers. The choice is yours.

Learn to relax: Anger can be a serious strategic error — you are displaying your weaknesses and inviting exploitation. Learn to make your anger an asset, and channelise your energy otherwise uselessly spent in doing something constructive.

Next time something or someone attempts to give you another ulcer, try this:

> *Tense each of your major muscles starting from your neck, shoulders and arms, and down to your legs for about five seconds. Take a deep breath to help pump oxygen into the blood vessels and body tissues and send refreshing blood to the brain. Drink a glass of water and close your eyes for a while. After about 10 minutes, think of pleasant things that happened in the past or those that are coming up in the future. You'll find your body feeling more comfortable and your breathing will become even and normal.*

It definitely is better than, say, reaching out for and lighting up a cigarette or drowning your sorrows with a bottle of whisky.

3. Siesta—the best stress buster

The U.S. scientists, after extensive research, have recommended a nap (a brief snooze) during the day as it improves the brain's ability to absorb new facts. This research was conducted on volunteers who slept for 90 minutes during the day. Their performance was better at cognitive tests than those who did not go far a nap. The latest study, from the University of California at Berkeley, has suggested that the brain may need sleep to process short-term memories, creating space for learning new facts. In their experiment, 39 healthy adults were given a difficult learning task in the morning, with broadly similar results, before half of them were sent for their siesta.

When the tests were repeated, those who had taken a nap outperformed those who had carried on without it. Checks on the brain's electrical activity suggested that this process might be happening in a sleep phase between deep sleep and dreaming sleep, called stage-2 non-rapid eye movements' sleep, when fact-based memories are shifted from the temporary storage in the brain's hippocampus to another area called the pre-frontal cortex.

The research was conducted under the leadership of Dr. Matthew Walker who said: "Sleep not only rights the wrong of prolonged wakefulness, but, at a neuro-cognitive level, it moves you beyond where you were before you took a nap."

4. Reason out stress

It happened about 25 years back. Almost every female operator in a Kolkata telephone exchange complained of getting shocks from the imported telephone exchange equipment. All efforts by the management, even by an Australian medical team, failed to detect reasons behind this phenomenon. However, a team from the Defence Institute of Physiology and Allied Sciences successfully found out the reason. Their finding was that the reason of the complaints was the stress caused by the fear of losing jobs because of automation.

Stress is a strange phenomenon. It, many a times, causes unusual behaviour like the feeling of receving a shock from the telephone equipment that was well tested and was totally safe. It is necessary to understand stress before we look into stress management.

In simple words, stress is physical or mental tension. Stress is an internal response to external influences that invade and disrupt your equilibrium. It is felt when you feel uncertain whether or not you will accomplish what you had planned. It is caused by factors that tend to alter the existing mental and physical equilibrium in the body. The main cause of stress is anxiety. It is an uncertain uneasiness of the mind because of a bleak and uncertain future. Stress and anxiety are aggravated when pressures are put to achieve quick results. It is confined mainly to urban areas and is the outcome of complex and competitive living of the modern times. It is widely prevalent among administrators, managers, and politicians, though everyone, sooner or later, may suffer from it. Students were free from it as they lived a carefree life and had nothing to worry about. However, the situation is fast changing, and more and more students are suffering from stress due to the excessive competitiveness they face during their exams. The phenomenon is more visible among those who are preparing for their class XII board examinations and competitive tests, or in those students who are worried about failing to seek admission in premier institutions after class XII.

Stress is natural as it is the normal manifestation of the body's adaptation to the demands of the external environment. Therefore, one should learn to face it and not run away from it. You can always overcome stress by following a stress-management strategy. This is a three-step strategy.

First step: *Identify major stress areas and measure the intensity of each area.* Try to recollect major tensions and stresses that were felt by you during the past week or month. Now you have with you a mental inventory of various stresses. After this you should write down the items that caused you stress and rate their intensity on a scale of one to ten. Point one would be the lowest stress point and point ten would be the highest. Now you can assess the causes for your stresses over a short period of time.

Second step: *Muscle relaxation*. Hans Selye, a noted stress researcher suggests breaking the spiral of tension by using simple relaxation technique. He suggests progressive muscular relaxation:

> Sit comfortably and not lazily in a chair, in a dark quiet room. Close your eyes and mentally focus on the top of your head. Imagine loosening of muscles around that point. Slowly move your mental focus to your face, forehead, eyes, cheeks, mouth, and jaw. Simultaneously feel that these muscles are relaxing and the tension is melting out. Move to your neck and other parts of the body visualising the muscles becoming less rigid and less tense. You will feel the stress draining out of you. Regulate your breathing to a deep, rhythmic motion of smooth and graceful inhales and long exhales. This complete exercise of moving from head to toe should take about ten minutes, making you feel completely relaxed and calm. Try this twice a day, morning and evening.

Hans suggests a second exercise called "mental-imagery". You can begin it after practicing the first one for two weeks. This exercise expects you to visualise a vivid mental image of a completely calm place. You can see the sights, hear the sounds, and sense the entire setting. Use this imagery in your relaxation exercise to focus upon yourself after you have journeyed through your body during the first exercise. By doing this you will condition your mind and body to react to the mental image developed by you by becoming calm and relaxed. Once you have accomplished this over a week or so, you can use this imprinted image during the working day also to bring about tension reduction.

Third step: *Find a "shoulder to weep."* Friends willing to listen to you are the best stress-busters. Psychologists and counselors do nothing but offer their shoulders to weep and charge hefty fees for that. Your friends can provide it for free. If you do not want to share your worries with someone else, write down your feelings and factors that caused you stress and troubled your mind. Keep a diary to release the stressors and strains you had faced during the day. It is the second best and free stress buster.

Probably, now you find yourself ready to fight stress and feel a stress-free person.

Decide well

Sudha, an antiquarian, bought an ancient lamp from a scrap dealer. On reaching home, she rubbed to clean it and *BANG!* A strange looking creature suddenly appeared in the room. Terrified, she yelled, "Who are you?"

"I am *Chrag Jin*. Whoever owns the lamp is my master," the Jin bowed and replied.

"But what do you want from me?" the bewildered lady asked him.

"I am at your command, ma'am. Whatever you desire will be done".

The lady ordered him to clean the house. He did it in no time at all. She gave him another assignment that also he finished in a jiffy. Quite stupefied and dumfound she could not think of any work for him. Soon she saw a heap of apples in the kitchen and ordered him to sort them out into three sizes, large, medium, and small. Then she left the house for shopping. When she came back she was surprised to see the Jin sitting in a corner and looking vacantly at the apples. "Why haven't you finished the job as yet?" she demanded. The Jin explained that he was unable to decide between the larger and the smaller apples.

The almighty Jin was unable to take a decision and therefore he was not able to perform. Most of us are not able to reach a decision because we don't know how to decide. Decision-making is a vital factor in effective planning and execution. You have to take decisions at every step in your career. You move up the ladder of success only when you are able to take correct and timely decisions. At a higher level decision-making involves more responsibility, because your decisions affect a larger number of people and involve utlilisation of valuable resources. Managers, officers, and administrators are paid for taking decisions. Their efficiency is judged by the quality and speed of their decisions.

Decision-making is a skill in which some people excel more than others. However, it can be learnt and improved upon if you are willing to make an effort. You can learn it the same way you learnt how to add numbers in school or learnt swimming at the college pool. The secret is regular practice and learning from earlier work experiences.

Just like any other skill, decision-making too can be learnt with the help of certain techniques. These can help you master this skill. The following four-step formula can be useful in arriving at a good decision—identifying the problem; making an inventory of your resources; identifying alternate solutions; and idea-evaluation.

Identify your problem: Every decision is related to one or many issues. Find out the root cause of the problem. It is important to identify the problem clearly and exactly. If you cannot, you will not be able to arrive at the correct solution. You should not be vague and negative in identifying the problem. A clearly identified problem is half the battle won.

Make an inventory of resources: Second, you should know the resources that would be available to you for implementing your decision. This is done by making an inventory of the available resources—physical and financial. You should be clear about all assistance that you would be getting from the management. If you only have a vague idea about your resources, you may probably end up taking a wrong decision.

Brainstorming: The third step is to let your imagination run free and come up with as many solutions as possible. Do not discard any solution because it does not seem practical. The reason is that evaluation inhibits the discovery of new and creative solutions. When you think you have exhausted yourself, try for a few more. It is correct to say that the quality of the final decision will be proportionate to the number of possible solutions you first encountered. Sometimes the solutions that you initially discard as doubtful prove more valuable than those you considered conceivable.

Idea-evaluation: Arriving at the best possible solution is the final stage in decision-making. Before reaching the final solution you should assess the pros and cons of each solution from two angles — how close it comes to achieving the goals you have set; and, the amount of available resources that it would utilise. At this stage, invite responsible criticism and do not get overwhelmed by appreciation. Do not bother about who gave the solution, that is, delink the solution from the person who gave it, however, insignificant they may be. Sometimes the lowest person in the organisation gives the best solutions.

Let me share one of my personal experiences. When I was editing a magazine in the early 1980s, the wife of the Chairman of the newspaper house, who had become the President of FICCI, wanted to call a meeting of 25 prominent persons in Delhi. She wanted to interact with them on a new organisation that she was planning to form within FICCI. She gave me a notice of just three days. It was an almost impossible task to reach such a large number of persons and get their consent. As we were discussing the various ways to handle the crisis, the peon, Naina Ram Savaria, as he was serving tea sheepishly wanted to give us a suggestion. He offered to deliver all the invitation letters by the same evening. When asked to explain how he would do it, he gave the details thus.

He would make a route so that he could move in a circular way. He would go by bus to the first point and hire a cycle and deliver letters in that area. Then he would move on to the next point and follow the same pattern. Where required he would hire a cycle-*rickshaw* or an auto. He estimated a total cost of Rs. 100. Even if the letters were delivered by mail they would have cost the same amount and would have reached not the same day but the third day. And there was a great chance that many would not have reached.

We were all wonderstruck. There was no question of not agreeing to his suggestion. He was given the task and the next day he reported hundred percent deliveries. That day two persons contacted all the invitees by phone to get confirmation. Twenty persons agreed and turned up for the meeting. The Chairman's wife could not believe that this could have happened. After that we got all the difficult tasks to handle and much more than the appreciation of the Chairman.

Consider possible, probable, and preferable solutions. Consult a few knowledgeable persons. But do not waste much time as the Crisis Management Committee did in taking the decision on the Indian Airlines hijacked airplane. By the time they reached a decision, the plane had reached Dubai. If you take too much time, probably the crisis will worsen to a level that your decision will be irrelevant. The final decision should be reached quickly, and it should provide maximum returns utilising minimum resources. The Israelis are one of the best decision-makers.

Decision-making should not end with just deciding what is to be done. Two more things are important—an implementation plan and work allocation. You must decide how the decision is going to be implemented. Also who is going to do what, when, and how. Distribute work and fix specific responsibilities on different persons. This is very important, as a badly executed decision is worse than the best decision. The army is the best implementer of its decisions.

Taking decisions

It was a fine morning. Somewhere in the distance a band was playing a popular number in a park. Nearby was the king's palace where he was holding interviews for selecting the new Prime Minister.

The interview began on time and the king called the first candidate. The king asked him to find out where the band was being played. The person went, inquired, and came back with the reply to the king. The king then asked to find out why the band was being played. The candidate went again to find the reason and report to the king. Then the king wanted to know the number of persons in the band. The person went again and came back with the information and conveyed it to the king. And so the king kept on asking more and more questions and the candidate went again and again to find out more and more information. And so the interview progressed.

The king interviewed several persons for this top position and each one behaved the same way. Towards the end came a young smart person in his early forties. He was asked the first question; where was the band playing? He went out, took about fifteen minutes, and came back to answer the question. Then the king asked him all the same questions that he had asked the earlier candidates. The person gave all the replies without going out again and again to find out the answers. This candidate answered all the questions of the king then and there because he had collected all the relevant information when he went out the first time. The person was selected and became a successful and popular Prime Minister.

What can you learn from this story? The lesson is simple. You should always be thorough in your approach to problems. At every step you are faced with problems that you have to solve at the earliest. If you do not do that the consequences can be far-reaching, even detrimental. The decisions are related to professional aspects. Many a times these may concern your personal matters also like the selection of a career, a job, or even your life partner. Whatever may be the situation, you have to choose one out of the many alternatives open to you. Quite often some of the decisions you make are irrevocable, for example if you decide to study commerce in school you cannot shift over to science later. Therefore, it is imperative for you to collect detailed information on all the possible alternatives before you make your final choice.

The question of paramount importance is how should you make the right choice? We decided to discuss with a number of persons who were successful in their respective careers. We analysed their strategies before writing the following suggestions. Our feeling is that most of them have adopted a "four-pronged strategy." It involves four steps—finding out the various alternatives, collecting information on each alternative, evaluating the merits and demerits of each alternative, and taking the final decision.

Various alternatives: The first step is to find out the various alternatives available to you. You should not begin evaluating then and there. It is a common mistake that is made by most of the persons. Take the example of Rahul who has appeared in his class XII examinations and wants to become an engineer. He has to make two decisions. One, which field of engineering he should opt for; and second, which engineering college should he join? For the former the various alternatives are mechanical, electrical, mining, chemical, civil, electronics, computers, civil aviation, and marine. For the latter he would have to choose from the various IITs, regional engineering colleges, BITS, and some newly opened private colleges. This method of option formation can be adopted whenever an important decision had to be made.

The whole exercise may look highly theoretical and academic, but it is not. There is no need to pick up a paper and pencil and jot down the different choices available to you. The entire exercise may be mental. An alert experienced mind can critically analyse the various options.

Collecting information: The next in decision-making should be to collect all information on the various aspects of all the options. The moral of the king's story is most relevant at this stage. You must collect comprehensive information from different sources. You should find out the employment and promotion prospects in India and how the demand for the option would grow in the coming 30 years. You should also find out the possibility of going abroad. The cost of the course is an important area that you would like to consider at the time of decision-making. What are the best institutions for the options, what are the salary patterns, and which are the major companies that can offer employment are other areas on which information should be collected.

The information should be collected from different sources. You must talk to your teachers, friends, and students engaged in those studies for which you want information as well as from your business friends. It may not be possible to tap every source but as many as possible should be tried.

Evaluation: After collecting information from different sources you should evaluate the different options available to you. At this stage you should weigh the pros and cons of each option. Consider possible, probable, and preferable consequences and select the option that is most likely to have the best consequences. Do not hesitate to seek the counsel of knowledgeable and experienced persons.

Decision-making: Now comes the final stage of taking the decision. List all the evaluated choices priority-wise. This has to be done carefully. Now select the choice that you think will suit you the best. Your decision should help you accomplish your aim in life and also be acceptable to those who matter in your life.

Once you take the final decision, stand by it and work hard to make a success of it. True determination will get you results that will take you in the right direction and to the top of your career.

Bottom-upwards approach

Shankar, a wealthy merchant, was leading a comfortable and carefree life. One day when he was getting dressed up for the office he had a strange feeling. His eyes were popping out. After some time he had a sensation of ringing bells in his ears. Both the feelings recurred. First it was at long intervals but after some time it was prolonged. Fearing that he might be suffering from some serious illness, he sought an appointment with his doctor who after examining him referred him to an ENT specialist. The diagnosis was enlarged tonsils for which he had to go for an early surgery. Shankar got himself operated. He was feeling better after that.

After about eight months he again started feeling the same sensation in his ears and eyes. Shankar went to the same ENT specialist who had operated him. He checked him and pronounced that his throat was all right but that he needed to get his teeth checked as he could be suffering from pyorrhea. Shankar went to see a dentist. After a thorough check up, the dentist confirmed that he was having acute pyorrhea that was causing the funny sensation in his eyes and ears. He recommended extraction of a number of teeth, root-canal treatment to a few and taking medication for some time. The treatment continued for about two months and Shankar became all right.

Shankar remained all right for about seven to eight months and again as the winter set in, the same feeling in his eyes and ears recurred. This time Shankar went to a five-star hospital, the best in the city. A panel of doctors examined him and pronounced that both the doctors were correct in their diagnosis. But, they said, he had gone to both of them quite late. The infection had spread to the whole body by then affecting most of his vital organs. They told him in a concerned voice and apologetic tone that his life was of a few months only. The dejected Shankar came out of the hospital cursing his luck and the delay he had made in going to the doctors.

Thinking that his life was drawing to a close, Shankar decided to live his few last days in style. His first plan was to buy himself a new wardrobe and live dressed smartly. He went to a fabric store and bought the most expensive suit lengths and shirt pieces and went to the best and the most expensive tailor in town. The tailor, while taking down his measurements, told his junior to note them down. "Collar size, 14½ inches."

"But my collar size is only 14 inches," interjected Shankar to tell him the correct size.

"No sir, it is 14½ inches", the tailor checked again and told Shankar.

"But I have been wearing shirts of 14 inches collar for the last three years. Why should I change now?"

"I would stitch shirts for you of 14 inches collar size. But do not come to tell me that your eyes were popping out and you were feeling ringing tones in your ears!" told the tailor to a dazed and shocked Shankar.

The predicament in which Shankar found himself can be avoided if we do not avoid thinking in extremes and jumping to conclusions immediately. Rather than taking the most serious reason in the beginning as the cause of the problem, we should start from the most insignificant one. For example, if the electric lamp is not working check if the wiring is loose in the plug, socket, or switch. Also check the MCB as it may be off. If you find everything in order only then should you call the electrician. If you do not care to do that you will not be working till the busy mechanic arrives. He might come after a few hours. Also think of the money you would be saving. The habit of thinking in extremes can be expensive and painful as Shankar realised after losing everything in life to his utter dismay and suffering.

You have to take a rational approach of solving a problem from the simplest cause to the extreme one and not the other way around. Start from the basic one and do not presume that the entire system has failed. Start with the most unimportant cause and move to the serious ones in a systematic way.

The "bottom-upwards approach" is not only sensible but also economical. You move up step-by-step, checking the less important causes till you reach the most appropriate one. In this process you may identify many minor defects that might create problems in the future. If you are checking the various electric points and fuses, you will tighten many others that you would not have cared to check ordinarily. These could have created a problem in the following days and prevented you from doing many important tasks. Above all, you escape the misery of feeling that you have been cheated and taken for a ride.

The "bottom-upwards approach" can prove to be both interesting and informative provided you follow it up step-by-step. You will find that it is like carrying out an investigation. In the process you enrich your experience as you learn many new things about the problem. It also makes you self-sufficient and you need not depend on outside help every time the problem arises. The approach will develop in you the habit of paying attention to the small things in life.

Do not get too impatient if you do not follow this practice in the beginning. This attitude cannot be developed overnight. You should begin following it in taking care of your problems every day. Soon you will find that it has become a part of your work style. In moments of emergency you will become the best person to handle it.

So why delay. Start making the "bottom-upwards approach" a way of life.

Managing difficult persons

A modern workplace is getting bigger and bigger because of expanding businesses. In such organisations a problem normally faced by managers is—how to deal with those who are not cooperating. There is no problem with those who give full cooperation to the manager in attaining the target. But the problem is with those only who are in the habit of shirking work and obstructing the process of work. These type of workers are the biggest problem for a manager because they not only do not work but also do not let others work. Handling such difficult employees becomes the most difficult task for a manager. The first impulse, normally, is to get rid of such persons but that is not the solution because the new employee may be more difficult than this one. Moreover, there is the cost of hiring and training a new employee that is incurred. Therefore, a wise manager will always try his best to handle difficult employees by using some creative ideas. A successful manager is always able to handle such persons in a positive way and turns them into productive workers. Such managers become a valued asset to an organisation and are sought after by other organisations.

The secret

What is the modus operandi of such managers? Here are a few techniques that have been used by such managers who specialise in turning non-productive workers into productive ones.

The first process is to change the job profile of the person who is difficult to handle. He should be separated from others so that he does not create a negative impact on those who are working hard to achieve their targets.

The second step is to watch the work style, work pattern, and the routine of the person. Try to find out whether his behaviour is inappropriate or desirable. Try to find out if has spread the rumour that he was being dubbed a difficult employee just because the manager does not like him.

The third action is to develop a regular and healthy conversation with the person. The objective should be to find out whether his behaviour was work related. It could be that he did not like the work assigned to him. There could also be some personal reasons responsible for his inappropriate behaviour in the organisation. Try to understand his problem if his negative attitude toward work was due to personal reasons. As a worker is a human being, his work is bound to be affected if he has a problem in the family. If he can be helped you should try your best to pull him out of his mess as far as possible.

If the problem is work related, it should be addressed in a reasonable way. The person may be asked about problems he was facing in doing the work. Sometimes it may so happen that the employee himself may not be aware of the problem. In that case the manager should make him understand the work in a simple way. He can also show him how to organise the work and do it.

If there are behavioural problems the employee should be made aware of those problems. He might not agree but the manager can give examples of his unwanted behavior and how that creates a negative impact on others. In many a cases the employees do not understand how they cause problems for others.

The fourth step is to develop a personal contact with the employee. The manager should meet him more frequently so that he is able to understand him and his problems. The employee would also develop closeness and may reveal certain facts that may help the manager in improving the person. Using this technique, the manager can open a two-way communication with the employees. It will help in eliminating the communication gap and he also would understand what the organisation expects from him.

The manager has to understand that a difficult person has some abnormality in his personality. Therefore, in the beginning while handling such a person his inappropriate behavior should not be taken as an offence. It has to be kept in mind that his problematic personality is responsible for his peculiar behaviour. This will help the manager in not becoming emotionally reactive or stressed. Therefore, in handling such persons the manager should be objective and professional.

The difficult person has to be kept under observation for a certain amount of time. That would depend on the nature of the difficult element in the person. During this period three developments are possible. One, the person may change his behaviour and begin to perform appropriately. Second, he may decide to leave the organisation because of continuous monitoring. Third, he may neither change his behaviour nor leave the organisation.

The first two developments cause no problem. The first one is the best as the non-productive person becomes a productive one. In the second possibility the organisation can get a better person. There is no purpose in keeping a person who does not have a sense of belonging towards the organisation. The third one is difficult because the manager will have to take corrective action. It may ultimately lead to firing the difficult employee. If there is no other option than firing the employee then make sure that the correct procedures have been followed. The manager must document all the corrective actions taken by him. A reasonable and proper opportunity should be given to the errant person to defend himself of the charges. Finally, the proper termination procedures should be followed so that the company can defend its action if the person goes to the court.

It is psychological for the manager to feel guilty after terminating the employee. But management is not possible with impulsive and emotional behavior. The first responsibility of a manager is to ensure that the company grows at a fast rate. If a person does not fit in the corporate culture and does not add to its growth, he has no business to continue there. Therefore, if all opportunities have been given to a person to improve himself and the person has refused to improve his work or behavior, then the manager should not feel upset in showing the person the door. In fact, it will improve the work environment in the company and will keep the other employees' morale intact and the working environment stress free.

> Managers have to be leaders to move to the fast lane. They have to have vision, intellectual drive, and knowledge to perform managerial functions like planning, organising, recruitment, directing, coordinating, budgeting, and administration. To be an effective manager one has to be the harbinger of change, be able to deal with conflicts, solve problems, be a strategist, and a problem solver. He has to lead his team to win. For that he has to know and understand the team mates, not pass on problems to others, and develop entrepreneurial skills. He has to be down-to-earth and not an egocentric person. He should avoid flattery and try and make friends and not enemies. Networking helps; for this he has to meet people, create an impact on them, and develop friendships. He has to be an effective public speaker for which he has to develop confidence. Conflict management is an essential part of the duty of a manager. It causes stress and he has to learn to manage it effectively and coolly by learning how to relax. He has to be a good quick decision-maker. Finally he has to manage difficult persons.

Chapter 8

Learning from Peers

Life presents us many teachers, each with some definitive strength. We could perhaps contribute so much more, if only we kept observing, learning, changing, and implementing.

WALE E. VIERIA
Chairman of the US-based International Council
of Management Consulting Institutes

As the saying goes, "Fools do not learn from their mistakes, wise men learn from others;" and it is also true. We know about the life and work style of a number of highly success-oriented persons. How they all struggled hard and reached dizzying heights in their careers. We would present to you a few case studies. These are of Mr. Konosuke Matsushita of National Panasonic; Sardar Vallabhbhai Patel, the first Deputy Prime Minister of India; Mr. Mohan Singh Oberoi, the late chairman of Oberoi Hotels; Mr. Lee Iacocca, President of Ford Motor Company; Mr. Shanti Prashad Jain, the late Chairman of the Times of India Group; and Lal Bahadur Shastri, the former Prime Minister of India. They all have much to tell you about how to lead a full and effective life—an effective success system.

Rags to riches—the Oberoi story

On 15 August 1922, a 22-year-old young boy alighted from the train in the picturesque hills of Shimla, the then summer capital of British India. He was a stranger to the town, penniless, and jobless but had a mind full of hopes and aspirations. He also had a wife and a little kid to fend for. In the following 50 years, he made for himself a room at the top of a chain of about 30 hotels in India and abroad. He was Mohan Singh Oberoi, the internationally reputed hotelier whose phenomenal rise from a hotel employee to a hotel magnate provides an ideal for success. Six years after his death, in 2007, his Udaipur Hotel, Udaivilas was adjudged the best in the world.

> **Learn from success-oriented people to take a shortcut to the top of your career.**

Hard work is the first characteristic that is likely to be found in the personality of every successful person. Oberoi had it in plenty. Even in the last years of his life of 102 years, he worked six hours a day, four days a week.

Oberoi started his career as a clerk in Cecil Hotel in Shimla and soon became the Chief Clerk. Being the best hotel worker in the town he was offered a job by Clark's Hotel that he joined as Assistant Manager. He became the owner of that hotel within a period of 12 years. Then onwards success chased him. In the following four years, he took the Grand Hotel in Kolkata on lease. Oberoi's greatest asset was that he never shirked work and was always willing to take up extra tasks to the utmost satisfaction of his bosses.

Winning the confidence of his superiors as well as colleagues was the second trait of his personality. Oberoi was not only his boss's favourite, he was the darling of all his colleagues, without any exception. Everyone at the hotel wanted to work with him. He enjoyed so much confidence of the owner that he asked Oberoi to manage the hotel when he went away to England for a year. When he came back he was surprised that the hotel had made more profits during his absence. That spoke high of the efficiency and honesty levels of Oberoi.

Oberoi never stopped learning. He always kept his learning process alive. He maintained two things in mind. Never become self-righteous as it gives arrogance and egoism. He always analysed his behaviour and decisions, and changed them if he found that he was wrong. Secondly, his mind was always open to new ideas, concepts, systems, and practices. He never hesitated to learn from his juniors. At the age of 50, he spent three months in Europe and America to minutely study the functioning of hotels in those two countries. He closely studied their strategies, methods, and customer relationships and gradually implemented a novel methodology unheard of in the Indian hotels. The impact of this was that the foreign guests always went back so satisfied that they always stayed in his hotels. And because of this his hotels were included in the 300 Best Hotels in the World, a publication of Harper and Queen magazine from London. This gave him added clientele. In fact, the learning process stops when a person becomes self-righteous and closes their mind to new things.

Right decisions at the right moment and acting at the appropriate time is very important in life to be successful. One should not only make the right move but also act fast. A person with a wavering mind cannot take timely decisions and, therefore, success runs away from them. Oberoi had this unique quality in his personality. He decided to buy hotels when they were going very cheap and at favourable terms. The first in Shimla was bought by him at a throwaway price. Paucity of resources did not deter him. When buying the first hotel he was short of money. He managed help from friends and relatives and even mortgaged the jewellery of his wife. During World War II, his hotel business progressed in leaps and bounds when he decided to offer attractive deals to American soldiers offering them a buffet lunch at Rs. 5 per head. He was hosting 2,000 soldiers per day making a staggering sum of Rs. 10,000 per day only on lunch. It was a colossal sum in those days.

Oberoi believed only in the best. He made every effort to be the best and in fact he became the very best. He maintained the same record throughout. His hotels in India and abroad have a brand, a standard, and carry a touch of class. He took care to offer hospitality amidst elegant surroundings to his customers and never compromised as far as quality was concerned. Today his hotels have a regular clientele, guests who stay only in his hotels and no where else. In the post-Asiad period many of the city's hotels had a low occupancy ratio. But Oberoi's occupancy rate was high, almost full in the season. Despite high rates and expensive rooms, the normal occupancy rate in the Oberoi Hotels varies from 75 to 90 per cent. The reason of this has been not only the efficient service but also the presence of larger rooms with more amenities. Oberoi introduced many facilities that now are common in hotels across India. These were the provision of three telephones in each room (at the bedside, on the writing desk, and in the bathroom), direct dialing facility (local, national, and international) from rooms, channeled music and international temperature controls in rooms. These, plus the hospitality make Oberoi Hotels the best place to stay for busy executives, rich businessmen, and well-to-do tourists.

Oberoi laid special emphasis on the quality and authenticity of the food served in his restaurants. This created a staunch faith in discerning guests in his hotels. His 109-item buffet spread was once the most popular haunt in Delhi. When many hotels offered cheaper but heavy lunches, Oberoi raised the price from Rs. 55 to Rs. 60. His managers were not in favour of this change because they thought the guests might shift to other hotels. But Oberoi was sure of his quality. Rather than reducing the price, he added a few more items to the buffet and that attracted more guests. In fact, guests shifted from other hotels to his hotel as the food was not only better but it had more variety. While other hotels could not attract customers even at much lower rates, Oberoi's venues were overflowing.

A deep faith in "permanent shop strategy" instead of "railway platform strategy" gave Oberoi a roaring success. He did not practice the latter strategy because at the railway platform the passenger buys only once. So the seller does not bother to satisfy the customer knowing very well that they would not come again. He fleeces them to the hilt and provides inferior quality material and service. In the former, the seller is careful to serve the customer with his best ware and service. The seller is interested in building up a permanent clientele and wants the customer to come again and again. This strategy is true in networking too. If you want permanent friendly relationships you cannot exploit them for your self-interest. If you do so, you close the door after the first contact. But if you develop warm and friendly relations, you can go to the person again and again for favours. Oberoi understood this right from day one and succeeded in building up a permanent clientele.

"Be in touch" is a good lesson to learn from Oberoi. Normally people forget about a person after the work is completed. But Oberoi was different. He maintained regular contact with anyone who stayed in his hotel once. The computer system stored the names of guests for five years after their first check in. He personally used to go through all comments and complaints registered by the guests and even wrote to them if he felt the need of it. To ensure that the complaints and suggestion reached him, the Finance Department and not the front office was asked to keep the key of the suggestion box.

Effective organisation and management is possible only when you develop an effective system that can work under every situation, circumstance, and crisis. Such a system can be developed over a long period after learning from the past mistakes. Also the system should develop multi-partisan support from superiors, colleagues, clients, and the public. This was the secret behind Oberoi's success.

Success lies in making a sincere effort to cultivate the "Oberoi spirit" because that is what took him to the top of the hotel business not only in India but also overseas. Oberoi is a much-respected word in the hotel business globally. He has left behind him a solid system and the best and the most profitable hotel chain in the world.

How you too can strive to be Indra Nooyi

The *New York Times* business columnist and author Joe Nocera believes that the Chairperson and Chief Executive Officer (CEO) of PepsiCo (since October 1, 2006), Indra Krishnamurthy Nooyi is the most effective female CEO. PepsiCo is one of the world's leading food and beverage companies. Besides that, she is a Successor Fellow of the Yale Corporation and a Class B director of the Board of Directors of the New York Federal Reserve. She also serves as a member on the boards of the International Rescue Committee, Catalyst and the Lincoln Center for the Performing Arts, and on the Board of Trustees of Eisenhower Fellowships. Nooyi is the Chairperson of the U.S.–India Business Council.

She is the only Indian woman to become the Chief Executive Officer of the more than $25 billion multinational, and perhaps the first Indian to reach to this level. Being a highly successful corporate person of Indian origin, she is rightly the role model of every corporate manager not only in India but across the globe. What is important is that she has proved that being mediocre (a faculty member of IIM Calcutta has brought out this fact to the media) from an ordinary Indian middle class family is no obstacle to reach the top of one's career at a very young age. Like her, the present generation of managers can rightly aspire to be in the fast lane and make a dent in the corporate sector. It should not be a difficult task provided they try to understand how she moved upwards leaving others far behind. If she can achieve this, nothing is impossible for an average determined and strong-willed person like you.

What can we learn from her career path

One, she is **simple and does not make a trivial matter a prestige issue**. Sometime back she delivered a much talked about speech at the graduating ceremony of Columbia Business School. In her speech she said that when she was in school in India, remembering the names of the five continents was a difficult task for her in the geography class. She devised a simple formula to remember — Africa for the small finger, Asia for the thumb, Europe as the index finger, South America for the ring finger, and North America as the middle finger. She justified the analogy of the five fingers with the continent based on their economic and political standing in the world forum. This immediately set off rumpus and she silenced everyone by apologising immediately.

Second, she is a **quick and determined decision maker** and sticks to the work until it is finished. Those who have worked closely with her say that if she gets an idea, she goes after it and nothing can stop her. This firmness and go-getting attitude has won her approbation. This has helped her build a strong image to reach the top echelons in the organisation.

Indra is known in PepsiCo for her determined style. It became apparent soon after she joined the company as its chief strategist. She won over Roger Enrico, the then Chief Executive of the company, to drop Taco Bell, Pizza Hut, and KFC in 1997 because she didn't feel PepsiCo could add enough value to the fast food business. Later she was the main force behind the purchase of Tropicana, the spinoff of Pepsi's bottling business, and the $13 billion merger with Quaker Oats Co. Each of these acquisitions were profitable. "Indra can drive as deep and hard as anyone I've ever met," said Enrico "but she can do it with a sense of heart and fun."

Third, Nooyi is **a family person and has strong faith in traditions**. Though she is extremely busy, she is able to achieve a balance between the corporate job and family responsibility as a mother and a wife. She is a strict follower of traditional practice at home be it the practice of taking off shoes before entering the *puja* room or any other simple Indian beliefs and practices. She attends PepsiCo board meetings in a sari because she believes that the corporate world recognises the value of people who are genuine. She has an ability to blend a high-powered career with her family and her Hindu heritage.

She views PepsiCo as an extended family and everybody at the company is there to help in every way possible, "I love my family, but PepsiCo's also my child. So really I don't look upon it as a chore," says Nooyi. Sometime ago, when Indra was traveling, her daughter would call the office to ask for permission to play Nintendo. The receptionist would know the routine and ask: "Have you finished your homework? Have you had your snack? OK, you can play Nintendo for half an hour". She then left a voice message for Indra saying, "I gave Tara permission to play Nintendo".

Fourth, she has developed **innovative ideas and has implemented them** to achieve high goals. One of her high goals is the development of a diverse and inclusive workforce. She believes that the best results can be achieved only when you hire a broad spectrum of people who are the best and the brightest. She also believes that parity must exist in promotions both among men and women and among diverse employees.

Fifth, she has an **open mind and learns from wherever she can**. Nooyi is a passionate sports fan, particularly of basketball. Once she spent hours studying videotapes of the final championship games that the basketball great Michael Jordan played with the Chicago Bulls for lessons on teamwork. This enabled her to fight hard for PepsiCo's successful $3.3 billion acquisition of Tropicana in 1998. With this acquisition she was able to increase PepsiCo's earnings and enhance its image as a premium brand for convenient foods and drinks.

Under the leadership of Indra Nooyi, PepsiCo has seen tremendous growth. She attributes success to commitment and diversity. She has incorporated a philosophy of diversity in every aspect of PepsiCo's operations. Nooyi describes the concept of diversity as a "universal good" with "no downside." This philosophy has led to a corporate entity that is not only profitable, but is also a nurturing environment for its workers.

> Addressing *The Indus Entrepreneurs (TiE)* at Burlington, Marriot, in October 2004 she suggested a "Seven-Point Leadership plan" for getting into the fast lane to move up the ladder in the corporate sector.
>
> One, **identify your core competency**. "In my case my core competency is my ability to be able to demystify any complicated problem." Continuously strive to enhance that core competency.
>
> Second, have the **courage and confidence** to stand up and defend your ideas.
>
> Third, **always be yourself**. She narrated her own example about wearing a saree to an important first interview and getting the job despite her being dressed differently.
>
> Fourth, develop **effective communication**. Clarity and conciseness are critical for effective communication. She suggested reading speeches of great leaders like Abraham Linccln or John F. Kennedy to see how they were able to inspire people.
>
> Fifth, **consistency** in behavior would help you build trust in those who want to follow you.
>
> Sixth be **compassionate** and work both on empathy and sympathy. She also stressed the value of an inner compass. You can call it faith or conscience to help make difficult decisions while addressing personal conflict.
>
> Seven, you must have either a coach or mentor. It is very important. They could be anyone—your parents, other family members, or your boss. But you cannot pick them. They will pick you.

The innovator—Lee Iacocca

Lee Iacocca, son of an Italian immigrant, was a combination of hard work and ambition. Medical problems and anti-Italian prejudice did not deter him from reaching the top in his career and changing the concepts of marketing in the United States. Rising through the ranks of the Ford Motor Company he became, after 32 years of slogging, President of the company. How did Iacocca rise to this exalted position? What was it that rescued this man of steel from an ungracious fall?

The art of communication is *sine qua non* to success and in leading people to achieve the ultimate objective. A good leader is a resolute decision-maker, who forms a team of the right type of people, communicates with them, and motivates them into action. Maintaining cordial relations with co-workers and with those who are at the grass-roots level is vital. Workers need to be motivated by a two-way process of communication. It implies talking to them in a group. It is not merely the kind of public speaking without a personal touch and listening to the workers' woes with all the patience one has. It entails that an efficient leader must do his homework well by having a solid grounding in reading and writing, in order to take the right kind of decisions. If based on intuition, the decisions must be supported by facts.

An organisation has to work as a team and not as a pack of individuals taking independent decisions and not caring for others. When Iacocca moved to Chrysler, after being sacked from Ford, he found, to his horror, that the problem was not confined to top management alone but throughout the company. People, by and large, were scared and despondent. The vice-presidents were square pegs in round holes. There was no team, only a collection of independent players.

An effective and efficient leader has to manage his time effectively. He must give his best for the task in hand during the assigned period of time. He must also be a trendsetter and a person who is emulated in thought and action by the team members. He must act fast because the speed of the leader sets the speed of the team.

The idea of teamwork and leadership is effectively and ruthlessly followed in the game of football. Vince Lambardi, a close friend of Iacocca and a legendary football coach believes that for teamwork and leadership: "You have to start by teaching the fundamentals. A player has got to know the basics of the game and how to play his position. The men have to play as a team. There is no room for *prima donnas*. You've got to care for one another. The difference between mediocrity and greatness is the feeling these guys have for each other. When the players are imbued with that special feeling, you know you've got yourself a winning team." Lambardi's idea of teamwork and leadership is not only valid for football, but is equally valid for the business world too.

Another quality that added vigour to Iacocca's personality was his innovative ability—essential for every successful leader. As a key figure in the competitive automobile industry, Iacocca had to constantly assess the likely changes in the market and prepare his own strategies to help the company face the emerging challenges. Often he had to mould his decisions to suit the objectives of the company. Iacocca's innovative talent came to limelight in 1956 when the sales in Ford Company were at the lowest ebb. The district under Iacocca was in fact the weakest in the entire country. So he threw in an attractive bargain—a modest downpayment of 20 per cent, followed by three years of monthly payments of $56. This "56 for 36" scheme facilitated people to buy cars in easy installments. The company's sales skyrocketed. In Dearborn, Robert S. McNamara, Vice-President in charge of the Marketing Division was so impressed by the plan that he made it a part of the company's marketing strategy. The scheme was so successful that the company sold 75,000 extra cars in a sagging market.

Iacocca had taken a leaf from Henry Ford's strategy as an innovator. Way back in 1914, Ford offered a 5-dollar-a-day wage to his workers. It was double the amount of what was being offered in the automobile industry. When asked about the exorbitant high wage, Ford's response was that besides getting the best workers, his workers would earn enough to buy their own cars. In a way, Ford was creating demand for his own product by offering a higher wage than the prevailing market wage. He was also able to attract the best workforce in the industry who offered him a high productivity. It automatically reduced his cost, and he was able to sell better cars at lower prices. This strategy of Ford was responsible for the birth of the prosperous middle class and the beginning of a wide market, the two primary factors responsible for bringing affluence in the United States.

Close family ties gave him a strong emotional support system. The support he had from his wife and children were the strength that helped him achieve the inevitable. Hard work does not mean toiling in a labour camp. One must snatch some time for rest and relaxation with the family. "If you don't do these things while the kids are young, there's no way to make it up later on," he warns. Two-sevenths of his whole life, weekends, and a lot of evenings were devoted to his wife and daughters. It was responsible for the extraordinary success that Iacocca achieved first in Ford and later in Chrysler. "I learnt about the strength you can get from a close family life. I learnt not to despair even when the world was falling apart. I learned about the value of hard work. In the end you've got to be productive," Iacocca accepted in a newspaper interview.

Iacocca's is a never-ending success story. But now it is time to tell yourself—"I've given this my best shot. It's time I set this work aside and go on a short holiday".

Indomitable Cyrus

The United Sates of America after the Louisiana Purchase in 1803, was fast expanding towards the West. Measureless tracts of land lay before the farmers, waiting for some entrepreneur to clear them. An American could stand in the middle of his field and see miles and miles of field lands on all sides extending till the horizon. An adventurous farmer could cultivate as much land as he wanted since there were no barriers on him. And every farmer, true to the American spirit, ploughed and seeded acre after acre. His trouble, however, began at the harvest time.

The fields were so extensive and the crop so plentiful that the farmer could not garner the entire grains even if he worked for 24 hours a day. And it was not possible to leave fully ripe grain for more than a day in its strains. The delay caused the heads of the grain to crumble on their stalks, ruining the unharvested crop. The small population that the U.S. had at that time, made it impossible to get extra hands. Every spirited farmer helplessly saw his grain withering under the hot sun and asked: "How can I harvest what I planted?" He definitely needed either huge manpower, which was not present, or a machine that could harvest his crop fast. Some innovative inventor could have provided it. Cyrus was the American who converted this dream into reality by inventing the reaper that changed the whole farming scenario, not only in the United States but throughout the world.

When thousands of farmers in America were praying to know about some technique to harvest their entire crop, a young man was silently working on a machine. His father, Robert McCormick, started the project. Robert worked for 20 years on a mechanical reaper but was unsuccessful in his efforts. After he died, his son, Cyrus McCormick took the father's work forward. He perfected the reaper at his farm, Walnut Grove in Virginia.

Cyrus was not a highly educated boy. He had attended school for a short time and wanted to join the iron business. But he was not successful there. Not knowing what to do, he decided to work on his father's project. He picked up the threads left by his father, but he worked on an entirely different design and principle. He planned a machine with long rotating blades, fastened on an arm that revolved as the machine was drawn through the field. While moving it would cut the stalks. His father had designed the reaper imitating the arms and legs and the back of a man.

His machine, unfortunately, did not work satisfactorily. When he tried the reaper in a field at Steel's Tavern in Virginia the blades were moving but could not cut the standing crop smoothly and evenly. The moving blades chewed at the stalks and the stubble behind the reaper. He was ridiculed and hooted by a rowdy group of farm workers. Cyrus did not feel beaten, though he was disheartened. He re-worked on the machine and made some adjustments. When it was tried again in the oat field of a neighbour, the machine worked perfectly well and cut the standing crop of grain smoothly and evenly. In 1837, Cyrus got a patent for the machine in his name. This, however, is not the end of his success story. It is just the beginning.

With a workable machine to sell, Cyrus left his farm in the 1850s to demonstrate the machine's usefulness to farmers in the West. As he showed how to operate the machine to harvest the standing crop, word spread rapidly and farmers assembled from distant places to see his reaper. They saw the corn pilling up on the trucks without the help of any labour. The only manpower needed was the person who would drive the horse to pull the reaper. The farmers were ecstatic and thrilled to get an answer to all their woes. They wanted to own the machine, but unfortunately did not have money to straightaway pay cash. They had spent whatever cash they had in travelling to the West, where Cyrus was giving demonstrations.

McCormick realised that the farmers' excitement was not sufficient for them to buy the machine. It was no substitute for money. They would have to have the money to buy the machine and only then could he sell the reaper to them. A brain wave struck Cyrus. He realised that when the farmers were able to possess the reaper they would increase their income several fold. So if he could offer them the reaper now and collect the money later it could be the start of a roaring business. He decided to loan the reaper to the farmers and collect the payment later. Thus, he introduced the "buy-now-pay-later" system in the U.S. It was a significant marketing revolution and became an important marketing strategy all over the world. It, primarily, has been responsible for the great market expansion globally.

The new strategy introduced by Cyrus was a tremendous success. He was soon flooded with orders for the reaper as farmer after farmer bought the machine. Farmers were reaping much bigger harvests year after year. This changed the agriculture scenario from subsistence to commercial farming. They even started exporting grains in a big way. It became the starting point of the economic might of the United States.

Why shouldn't Cyrus be our role model? He belonged to that breed of men who changed the destiny of the United States. When the Indian agriculture was in the primitive stage, Cyrus was moderanising the American farming techniques. It was his reaper that played a consequential role in making the American farmer think in terms of exports. Within a span of 21 years, 1839–1860, wheat exports went up from 2 million to 29 million bushels (one bushel is equal to about 35.24 litres) and corn exports increased from one million to 24 million bushels.

What can we learn from Cyrus? First, his fighting spirit that made him think of how farmers wanted to buy his reaper but could not because of their lack of purchasing power. Second, his innovative trait that made him think of how to go about re-designing the reaper so as to make it workable and efficient. He kept on changing the design till it satisfactorily worked. Third, the desire in him to achieve the goal he had set. He wanted every farmer to buy the reaper. When they could not buy it, he came up with a plan that worked. And last, his ability to organise and not getting disheartened by carping. Hooting did not silence him. Rather, it forced him to make his project a success. Most of us, if ridiculed, would have left the project at that stage.

Cyrus did not believe that success was just good luck. He had a highly developed common sense and practical judgement system. Rather than waiting for success to fall in his lap, he worked hard for it with patience and persistence, and did not get discouraged by obstacles. Instead he used them to motivate himself to perfect his work and achieve his objective.

Most people just dream of becoming rich and successful, but only a few make the effort to actually achieve their dream. It is the Cyruses among us who initiate change and progress in society. They are ordinary persons like you and me.

Intelligent marketing—Matsushita

Horimota, an impoverished Japanese in ordinary clothes, approached a water spring at a street corner in Tokyo. He pressed the pedestal lever confidently, drank water, wiped his lips with the cuff of the right hand sleeve of his shirt, and walked back. He was a satisfied person. Konosuke Matsushita, the top boss of Matsushita Electrical Industries, the owners of National Panasonic brand, was watching Horimota from the top floor of his office.

This was nothing unusual. People kept coming throughout the day and at night to the water spring to drink water. Matsushita never concentrated on this normal activity on the street. Somehow, this time the poor man's behaviour attracted the attention of Matsushita. He started analysing his behaviour.

Matsushita asked himself two questions. Why did Horimota not hesitate when drinking water from the water spring? Why did he not drink some other drink? After some brief contemplation he concluded that Horimoto unhesitatingly drank water from the water spring because of four reasons.

First, the water was *always available* from the spring in adequate quantity. Second, he knew that it was *safe to drink* water from that spring. Third, it was *within his walking distance*. If he were to walk longer or if it were located at a place about which he had to inquire, probably he would not have gone there at all. Last, he *could afford* the water at a price it was available for (it was free). If the water were priced, the old man would have tavelled a longer distance to find a place where he could get free drinking water.

These four points made Matsushita design a mass marketing strategy that made his company the largest seller of its products. The four distinct pillars of the strategy were:

- **Ample quantity**: There must be *abundant supply* of the product to be sold. There should not be a scarcity of the product in the market. So you must ensure that it is always available in an adequate quantity so that the consumer gets it whenever he decides to buy it. If the product is not available at his askance, he will buy some other brand. Having abundant supply necessitates mass production and a good distribution system.

- **Assured quality**: Your product must have a *positive image* in the market. You should ensure that the quality is not only good but is continuously improving. This will convert the customer into a regular buyer of your product. Not only that, he would also recommend it to his friends and relatives.

- **Point of delivery:** The product *sale outlets should be conveniently located*. A consumer in a free market economy does not want to travel long distances and to obscure places for shopping. He prefers places that are easily approachable.

- **Affordable price:** The product should be *reasonably priced*. It should be within the reach of an average consumer. If the price were higher than what the middle class can pay, the commodity would become unreachable and unsalable. Such a product would have restricted sale and its market would become narrow. A company producing for the mass market cannot earn profit in such a situation.

The "Q2P2 strategy" has four essential conditions for corporate success. The first condition is a surplus and not a scarcity economy. A surplus economy has abundant supply of goods and services so that the consumer does not go back empty handed from the shop. He should have a wide choice also to feel that the best has been bought. It encourages buyers to buy more and to buy regularly. The scarcity economy restricts choice and consumers have to buy whatever is offered to them. Such an economy will always operate at a low level and can never bring prosperity to its people.

The second condition is that consumer satisfaction should be the prime objective of the producer. The motto should be that "the customer is always right" and not, as in India, that the "customer is invariably wrong." A satisfied customer would mean a larger market. Disgruntled customers will shrink the market as they would drive away customers from the market.

The third is that the distribution system should be efficient. In a large economy consumers are scattered all over the country. Though they have no contact with each other, their interaction is through the media. A bad distribution system will not deliver goods when needed and would get adverse publicity in the newspapers. When this happens, consumers shift their loyalty to other products, which once gone may not come back. This damages the image of the company.

The last is that the product should be of good if not excellent quality. A bad product may sell but only up to a certain point. No one buys an inferior product a second time. Only a good product can survive in the market in the long run. Products like Lifebuoy and Lux have existed in the market for more than 80 years. Many products could not last for more than a few months.

Matsushita understood the secret of success from the behaviour of a poor person on the street. He translated it into a strategy and built up a huge corporate empire following that strategy. We should learn to pick up ideas from common people around us and convert them into our success formula.

Decide to learn from mundane and routine situations, and improve your market value.

Jack Welch—The best known corporate captain

Jack Welch, known as the CEO of CEOs came from oblivion. He was born and brought up in an ordinary middle class American family of quite modest means. He did not have any extraordinary quality. In fact he had several handicaps like he was short-statured and had a speech defect. Nevertheless, he converted himself into an extraordinary corporate personality and converted General Electric into a corporate powerhouse. His remarkable story is truly an inspiration to leaders from all walks of life.

Jack Welch joined General Electric in 1960. Not very happy with the job he wanted to leave the job only after a year. But his boss Reuben Gutoff, a young executive, saw the potential of an upcoming business executive in him and persuaded him to stay back. Thereafter there was no looking back. He made a mark for himself and within 12 years became vice president. He moved up the ranks to become senior vice president in 1977 and vice chairman in 1979. In 1981 he was made the chairman and became GE's youngest chairman.

The secret of Welch's steadfast rise to the top was his aggressive marketing of the company's products and services. During his 20-year tenure as CEO, Welch was credited with giving new dimension and direction to the company as well as enhancing the company's market value 23 times, from $12 billion in 1981 to $280 billion in 2001.

When Welch took charge of the company, it was widely believed that GE had already hit its highest point and there was no further scope for its growth. He not only took the challenge but showed the corporate world that there is no end to growth. His simple formula was that if you have reached the top rung of the ladder, build a whole new ladder to climb further up. He showed that it was not possible by just managing the company; a strong leadership was sine qua non. He took GE rung by rung, observing each rung and learning from the journey. The leadership that he provided enabled the whole team to climb at a breakneck speed of an annual average rate of 115 per cent.

When taking GE to higher heights, Welch's major focus was people. His guiding principle was: "That if you are in business development then you're in the leadership business and in fact you're in the people business. That means that your main focus areas have to be your employees, your customers, and your products." Those who have analysed the functioning of Welch believe that Welch had a profound grasp on GE and it stemmed from knowing the company and those who worked for it. More than half his time was devoted to "people issues."

His leadership style was to push the managers to become more productive. Welch worked to eradicate perceived inefficiency by demobilising non-productive persons in the company. Welch would fire at least ten per cent most inefficient and least productive employees every year. This earned him the sobriquet of the "toughest boss in America." By 1987 Welch had fired 25 per cent GE workers and reduced the workforce by 100,000. During the same period revenues grew 48 percent. With this he proved that change is the only way to go up. His slogan was: "If you don't love change, it won't love you — and it might just eat you alive." This management style of Welch became legendary during his 20-year reign of General Electric. His "no-nonsense leadership style" gave him a reputation of being hard, even ruthless, but also fair, when making business decisions.

Welch led the company not by speaking but by setting examples. He created a new concept of "stretch culture" so as to instill an approach of churning new ideas and driving for the impossible in his employees. According to him "stretch" means "moving beyond being as good as you have to be — "making a budget" — to being as good as you possibly can be: setting "impossible" goals and going after them." His belief is that a stretch atmosphere "replaces a grim heads-down determination to be as good as you have to be, and asks, instead, how good can you be?"

There is no doubt that Jack Welch is the greatest success story of the corporate world. The main factor that caused his grand success was his leadership style. He gave not only a formula for an effective leadership, but also suggested a mode of personal behavior. His management ideas and leadership skills are both admired by the business community and imitated by business leaders all around the world.

GE and India

GE entered India in 1902 and installed India's first hydropower plant and slowly extended all its global businesses in the country. Today GE has four partnerships with state-owned Bharat Heavy Electricals Corporation, State Bank of India, Wipro, and Triveni Engineering. But slowly and gradually GE is falling short of its target for India. There have been few reverses. But GE India's President and CEO, John Flannery, is satisfied with what GE has achieved. Though there are some glitches, Flannery is sure that he would be able to resurrect the company's fortunes. This would be possible by localising operations.

What Indian corporate leaders can learn from Jack Welch

Jack Welch has earned an undisputed place in the gallery of business leaders. Today, GE with its unique learning culture and unbound organisation, is one of the most admired companies in the world. Surely Indian captains of the corporate sector can learn from him. We mention here some of the lessons that they can consider:

- Be a strong leader and manage less. His advise was: "Weak managers are the killers of business; they are the job killers. You can't manage self-confidence into people.
- Be clear about your vision and articulate it precisely to those who are working under you. "Leaders inspire people with clear visions of how things can be done better."
- Do not complicate issues and problems. Keeping things simple is one of the keys to a successful and prosperous business. "Simple messages travel faster, simpler designs reach the market faster, and the elimination of clutter allows faster decision-making."
- Do not resist change. See it as an opportunity. "Willingness to change is a strength, even if it means plugging part of the company into total confusion for a while... Keeping an eye out for change is both exhilarating and fun."
- Do not block new ideas and thoughts. These are the lifeblood of business. "The operative assumption today is that someone, somewhere, has a better idea; and the operative compulsion is to find out who has that better idea, learn it, and put it into action — fast." Encourage arguments because arguments bring people together. A creative conflict is such where all the members of the team are encouraged to contribute ideas, knock down old practices, and stand up to peers and superiors.
- Give managers the opportunity to operate in a free environment. The best only way to harness the power of your people is "to turn them loose, and get the management layers off their backs, the bureaucratic shackles off their feet, and the functional barriers out of their way."

- Do not open too many fronts at one time. Select one issue and settle it forever. "Pick only those battles that can be won." Stay on top of your game until the very end.
- Build a meritocracy and cultivate leaders by taking a personal interest in the best and get rid of the worst. Involve everyone. A leader is really a teacher, a trainer, and an idea generator.

The Welch era at GE: 1981–2001

Jack Welch was the CEO of GE Electricals from 1981 to 2001. During his 20 years of leadership, Welch turned the slow-moving company into a dynamic growth company. When he left in 2001, GE was the most-admired company of the United States. In 2000, *Fortune* named General Electric the most admired corporation in America for the fourth year running, while the *Financial Times* named it the most admired company in the world for the fourth time. The follow data speaks for itself:

- In 1981 per employee sale was $69,000. By the end of his tenure, it reached $382,000.
- In 1981 market capitalisation was $13 billion; in 2001 it was $494 billion.
- Revenues in 1981 were $28 billion. In 2000 the revenues totaled $130 billion.
- GE stock traded at nine times the earnings in 1981. In 2000, the company's price-earnings ratio was 40 to 1.
- In 1981 less than 20 per cent of the company's revenues were derived from overseas operations. Under Welch, international business grew to generate 41 per cent of the revenues.

Humility paid Shanti Prashad Jain

The third November of 1838 was a historic day. Two publications, *The Bombay Times* and *Journal of Commerce* came out of the printing press in Bombay, now Mumbai. Later the two were converted into one newspaper — *The Times of India*. Two Englishmen, Bennett and Coleman made *The Times of India* possible in 1861. However, for another 89 years, it remained confined to Bombay along with its sister publications, *The Illustrated Weekly of India* (it came out of the press in 1880). *The Times of India* remained a regional newspaper till Sahu Shanti Prashad Jain (SPJ) and his wife Rama Jain came on the scene in the early fifties. Then began an era of rapid expansion. Today *The Times of India* is the largest circulated newspaper in the world. In the early 1980s it was a Rs. 80 crore company. Today its top line has crossed Rs, 5,000 crore. How did SPJ and later his son Ashok Jain and now his grandson Samir Jain convert the pigmy into a giant?

Imagination, vision, and hard work were the three prominent traits in SPJ that made him the success icon of the third quarter of the 20th century. He adopted a unique management strategy for running the Bennett, Coleman & Co. Ltd. (BCCL). Three cardinal principles of his management strategy were lifetime employment, providing a family environment, and teamwork. He adopted these principles much before the Japanese adopted them as an integral part of their management strategy.

During his more than 27 years of stewardship of the company, SPJ nurtured the group like a family. His God-fearing religious disposition, calmness, and cool temperament created a feeling of fraternity among all the employees. He promoted this feeling in several ways. He would discuss their problems, even personal and family ones like a head of the family. Jagdish Prasad Saxena, a lifelong employee never thought that "he [SPJ] was the employer and I was the employee". SPJ cemented the family bonds by meeting even the junior-most employees, talking to them and inquiring about their problems whenever he visited any of his establishments. Once he suffered a massive heart attack in Patna and had to be hospatilised. When he left the city a couple of weeks later he personally thanked each and every employee. On another occasion, an employee lost his son-in-law soon after the marriage of his daughter. The hapless man wanted to rehabilitate his daughter but the conservative community would not permit this. Sahu not only took the entire responsibility of her marriage but also supervised all other marriage ceremonies personally to ensure that no one created any problem.

SPJ believed in teamwork and devised his own unique ways to generate *esprit de corps*. He developed the system of mass recitation of *meri bhavna* by workers and suggested that Ramaji conduct it. When other industrialists ignored welfare activities, Sahu gave top priority to schools, hospitals, and clubs. He was particular about the club as it strengthened social interaction and a team spirit.

What gave SPJ a leader status was that he never ran away from his responsibilities and problems. He was a known troubleshooter. Here is an example. An emotion-charged procession of workers who were shouting aggressive slogans marched toward his office in Calcutta (now Kolkata). His aides advised him to leave the office and go home. Brushing them aside, he went to the main door to welcome the workers. Not expecting him there, the workers were overwhelmed and agreed to send a delegation to discuss their problems. You can imagine the goodwill this gesture created among the workers. This was not unusual. It was his normal style of functioning. He believed that "a man, who enjoys responsibility, usually gets it. A man who merely likes exercising authority, usually loses it," say Prem and Padma, his two grandchildren.

Though more equal than others, he believed that "all are equal". He exhorted his grandson not to have a separate bathroom in the office and to use the common one. It was to ensure that the common bathroom does not stink. Firmly but affectionately he made his 11-year old son, Alok, apologise to Sardar Singh, a *durban* (doorman), whom he had insulted.

Sahu always gave life-long employment and never dismissed any worker even when moderanisation necessitated retrenchment. On one occasion some employees from a coal mine were to be retrenched. He instructed that surplus employees be transferred to Calcutta. His son objected on the plea that better qualified persons were available in Calcutta. He looked sternly at his son and the message went home. No one was dismissed.

Calm as the sea, he seldom rebuked anyone, yet he generated fear in every one, not because of the authority he wielded but out of respect. Naturally, every one gave their best to the company. Wrote Saroj Goenka, the niece and the daughter-in-law of Ram Nath Goenka, owner of *The Indian Express Group*, in her reminiscence:

> *Forever tender*
> *Soft and tremulous*
> *In form and face*
> *Himself angelic and divine.*

He was the man behind the phenomenal growth, vertical and horizontal, of *The Times of India Group* of publications.

Never say die—the Tojo approach

Every boy in Hidebi Tojo's class was asked to teach an illiterate member in his family. Tojo, the 12-year-old boy had only one illiterate person in his family, his grandmother. When he approached the 75-year old granny, she laughingly brushed him aside saying, "Why should I study at this age?" Tojo was dejected. But he did not want to tell his teacher that he had failed in his mission. He kept on thinking on how to make the granny agree to learn, read, and write. She was a stubborn lady, as old persons generally are. Tojo's mind kept on thinking of various ways and a brain wave struck to him.

The next night he was sitting in his granny's lap, listening to the story she was narrating. When she finished and asked him to go to bed, Tojo asked her, "Granny, do you want to go to hell or heaven?"

"Why should I go to hell, you stupid fellow? I definitely will go to heaven."

"But you can't, Granny. There is a register at the gate to heaven and you have to sign your name. No thumb impression is accepted," Tojo said, giving a meaningful look.

Next night there was no story session. It was literacy class for Granny.

Tojo later became the famous General of the Japanese Army that fought the Second World War and knocked at the door of India giving sleepless nights to the British. He was also the Prime Minister of Japan from 1941 to 1944. His secret of success was, "never accept defeat".

This motto has become more apt with increasing competition in every sphere. At every step, whether it is admission to a school, finding a seat in a professional institution, or getting a satisfactory job, you face tough competition. It is becoming tougher every passing year. Only those who adopt the Tojo approach can be the ultimate winners. What is the "Tojo approach?"

The essentials of the Tojo approach are determination, planning, and the capacity to work hard.

Determination is the tenacity to do what you want to do. The primary requirement for this is a firm mind, a clear perspective, and knowledge about your weaknesses. A firm mind will lead you towards a definite path. A clear perspective will make you think maturely, objectively, and pragmatically. You would be able to establish a relation between the different aspects of a problem. If you know your weak points, you can make efforts and develop ways and means of overcoming them.

A good example of strong determination is Maharaja Ranjit Singh. Once when his army was marching towards Kashmir, it reached the banks of the Sutlej River, and found that the river was overflowing. The commander gave orders to stop. He was perplexed because the army could not cross the swollen river. As he was contemplating his next action, the Maharaja came galloping from the rear and jumped into the river saying. "*Sabaha bhoomi Gopal ke, ya mai atak kahan; ja kai mann me atak hai, wahi atak gaya*" (All the universe belongs to God, there cannot be any obstruction here. Only the ones, who hesitate, will not win). The soldiers followed the determined king and the whole army had soon crossed to the other side of the river.

Coming to more recent times, we have the example of the former Chief of the Air Staff, Air Chief Marshal P. C. Lal. An average student, Lal was timid and lacked self-confidence tells Khuswant Singh, his intimate friend and a known journalist and author. However, his determination made him "a man of enormous rectitude and courage, the likes of which has become all too rare today".

Planning is the second essential ingredient of the Tojo approach. It is the desire to direct our actions to achieve predetermined ends. The importance of planning arises from the fact that actions must be properly organised and implementation should be so timed that the desired objectives are achieved. If you believe in *ad hoc* efforts you may win but the chances are that you may not. I can give you a real life example of success due to good planning.

My friend Navin was very keen on going to the United States for higher studies. Though he got admission to several universities, he could not make it because of certain family constraints. However, the desire to go to the U.S. remained latent. As soon as the constraints weakened he planned his move. He joined a prestigious university for research and selected a topic on which not much work had been done. As there was not enough material in India, a visit for the U. S. was imperative to collect material. Within two years he was sent to the U. S. to collect material for his research. During the visit he cultivated several contacts in a number of universities. Within four years, immediately after finishing his research, he got an invitation from an American University offering a visiting professorship for one year. Had he not planned well, he would have not been able to achieve what he wanted to.

Finally, if you want to see your dreams become reality you must develop the capacity to work hard. I have seen many ordinary persons reaching the top only because they were hardworking and imaginative. They never gave up learning. In fact, they always made an assessment of themselves whenever they fail. You should also remain alert and be guided by the experiences of others.

The people's PM — Lal Bahadur Shastri

I could not get an answer as to why my father, till he died in the late seventies, missed a meal every Monday.

The beginning of the seventies solved the food problem that had prompted Shastriji to give the nation a call to miss-a-meal every week. Naturally no one was continuing with the practice that every Indian began to follow in 1964 on a call from late Lal Bahadur Shastri when India was facing acute food crisis. I got the answer a few years back when I met an old classmate, an avid fan of Shastriji. I wanted to invite him for dinner on Monday when he visited Delhi. Politely he suggested fixing some other evening. On my enquiry of why not Monday he told me that he was maintaining the practice of missing dinner that he had started in 1964.

"What is the need now?" I asked, flabbergasted.

"You know Shastriji never withdrew the call he gave to us," he replied.

"But he did not survive to see India turning self-sufficient in food.

So how could e have given a call?" was my question.

"You know for all of us he was like an elder family member. I am a conservative old-timer. If I give a word to an elderly person of my family, I follow it till I get his or her instruction to discontinue it. You know that."

He was correct. A fanatic, as I used to call him, he was like that.

And that gave me the answer to my question: "Why my father missed a meal till his death."

Lal Bahadur Shastri was probably the only leader in the post-independent era who, even after becoming the Prime Minister, lived like an ordinary middle class person. He firmly believed in the same value system he had faith in.

Indeed Lal Bahadur Shastri lived like a middle class person throughout his life. He did not dress expensively and wore simple and neat clothes like any ordinary Indian in the street—inexpensive *khadi kurta* and *dhoti* and simple *bundi* (waistcoat without collar)—and did not change his style even when he visited foreign countries. His simplicity in dress and deportment won the hearts of every middle and poor class Indian who identified with his personality.

He carried an air of refinement, true culture, and absence of any harshness in his behaviour. He was a true gentleman in every sense of the word. His closeness with common people and a sense of human equality came to him naturally, without any conscious effort.

Humility and honesty were his two prominent trademarks that every common Indian liked. The extent of humility and care for the public money was so intense that when he traveled out of Delhi on official tours, he avoided staying in VIP government guesthouses. He preferred to stay with some close friend or relative or in some other moderate lodging. When he lost his ministry because of the *Kamraj* Plan, he moved to a small house, started washing his own clothes, and reduced his expenditure on food. In 1962, when he was Home Minister, he willingly vacated the rented house in Allahabad to the owner who wanted it back. Next morning he read the news with the heading, "The Homeless Home Minister" in the newspaper.

The whole life of Shastriji was the life of an average Indian. Like majority of Indians of today he had a humble beginning and followed the right course of action throughout his life. He always thought deeply about the right course of action, and once he had made up his mind, he stuck firmly to his decision. This is what is followed by the large multitude of people in our country.

No doubt he is still in the hearts of so many people, even those who have never seen him.

> *Learn from peers like M. S. Oberoi, Indra Nooyi, Lee Iacocca, Cyrus McCormick, Konosuke Matsushita, Jack Waltch, Shanti Prasad Jain, Hidebi Tojo, and Lal Bahadur Shastri.*
>
> *Oberoi took the right decisions at the right moments, believed only in the best, and developed an effective and responsive management system. Nooyi is a quick decision-maker with innovative ideas and implements them. She has an open mind and is a good learner. Lee Iacocca has been a good and effective team leader with excellent innovative abilities. A hard worker, he is a good family head. Cyrus, though not very educated, had an innovative mind and was a good strategist in designing marketing plans in selling his product. Matsushita understood the secret of success from the behaviour of an impoverished person. He designed the strategy of creating a surplus, ensuring consumer's satisfaction, developing a sound distribution system, and offering the product at an affordable price. Walch believed in aggressive marketing and pushed his managers to work for more productivity. He did not believe in sermonising but in setting examples. Jain's success depended on three traits — vision, imagination, and hard work. He believed in team work and that all were equal. Calm as the sea he never rebuked anyone. Tojo had strong determination, was a good planner and a hard worker. Shastri had two virtues —humility and honesty.*

Chapter 9

Leaders' Legacies

Unlimited power lies sleeping within you. Let it slumber so more.

ANTHONY ROBBINS

Now you know how to develop a success system to be a winner and reach to the apex of your career, "number one" in your profession.

Whatever you achieve in your career entirely depends on the external environment and ethos. This you have to accept in your stride, because you may not be able to change it. But you can be a dynamic person—a catalyst. You can be a change agent and influence the polity and society. It should be your mission as a young member of the society. How can you do it? Very briefly, by deciding to be a leader in the true sense of the word—to change society in a positive way to make it a better place to live in.

Today India is facing its greatest challenge of contemporary history—the need to create a new environment to live and work in. Sooner or later, the political leadership that would emerge in the coming years, we hope, will be in the young hands. It would establish a corruption-free, law-abiding, production-oriented society. When it happens, you will have to play a major role because the challenge today is not national but global. The economic interdependence is a fact of life in the present society, whether it is the old Soviet system or the emerging market-based economics. Are you, as a young leader of the polity and society, prepared to accept this challenge? If not, how would you equip yourself to face the massive changes in India in the next few decades?

Do not get entangled in the quagmire of the first question. The second one is more significant. You must prepare a blueprint for improving your competitive power. We suggest a four-way strategy of doing this.

Develop a work culture in your personality

You must change from a rigid, slow-moving and centralised work system to a flexible, fast-moving, and decentralised one. It would hasten your decision-making process, which is the need of the hour. This is easier said than done, particularly in Indian conditions where change is not only slow, but is not acceptable to the older generation. But being the younger member of society you should foresee the requirements of the prospective global society. You must acclimatise yourself to the requirements of the global society and not to the Indian society alone. You have to understand the need for change in attitudes and the style and structure of social, economic, and political management. In a fast-moving world you cannot postpone it for a long period because you are competing with countries like Japan and China. They have the history of producing the best at the lowest cost. Therefore, you need to combine the Japanese cooperative spirit with the American ability to think for one's own interests.

Expand opportunities

You must learn to spread your wings, even beyond your capacity. These are the times of expanding opportunities. New openings are emerging every year and you have to be aware of them. You cannot prosper in the coming decades if you continue to do things the same way your forefathers were doing or the way they were done in the past. You have to adopt the best systems and methods of functioning. You must be in touch with knowledgeable persons and interact with them to strengthen your knowledge base. It will enable you in speeding up your decision-making ability, cutting costs, improving quality, and reacting swiftly to the changing situations. Follow the Japanese philosophy of Kaizen of "constant search for improvement". Your effort should be to train yourself and motivate your team to find new areas of work and improve on the existing ones. The team must be trained for better results through a cooperative problem-solving process and team commitment.

Get the best

Your effort should be to get the best deal by improving human relations and work methods. Roger B. Smith, former Chairman of General Motors had suggested "four absolutes of quality management". First, quality is not how well you do a job; it is whether you do the job that is needed to meet your requirements. Second, you must change the work methods so that what you do is appropriate right from the beginning. Do not wait for the problem to arise and then try and fix it. Third, your standard must be zero defects, something more than six-sigma. It is definite that nothing is perfect and only the Almighty can reach the state of perfection, but if you believe in perfection your achievements will almost be closer to that. Last, the measure of quality is the "extra cost" because of defects. The less is the "extra cost", the higher will be the quality. The slogan should be "we will do it right, so that we can compete with the best in the world".

Develop human resources

In the past the capital, equipment, and technology received the maximum attention from entrepreneurs and managers. Today it is the quality of human resources. Global competition cannot be won without an efficient, productive, and innovative workforce. India never gave any importance to these aspects. The system for years has been authoritative and imperial. Therefore, the needs and requirements of the people were never given any importance. But today Indians, even in villages, are becoming more aware of their rights. They are empowering themselves and are demanding better service from the civil servants, businessmen, and traders. As the economy becomes more and more affluent, mature, and competitive, demands on administration, trade, and industry for better services will gain momentum. It requires an attitudinal change and a different *modus operandi*, more so if you are working to serve ordinary people. Develop the ability to quickly respond to a new scenario.

In fact, individuals alone cannot bring about rapid and far-reaching changes. The governments — state and the Central — too have to undergo a change in their roles and attitudes. In the contemporary world no government, even the military dictatorship, can place total restrictions on human freedom and activity. Not only that governments, whatever their form, have to create economic conditions favouring all-round development and productivity in the country. Unfortunately, the governments do not seem to be enthusiastic for either of these requirements. As a result, we have failed to take advantage of the global boom. India's share in world trade has fallen from 2.5 percent in 1950 to less than one per cent in recent times. Consequently, less proportion of money is left for productive and developmental activities. No doubt we are faced with low productivity, bottlenecks, and higher costs that are progressively weakening our economy. No doubt the youth feels frustrated and discontented. It is reflected in the increasing violence, road rages, and anti-societal activities.

The present day youth will live in the modern future India. In fact, they have a stake in the India of the next fifty years and not the vanishing generation of pre-independence and licence-permit *raj* era. They have to ensure that the society and polity develops in a healthy way so that an economically, socially, and politically strong nation emerges. It should be minus corruption and criminalised leadership. It should be a merit-oriented society, free from mediocrity.

The ultimate strength of India depends on the ingenuity and determination of its youth — the young boys and girls who have their future at stake. What Robert MacNeil said about the U.S. long ago is true about India too. He said, "The country's future success in the world is in a large part going to be determined by business. The military strength cannot ensure a higher standard of living. Diplomats and politicians cannot negotiate it. Business is the bread and butter of democracy. It is what feeds, clothes, and houses us".

The sooner you understand it, the happier you would be.

Where others fail, Indian managers succeed

One recent trend in global corporate scenario is the increasing role of Indian managers at various levels. A few, like Anshu Jain, Gurucharan Das, Indra Nooyi, Vikram Pandit, and Arun Sarin have reached the top managerial positions leaving hundreds of thousands Europeans and Americans behind who, nevertheless, enjoy a dominant position in their domain. Graduating from premier institutes like the IIMs and the IITs, the Indians managers are reaching the top management level in global organisations and continue to work abroad drawing handsome salaries. The *Fortune* Magazine realised it ten years back when in its May 15, 2000 issue it declared that Silicon Valley would not have been what it is today without Indian managers. It placed the wealth generated by them at $250 billion, more than half of India's current GDP. The U.S. Census Bureau has also estimated the Indian median family annual income at $60,000 as against the national average of $38,885. The annual buying power of Indians working abroad is calculated around $20 billion.

Yet the high-flying Indians are humble about their success. Adobe CEO Shantanu Narayen casually says, "It is not a big deal, because America is an egalitarian and meritocratic environment." Harvard Business School's, Nitin Nohria gives credit to IIT. Pepsico's Indra Nooyi modestly says, "I am a mother first and then a CEO."

The dominating Indian manager

The rise of Indian manager at the global scenario has not come all of a sudden. It is the outcome of decades of hard work and the capability of attaining a high degree of professionalism. Besides that problem-solving ability, decision-making skills, cognitive skills, and social skills are the most prized generic skills that have made Indians the most sought after managers in almost all countries including China and East Europe where language is the major problem.

The upbringing of the Indian managers also helps them. It inadvertently grooms them for a good chance of success overseas. Sanjaya Baru, Editor of *Business Standard* corroborates it in one his columns: "Stories of extreme hardship, braving impossible odds and innumerable sacrifices, abound in the lives of nearly 90 per cent of the students in the country. But among them, some perform exceptionally well. Their academic laurels are so brilliant, that at times their CV looks intimidating. And each one acknowledges that it's the right education that made them what they are today."

Four professors at the Wharton School of the University of Pennsylvania, Peter Cappelli, Harbir Singh, Jitendra Singh, and Michael Useem, have researched on the success of the Indian manager and have co-authored *The India Way: How India's Top Business Leaders Are Revolutionizing Management*. After two years of study they found it in the uniquely "India way of doing business" that is essentially based on a simple philosophy—"think in English and act in Indian". It also is mainly responsible for fuelling an economy that even in perilous global times remains a dynamo.

R. Gopalakrishnan, Executive Director, Tata Sons, the holding company of the Tata Group, supports it in an article when he writes: "For the Indian manager, his intellectual tradition, his y-axis is Anglo-American, and his action vector, his x-axis is in the Indian ethos".

The Wharton professors say they found from their study of Indian business leaders that their "x-axis" is defined by four distinctive elements of managing:

1. Holistic engagement with employees. Indian business leaders see their firms as organic enterprises, where

sustaining employee morale and building company culture are critical obligations and the very foundations of their success. People are viewed as assets to be developed, not costs to be reduced.
2. Improvisation and adaptability are also at the heart of the India way. In a complex often volatile environment with few resources and maddening red tape, business leaders learn to rely on their wits to circumvent the innumerable hurdles they recurrently confront.
3. Creative value propositions. Given the enormous and intensely competitive domestic market and the country's discerning customers, most of them of modest means, Indian business leaders have of necessity learned to be highly creative in developing their value propositions, delivering entirely new products and services with extreme efficiency.
4. Broad mission and purpose. Indian business leaders place special emphasis on personal values and on having a vision of growth and strategic thinking. In addition to serving the needs of their stockholders, like CEOs everywhere, they also stress broader purpose.

The Gopalakrishnan theory

Gopalakrishnan has attributed four factors to the immense success of the Indian manager.

First it is the subsidised higher education because of which it is within the easy reach to middle-class people. It is the low cost of education even at the professional level like medicine, engineering, and management (leave out the private sector profit-hungry institutions) that several thousand pass out from the high quality institutions like IIMs, IITs, Regional Engineering Colleges, et al. Those who do not get into these institutions and can afford expensive education join institutions in Australia, USA, and UK. One advantage of facing high-pressure competition at the entry level is that Indians become "psychologically autoclaved".

Second, the struggle for survival in India, compared to elsewhere in the world, is tough. He lives in chaotic conditions, has very little privacy to study at home, and the burden of examinations is tremendous making life extremely stressful. It forces the Indians to learn to fight and be persistent. Naturally they develop a never-say-die attitude. This has been accepted by Judy Rosenblum of Duke Corporate Education: "In order for people to develop as professionals, they need to be immersed in problems. A problem provides the opportunity to grapple with and test one's ability to adapt."

Third, you can credit the British; the capability of thinking in English is a great asset to us Indians. Among the non-English speaking persons probably Indian managers are the only ones who can think in English and articulate it excellently. The MBA education is in English, case studies are mostly American or British, and language proficiency helps them to better understand English literature, music, and movies. The language of business in India is also English.

All this makes an Indian manager a commonsensical, linear-thinker, and communicative in his intellectual skills. "Bundled together, these principles constitute a distinctly Indian way of conducting business, one very different from other countries, especially the U.S. where the blend centers more on delivering shareholder value," four Wharton Professors believe. With such a blend in view how can an Indian manager accept a back seat in any global competition?

> Be a dynamic leader and try to change the society in a positive way to make it a better place to live in. This can be done by developing a work culture in your personality and expanding opportunities for yourself and others. You must develop better human relationships and working methods. The young managers of today have a stake in Indian's future because they are going to live for another 50 years. They are already making a mark for themselves in the world. Much more can be done and achieved.

•••